How the MIND Uses the BRAIN

(to move the body and image the universe)

Ralph D. Ellis and Natika Newton

How the Mind Uses the Brain

How the Mind Uses the Brain

(To Move the Body and Image the Universe)

RALPH D. ELLIS

and

NATIKA NEWTON

OPEN COURT
Chicago and La Salle, Illinois

To order books from Open Court, call toll-free 1-800-815-2280, or visit our website at www.opencourtbooks.com.

Open Court Publishing Company is a division of Carus Publishing Company.

Copyright © 2010 by Carus Publishing Company

First printing 2010

All rights reserved. No part of this publication may be reproduced, stored in a retrieval system, or transmitted, in any form or by any means, electronic, mechanical, photocopying, recording, or otherwise, without the prior written permission of the publisher, Open Court Publishing Company, a division of Carus Publishing Company, 70 East Lake Street, Suite 300, Chicago, Illinois 60601.

Printed and bound in the United States of America.

Library of Congress Cataloging-in-Publication Data

Ellis, Ralph D.
How the mind uses the brain : to move the body and image the universe / Ralph D. Ellis and Natika Newton.
      p. cm.
      Includes bibliographical references and index.
      ISBN 978-0-8126-9663-9 (pbk : alk. paper)
  1. Consciousness. 2. Cognition—Philosophy. I. Newton, Natika II. Title.
    B105.C477E45 2010
    128'.2—dc22
                                                                2009047669

Contents

Introduction: Searching for the Covert Agent
of Consciousness — vii

1. The Devil's Pact (Or, Why the Hard Problem Is Now So Hard) — 1
2. Action at the Macro Level: An Agent-based Theory of Intentionality — 25
3. Action Imagery and Representation of the External World — 49
4. Do We Need an Emergency Metaphysician? Action versus Reaction at the Micro Level — 63
5. Herding Neurons: The Causal Structure of Self-Organizing Systems — 83
6. The Paradoxes within Phenomenal Consciousness — 99
7. The Self-Organizing Imagination: Addressing the Mind-Body Problem — 135
8. Introspection and Private Access — 163
9. Action Imagery and the Role of Efference — 195
10. Connecting Physiology with Phenomenology — 217

References — 239

Index — 259

INTRODUCTION

Searching for the Covert Agent of Consciousness

Conscious beings understand the world either by acting in relation to it, or by imagining how we could act relative to it. That is the basic intuition at the root of the currently resurgent "organicist" and "self-organizational" approaches to consciousness and cognition (Ellis 1995, 2005; Newton 1996, 2000; and others to be cited later). Part of the motivation for such a theory is to make room for the difference between *non-conscious* information processing, which can be done by mechanical gadgets, and *conscious* and/or *"mental"* information processing (in a non-trivial sense of "mental"), which seem to occur only in living organisms. Conscious and fully mental systems manifest additional features beyond what digital computers and robots do. Digital information processors exhibit merely the ability to react to inputs and then process their logical implications. In our view, the extra ingredient in living organisms is grounded in their ability to *act,* an ability that is lacked by mechanical gadgets and even some types of brain structures that can only *re*-act in complicated ways.

This basic intuition can be conveyed by means of a simple thought experiment. Suppose we try to imagine a visible object in relation to which it would *not* be possible to perform any action. Typically, we might think of ghosts as such creatures. But even in the case of ghosts, we would not understand the creature as an existing being if we could not at least *imagine* acting in relation to it—bumping into it, grasping it, shaking hands with it, running away from it, and so forth. Also, our brains must act in certain ways to gear us up to *create* the image (and not merely receive and react to an input) in order to enable us to be conscious and mentally aware of the image of the ghost. The brain can execute this action whether it receives input from an actual ghost or not. We may not normally think of the behavior of neural systems as "actions," but we plan to argue in this book that *some* brain processes—including those that facilitate the purposeful creation of imagery—can appropriately be called actions rather than mere reactions. For now, our point is that, even if the ghost is only a mental image, the brain's action is remarkably similar to what it would do in perceiving an actual ghost. According to the self-organizational and dynamical-systems type of approach to consciousness that we are advocating, we would not be able to be aware of the ghost, and certainly would not be conscious of it, unless we did perform these real and imagined *actions* in relation to it.

But to pursue this ghost example a step further, some would charge that the very problem with the action-centered account is that it creates *metaphysical "ghosts"* of a different sort: it suggests that the mind itself has causal power and can act with its own force on physical objects; thus it makes consciousness seem like a metaphysical, "ghostly" entity. Moreover, such an "enactive" approach may seem to require a clear-cut distinction between action and reaction, whereas modern science teaches that actions are only complicated sequences *of* reactions. That is, as another well-known Newton put it long ago, nothing acts unless first acted upon. So the enactivist notion of an entity that acts *on its own,* or in other words, that initiates and organizes its own action rather than just mechanically reacting, seems like a metaphysical apparition.

And there are still other objections. For example, isn't it circular to explain consciousness of the environment as *derived from* the ability to imagine actions, when imagining an action is *already* a conscious act? What reasons are there to think that the ability to act on the environment can better explain consciousness and cognition than simply receiving and processing perceptual information? Does the action-centered approach really offer any theoretical advantages or specific new empirical predictions?

We believe it does. The purpose of this book is to develop and defend a coherent action-centered and self-organizational theory of consciousness and intentionality that emphasizes emotionally motivated *action imagery,* and to show how such an account can resolve the many facets of the mind-body problem.

We acknowledge that a vast number of books about consciousness have appeared in the past two decades. Yet we believe there is still crucial work to be done in developing a coherent self-organizational account of consciousness in its entirety, all the way from the emotional motivations arising from the self-organizing system—whose role is all too neglected—to the action imagery that is motivated, to the conscious perception and abstract thought made possible by this imagery. We plan to show how emotion and action imagery actually *ground* other forms of consciousness that are built up from them. This as yet unexploited line of thought emphasizing emotion and action imagery from a self-organizational viewpoint is important, not just because it is neglected, but also because of its as yet mostly untapped explanatory value. It offers solutions to a wide variety of traditional puzzles and problems that have baffled more traditional accounts. The emotivist self-organization theory could be called a Kuhnian "revolution"—a paradigm shift—in substituting an active for a passive account of mentality, in a way that is at home with the currently competing environments of phenomenology on the one hand, and empiricism and analytic philosophy on the other. This general type of proposal has been part of the scene for some time, in a mostly marginalized tradition leading from Merleau-Ponty to Gibson to Varela (see Gibson 1986; Merleau-Ponty 1941, 1942; Varela et al. 1991). Largely owing to the development of self-organizational explanations of organic processes, we now have the resources with which to establish a fuller version of this action-centered approach that is, we believe, both more comprehensive and more explanatorily adequate than other versions.

By a "self-organizational" account of consciousness and intentionality, we mean an account holding that 1. understanding of objects and concepts is primarily in terms of the possible actions they afford, and 2. active, self-organizing brain processes subserve this understanding. We should stress at the outset that this type of action theory is different from several other "enactivist" and "embodiment" trends that are currently being explored. Many theorists who hold that action underlies cognition, such as Thelen et al. (2001), suggest that we understand the world only by acting in relation to it, and that representations in the brain are not needed, or that representations play no important role in most cognitive processes (O'Regan and Noë 2001; Hutto 1999, 2000). We disagree. In our view, we understand objects not simply by acting, but more importantly by *imagining* how we could act relative to them. Correlatively, action imagery allows us to represent objects by entertaining action imagery relative to them. It is not necessary literally to act. Moreover, action imagery can be accounted for largely in terms of *brain processes*. Imagery that represents objects ("sensory" imagery) then builds on this action imagery (imagining how we could act), and both types of imagery are executed primarily by the brain. So even though there are no "pictures in the head," it is entirely possible to understand how representations of the environment, grounded in action imagery, are indeed enacted by dynamic and widely distributed brain processes.

What do we mean by "consciousness"? We are interested in consciousness in the sense of phenomenal experience, which in well-known parlance occurs when certain mental states are "like something" for the subject. We are concerned with *phenomenal* consciousness in Block's sense (1995) rather than his "access consciousness," which can occur without conscious awareness. Consciousness, in our discussion here, refers to what we can experience when we are awake or dreaming and not when we are in a dreamless sleep (Ellis 1995; Nagel 1974). In later chapters we offer more precise characterizations of phenomenal consciousness, and of the active agency that produces it. For now it is enough to identify our subject of inquiry as the familiar state of "phenomenality," in which we find ourselves in the midst of experiences of qualitative properties of the world with which we interact or can imagine interacting. (See Natsoulas 1978, 1981, 1990, 1993, 2000.)

Until recently, one heard little about the emotivist type of action-centered account of consciousness. Varela et al. (1991/1993), Ellis (1995, 2005), and Newton (1996) have moved in this direction, and there has been discussion of "embodied" (Clark 1997; Gallagher 2000; Humphrey 2000), "dynamical systems" (Freeman 1987, 2000; Juarrero 1999; Thelen and Smith 1994), "self-organizational" (Ellis 2000 a, b; 2001 a, b, c; 2002 a, b, c,), and "ecological" (Gibson 1988; Neisser 1976, 1994) explanations of the relationship between consciousness and cognition. Neisser has had more indirect influence on subsequent developments than is often acknowledged, and we shall return to him in our last chapter, in the context of integrating neurophysiology with phenomenology. With regard to the crucial role of *emotion* in supposedly non-emotional cognitive processes, Panksepp (1998, 2000) has suggested that the aspects of the emotional brain that gear us up for action could be the basis for all consciousness. Emotivist self-organizational theory, then, is a way to incorporate all these new approaches under one umbrella—the thesis that we understand the world in terms of actual or possible actions which in turn must be emotionally motivated by an organic, self-organizing system. Such systems, by the very nature of self-organization, function more holistically than as a piecemeal collection of parts.

In all these new perspectives, consciousness and intentionality arise from the organism's attempts to use its environment in the service of purposeful organismic action. In our version of the self-organizational view, all consciousness and understanding of objects is based on *imagining* how we could interact with them for organismic purposes (Newton 1996), and we do this primarily by actually *instigating efferent action commands* which are then *inhibited* (Jeannerod 1997; Stippich 2002). An efferent stream of neural activation, in one of the traditional meanings of "efferent," is one that goes "away from" the most central action-initiating core, to relay an action command to the body. This is the sense in which we believe, with Jeannerod, that *inhibition* of this activated stream in the vicinity of the motor cortex, before it is able to be transmitted to the body's extremities, is the way "motor imagery" is formed. The resulting understanding of objects in the environment relative to the imagined actions they could afford, and the subject's understanding of imagined actions themselves, can then be used to elucidate the intentionality not only of objects (Newton 1996), but also of language (as already hinted at in Rhawn Joseph's work on silent internal speech—see Joseph 1982), logic (Ellis 1995, Chapter 3), emotional situations (Ellis 2005), and other persons (Newton 1996); and it can also be used to organize neurophysiological observations about conscious and motivational processes into a coherent framework (Ellis 2005).

The self-organizational approach, as we have already hinted, presents many philosophical and scientific problems. One of the most serious challenges is to clarify what is meant by "action" as opposed to "reaction." Action theories of consciousness use the word "action" in more than one sense. For example, we will talk about *motor* actions involving overt limb movement ("macro"-action), and we will also talk about holistic or "organismic" actions on the level of *neural organizational patterns* that serve to maintain homeostasis and the well being of the organism ("micro"-action). This latter usage is less common, but any significant distinction between action and mere reaction seems to depend on it. Is it philosophically coherent and compatible with scientific accounts to say that the whole organism can (consciously or not) purposely "use" its micro-components rather than being a mere summation of their separate mechanical reactions? To answer this question requires not only looking at the way the brain self-organizes to enact patterns that are built up from the sum of its parts, but also at the way the whole self-organizing system appropriates, replaces, and reorganizes its own parts to make them fit the trajectory of a holistic, dynamical pattern of activity.

The recently elaborated concept of complex dynamical systems (Bunge 1979; Juarrero 1999; Kauffman 1993; Kelso 1995; MacCormac and Stamenov 1996; Minsky 1986; Monod 1971; Newton 2000; Prigogine 1996; Thelen and Smith 1994) is our starting point for such an understanding. Complex dynamical systems, in the terminology of these theorists, are structured so as to preserve continuity of pattern across exchanges of energy and materials with the environment. We suggest, in agreement with Bertalanffy (1933), Bunge (1979), and Monod (1971), that *living* systems are dynamical systems that have a special feature: unlike other self-organizing systems, they must *seek out and appropriate* the replacement components to keep the pattern of organization going.

The activities of living systems are not merely built up through the accumulation and summation of the causal powers of their micro-constituents. According to the dynamical systems account, there is also a causal power on the part of the whole system, to regulate—and in fact even to find and purposefully make use of—micro-components on an as-needed basis. Since emotions are expressions of this self-organizational tendency, we believe that a workable self-organizational account of consciousness must contain an indispensable role for emotion. The emotional contribution to human information processing is what makes it conscious, but to understand how it does so implies revising the old way of thinking about information flow in the brain, in a sense turning our understanding of it upside down, as we will explain later.

A natural first question to raise against all action-centered theories, such as enactivism and ecological psychology, has been well summarized by Kurthen (2001): What reasons are there to think of action as being any more essentially accompanied by consciousness than simply receiving information?

Our answer to this question will depend ultimately on developing a full story of why the enactive thesis leads to a more coherent solution to the various mind-body problems we shall discuss. But by way of introduction, we can get a preliminary intuitive grasp of why action makes so much difference by imagining a simple example. Imagine directing your gaze out toward a scene, but in a completely blank stare, without "paying attention" to what is there. Instead, you may be paying attention to the mental act of multiplying 237×2, for example. In this case, you may not be actually conscious of what the scene looks like (at least, not to much of an extent), even though the *information* from the scene is impinging on the perceptual system, and is even being transmitted to the "perceptual areas" of the brain such as the occipital lobe. But then imagine that suddenly you do "pay attention" to what is there. Now you are conscious of the information received, whereas before you were not. This suggests that the *action* of paying attention (whatever our brains have to do when we perform this act) is a separate process added by consciousness, above and beyond the mere *receiving* of the information.

The "paying attention" to which we are referring in this example is not attention merely in the sense of a *narrowing or shifting* of the field of attention, as the term is sometimes used. Instead, we "pay attention" to see what is out there in general, whatever it might be, in the entire breadth of the visual field. Conversely, we could also *narrow* the field of perceptual information on which the perceptual system is focusing attention *without* necessarily being conscious of it (without "paying attention"—for example, while we are multiplying 237 × 2). In this case we would have a narrow field of perceptual information in our range of (unconsciously) "attended" stimuli, yet we could still be "blankly staring" and thus unconscious of it (or at least very minimally conscious of it).

In fact, "paying attention" in this sense is essentially what happens in the Mack and Rock (1998) "inattentional blindness" experiments. In the Mack and Rock studies, the stimulus is presented near the center of the visual field, yet because the subjects' attention is preoccupied, they remain *consciously unaware* of the presented stimulus. So whether the field of attention is narrow or wide, we can either "pay attention" or not, and this is what determines whether we are conscious of it. For this same reason, it is important not to equate shifting attention simply with *saccading,* or redirecting the focus of the eyes by moving them. While saccading is one way to redirect attention, it is not the only way. We can redirect our attention to 237 × 2 without saccading at all.

This example also preliminarily shows how an action theory can address some of the paradoxical and "ineffable" features of consciousness. What is added to the perceptual process by consciousness is an *action* on our part—paying attention is something that we do, and even can purposely do. This action component of consciousness helps explain why it seems as if the content of consciousness can have the mysterious quality of being both "in here" and "out there" at the same time. The action of paying attention is purely *our* action, which we do "in here," with our own bodily system, not something that causally results from what is done *to* us from the outside. Thus it seems "in here" even though the intentional content or "aboutness" quality of the experience makes the content of the consciousness seem to correspond to something that acts upon us rather than being acted upon by us—something "outside" of us and our own enacted bodily system. Thus the red that is created by our perceptual system *seems* to be pasted to the surfaces of objects, yet as philosophers and scientists have known since the time of Locke, perceptual properties like color and the timbre of sounds depend on the peculiar activities of the human perceptual system. The red color of an object seems independent of us, even though in large part it is created by our own brain activity.

Notice also that this active dimension of consciousness is not subject to the infinite regress of "homunculi" that would present itself if we said that being conscious were just a matter of *receiving and processing the information.* In the traditional information-receiving model, we need a homunculus—a little man inside the head—to look at the perceptual input in order to make it conscious. Otherwise, the resulting brain state would be merely a physical replica of the external thing being represented (or merely a neural pattern isomorphic to it, structurally or functionally representing it in some way). Thus there would be no reason to assume that the homunculus, the neural pattern, should be any more conscious than the external thing *of which* it is a replica (or an isomorphic semblance). The replica or the isomorphic pattern, after all, is just another physical object, just like the perceptual object, and with nothing more to recommend it as having the property of consciousness than the physical object that is being perceived. So this replicating kind of theory requires that the replica—the brain state that is isomorphic to the object—must somehow be registered consciously by some sort of homunculus. But then to explain the consciousness of the homunculus, we would need still another homunculus inside the head of *that* homunculus, to somehow consciously register the nonconscious "copies" occurring *there,* and so forth, leading to an infinite regress.

The action model of consciousness is not subject to this problem. What is added by consciousness is not just another receiving of information in a different place in the brain, but rather a self-initiated, self-organizational process—an action—which *precedes and motivates* the direction of attention, and thus is presupposed by consciousness. The action is not merely a way to replicate the object being represented in consciousness, or create a brain activity isomorphic to it, but rather a self-organizing activity that is already ongoing prior to any mere receiving or processing of perceptual information. The act of paying attention to see what is there, as Mack and Rock show, must occur *before* we can be conscious of what is there. This act therefore is not merely a causal result of the receiving of the information. To a great extent, the act of directing attention determines what information we receive and how we receive it. Without the *motivational* dimension that determines the actions that we imagine we could execute relative to the anticipated object, the conscious state would not have a phenomenal "feel" or a "what it's like" quality. We have not yet shown our evidence for this position, but it is what we shall argue in this book if the reader will stay with us.

1. Some Preliminary Evidence

If our hypothesis is true—if we are conscious of objects by imagining how we could interact with them, and if we do so by forming action commands which then are inhibited to prevent overt action—then we might reasonably ask what would happen with a subject whose frontal inhibitory processes had been prevented by brain trauma. There are indeed such cases, and they are highly illuminating for our purposes. In a rare behavioral disorder called "utilization behavior," the subject becomes unable to perceive objects without actually performing overt actions relative to them (see L'hermitte 1986). For example, the subject sees the doctor's coffee cup and automatically picks it up and tries to drink (even if the cup is empty). Or the subject walks into someone else's bedroom and automatically lies down on the bed. Whatever typical action comes to mind relative to the particular object, the subject overtly does the action.

What is remarkable about utilization behavior for our purposes is that it is consistently found to be caused by a *deficiency of inhibitory neurotransmitters* in the *frontal brain areas* (for example, see Archibald et al. 2001; Eslinger et al. 1991). This is consistent with our hypothesis that, in normal experience, we understand objects by imagining ourselves acting upon them or interacting with them, while at the same time we inhibit those action commands frontally, so that the overt action does not actually occur. In the case where the frontal inhibitory process is deficient, the subject is unable to inhibit the imagined action, and as a result goes through with it instead of just imagining it.

Note that this finding also explains the long-debated Libet "readiness potential" paradox (see Libet 1999). The paradox is that the brain activity that presumably subserves an action is observable approximately 300 milliseconds before the willed action occurs, whereas the subject is *aware* of the choice to perform the action only 100 milliseconds before the action occurs. Libet assumes that this means that the actual choice occurs unconsciously 200 milliseconds before we consciously will it. The paradox, then, is that we feel that we are deciding to do an action that our brains had already unconsciously decided to do 200 milliseconds earlier, yet we feel that we are just now deciding between still-available options.

Our hypothesis explains this paradox. If the brain activity observed by Libet corresponds to the initiation of an action, then essentially the same brain activity also must correspond to the *imagining* of the action—in other words, the motor imagery of ourselves doing the action, even *in the absence of the overt action*. Typically, when we are deliberately deciding whether or not to do an action, we form a motor image of the action as a part of the deliberative process. Part of the question we form to ourselves has to do with what it would be like to perform that action. So we must *image* the action, in the sense of Jeannerod's (1997) "motor imagery," *in order to* decide whether to overtly do the action. And this means that the brain processes that would subserve the overt action have already begun, even before we have actually decided to go through with the action. The initiation of the action command is a part of the process of imagining ourselves doing the action, and normally we do this *before* we complete the process of deciding to do the action. The brain activity that subserves an imagined action is very similar to the brain activity that subserves the corresponding overt action. The difference is that, in normal deliberate actions, the point when we decide to go through with the imagined action is the point when the frontal inhibitory processes are damped down, and the action command, which was already underway, is now allowed to lead to overt action. This frontal inhibitory process is just what the victims of the "utilization behavior" syndrome are unable to perform, because of frontal brain trauma or chemical imbalance of frontal inhibitory neurotransmitters. (For further discussion of this point, see Ellis 2005, especially 142–49.)

The same conclusion is implied by the behavior of Donoghue's monkeys (see Donoghue 2002), who are taught to play a computer game, and then electrodes pick up the electrical signal from the brain activity that subserves the monkey's action command to facilitate moving its hand to move the joy stick. Now the monkey can merely *think* of moving its hand, and the computer cursor moves just as it would if the monkey had actually moved its hand, because the computer is now connected directly to the monkey's brain as it merely *imagines* moving the joy stick. More recently, the same technique has been used to electrically pick up a monkey's brain signals to move a robotic arm (Velliste et al. 2008), which has promising implications for the development of prosthetic devices for humans.

What is remarkable for our purposes is that such an experiment would not be possible if not for the fact that the brain activity that subserves action *imagery*—the image the monkey forms of what it would be like to move its hand—were not very similar to the brain activity that subserves the corresponding overt action. The difference is that in action *imagery* the same action command is orchestrated just as it would be for an overt action, but then it is frontally inhibited. So when Donoghue's electrodes pick up on the signal of the action *image,* they are picking up the same signal as when the monkey was overtly executing the action.

This further confirms Jeannerod's account of action imagery, in which *frontal inhibition* is the extra ingredient that makes the difference between *overtly* executing an action and merely *imagining* the same action. In the case of Donoghue's monkeys, the imagining of the action then becomes "sedimented"—it occurs on a gradually less and less conscious basis—and the monkey's conscious attention is directed only to the cursor on the computer screen (or to the movement of the robotic arm, in the Velliste et al. study). But in order to be conscious of what it wants the cursor (or the robotic arm) to do, the monkey is implicitly (that is, below or nearly below the threshold of consciousness) imagining moving its hand. The movement of the cursor is understood relative to the cursor's "action affordances" for the monkey. And implicitly imagining an action affordance corresponds to much of the same brain activity as explicitly imagining it, which in turn overlaps with the brain activity that would be needed to *overtly* move the monkey's hand, as Jeannerod (1997), Stippich (2002) and others had already shown. The monkey implicitly imagines the cursor's action affordances for the monkey's own hand in order to make the cursor move. If the monkey were suffering from L'hermitte's "utilization behavior" syndrome, it might not be able to imagine its hand movement without continuing to *overtly* move its hand, just as L'hermitte's subjects could not avoid overtly drinking from his coffee cup.

These findings also imply that there often can be *implicit* action imagery, even when conscious attention is directed only to the external object. That is, during the several-day period when the Donoghue monkeys are learning that they can move the cursor without actually moving their hands, they are learning to move the cursor only by deliberately *imagining* the hand moving without actually moving it. But after they have completed this learning process, they pay attention mainly to what is happening *on the computer screen*. Yet, even at this later stage, it is their own *unconscious* motor imagery of the corresponding limb movements that makes possible the playing of the computer game by making the cursor move on the computer screen. The monkeys at this point may not be aware of the motor imagery that they are using to move the cursor on the screen, but the brain imaging studies by Jeannerod and Stippich, plus the fact that Donoghue's electrodes are able to pick up on the motor cortex activity, show that the monkeys are unconsciously imaging the corresponding limb movements. Earlier in their learning process, when the monkeys were still moving their limbs to play the game, essentially the same brain activity had led to *conscious* motor imagery. But then the motor imagery became gradually "sedimented," and as a result the monkeys no longer needed to pay deliberate attention to it. So the Donoghue technique reveals not only the physiological similarity between overt and imagined actions, but also the role played by *unconscious* motor imagery in other cognitive processes.

Another type of clinical case that is highly suggestive in this regard is the recent experiment by Changizi et al. (2008) in which subjects are asked to track a moving object. As the object is moving, a light is flashed for just an instant at the exact location of the object. Amazingly, the subjects report that the perceived location of the object is actually slightly *ahead* of where the object actually is. That is, they see the object as already having passed the spot where the light was flashed, even though it has not. They see the object as being where it is *going to be* an instant later, rather than where it is.

This finding is consistent with our view that consciousness occurs not at the point when we *receive* data into the brain, but rather at the point when we *anticipate* receiving the data. We must anticipate what kinds of environmental objects could facilitate the actions we are imagining performing. Thus the anticipation of where the object is going to be is the foundation for our consciousness of the object. The receiving of the information *from* the object (where it actually is) is not the brain event that causes us to be conscious of the object. This is why we always see the moving object as being just slightly ahead of where it actually is. We are always on the lookout for what is about to present itself to our senses, and this "looking-for" aspect of brain activity corresponds to our consciousness, not merely the "looking-at" aspect (as predicted in Ellis 1995). Thus the subjects' consciousness of the object seems to be experienced as where it is *going* to be rather than where it is.

In our view, the act of "looking for" something is a self-organizational activity of the brain, not a reaction to an input. As the Mack and Rock inattentional blindness studies suggest, a perceptual input with no prior attentional gearing up to look *for* that type of input would not initially or immediately result in consciousness. Thus when a completely *unexpected* object is presented, a much longer period of time is needed for it to register in consciousness, because the subject must first gear itself up to "look for" an input of the kind that has unexpectedly been presented (see Aurell 1989, and fuller discussions later in this book). For these reasons, we need to develop a theory in which consciousness results only from self-initiated action relative to anticipated inputs, not from mere reaction to actual inputs.

Along the same lines, Summerfield et al. (2006) find that "the brain resolves perceptual ambiguity by anticipating the forthcoming sensory environment, generating a template against which to match observed sensory evidence. We observed a neural representation of *predicted* perception in the medial frontal cortex, while human subjects decided whether visual objects were faces or not. Moreover, perceptual decisions about faces were associated with an increase in top-down connectivity from the frontal cortex to face-sensitive visual areas" (Summerfield 2006, 1311, italics added). This finding, too, is consistent with our view that the brain first actively gears itself up to look *for* motivationally relevant kinds of information in a particular situation, in a self-initiated way, rather than merely responding by processing received inputs.

A number of objections will undoubtedly spring to the mind of the thoughtful reader. To be sure, the evidence we have just presented is limited, and is meant only to whet the appetite. Later we will see a vast amount of additional evidence for the action-centered and self-organizational perspective. But before getting into that, we should first address some of the most obvious objections to this type of viewpoint.

2. Objections to the Action Hypothesis

The most obvious objection against an action-centered approach has been pointed out by Aizawa (2006). If we insist that action must undergird all conscious states, then it becomes mysterious how a totally paralyzed person can still be completely conscious. The action-based account must make room for the *imaging* of action to play the same kind of role that overt action can play. This is why, in our view, an account of representation is needed in which the representation of the goals of actions, and also the representation of imaginary actions themselves, can play an important part in making cognitive contents conscious. Paralyzed patients may not be able to act in the sense of bodily movement, but they can imagine acting. Yet it seems equally obvious that in some contexts the patients, like the rest of us, will not necessarily be overtly conscious of the implicit action imagery relevant to their perceptions, just as Donoghue's monkeys were not—so there will have to be an account of *unconscious* or *preconscious* "action imagery."

An important implication of Aizawa's objection is that an account of imagined action must begin by acknowledging that *the brain is the substrate* of these imaginings. We cannot make the "know-how" arising from overt motor skills and overt action into a substitute for the brain activities that in effect give rise to consciousness. We cannot say that consciousness is "out there in the world" rather than "in the head." And thus we cannot say that consciousness is not a function primarily of the brain, or that consciousness does not involve representation of objects that are outside the brain by doing something *in* the brain. In other words, we cannot sidestep the problem of representation. Furthermore, we need an account of how imaginary action representations can take place on an implicit or unconscious basis when our attention is directed *outward to the external world*. Jeannerod (1997) has been a source of major insights about the role of action imagery, and it is commonly accepted that intentional activity requires some sort of internal modeling or representation of the external environment (Grush 2004). Ironically, those who call themselves "enactivists" all too seldom avail themselves of these insights. This point will be developed in more detail as we proceed.

But this response leads to still another objection, which challenges the claim that the way we are conscious of objects is by imagining how we could act relative to them. If we explain consciousness as being based on such "action imagery," are we not being circular, since "imagery" (even action imagery) is already a form of consciousness? We readily admit that "action imagery" is normally thought of as a rudimentary form of consciousness, and the crucial role of this type of consciousness is emphasized in our action-imagery approach.

But in our view, action imagery can also occur on a preconscious basis. By saying that something is "preconscious," we mean that it is unconscious and yet is occurring in such a way that it could quickly become conscious if certain minimal conditions were added to it.

On the other hand, to say that action imagery is preconscious is not to say that it is not mental. We distinguish between mental and non-mental forms of information processing, even in cases where the mental is no more *conscious* than the non-mental. That is, there are non-conscious yet mental events, as when we unconsciously calculate spatial and temporal relationships while driving a car. Yet we also don't want to define "mental" in such a way that just any old causal sequence in nature that yields an information output is dubbed "mental." We don't want to say that, when we run hot water onto a jar lid in order to expand it, the jar lid then "perceives" the temperature of the water and mentally "computes" the amount of expansion that is to be outputted. That would make the meaning of "mental" so all-encompassing that it would become what Hegel called a "night in which all cows are black."

Our distinction between the mental and the non-mental is therefore congruent with the definition of "cognition" offered by Jesse Prinz (2004, 45–46): the key component of the mental (or what Prinz calls the "cognitive") is the way a process relates to "organismic control." What is done by a nuts-and-bolts digital computer represents the mental activities of its programmers and users, but the actual physical electrical signals are not literally mental, because each electronic signal in the computer is only a pre-programmed mechanical response to another electronic signal. In living organisms, the situation is very different in that organisms act rather than just react. This is why some living organisms can perform acts that are preconscious and yet mental in a non-trivial sense, whereas non-living systems can only simulate or represent the mental acts envisioned by their programmers. So some types of living organisms, in our view, can process information in a non-trivially "mental" way, and in some cases they can also become conscious of the information, not merely by receiving and transforming the input, but by using it or attempting to use it in relation to purposes they aim to achieve.

Naturally, we do not mean to imply that *all* organismic processes are intentional in this sense, such as adjustments to maintain equilibrium, signals to feel thirsty, etc. Some bodily as well as brain processes are merely reactions.

We should acknowledge, however, that every term can be defined in different ways (as the dictionary shows with almost every word), and we are not upset when people refer to computer activities as "mental," because those activities do compute, just as an abacus does. So if "mental" is taken to mean anything that computes, then the meaning of the term is broadened to include many mechanisms, such as thermostats and thermos bottles, which are not "mental" in the stricter sense applied to conscious or even proto-conscious organisms that actually use information to achieve a goal. The important point for our purposes here is that to ground a theory of consciousness in preconscious action imagery is not circular, but it does require paying careful attention to the difference between mental and non-mental unconscious brain processes, and in particular between conscious and preconscious action imagery. We will provide a full account of this difference in due course, especially in Chapter 7.

The crucial question posed by the objection is how and in what sense the idea that consciousness is grounded in the imagining of actions "explains" consciousness. This is a complicated question that must await more detailed discussion, but our argument will be essentially that what the brain does when we have action imagery is the key condition beyond mere information processing that must be in place in order for there to be consciousness of any kind (in other words, to create the property of consciousness above and beyond non-conscious information processing).

Note however that these brain processes are very widely distributed and are not limited to the motor cortex, but also involve the hypothalamus, the emotional functions of the limbic system, and motivational areas deep in the subcortex that initiate action and control the release of most neurotransmitters. By contrast to our view, competing "explanations" of consciousness cite conditions that are neither necessary nor sufficient for consciousness, such as mere information processing, behavioral effects, or brain states that can receive, transform, or isomorphically replicate inputs. It is not clear that such conditions could not also accompany *non-conscious* information processing, as in blindsight or as in the information processing of digital computers. Therefore, such conditions cannot explain the mysterious property of being conscious.

The action-centered view should be sharply distinguished from a "higher order thought" (HOT) theory of consciousness, in which thinking *about* our thoughts is what makes them conscious (for example, Rosenthal 1996). Although both the HOT theory and ours suggest that consciousness adds something above and beyond mere receiving and processing of information, this is about the extent of the similarity. A major difference is that HOT theories attempt to explain consciousness, not by requiring that consciousness involves action by contrast to reaction, but rather by adding still another layer of passive "receiving" to the information that has already been unconsciously processed. For example, in the HOT approach, unconscious pain becomes conscious when we "know that" the pain process (which was originally unconscious) is occurring. Also, HOT theories do not take consciousness as affecting the *content* of what is experienced, but merely as *observing* what the content is. Such theories make consciousness seem to be another passive reaction, a final station at which the processed information is received. This approach continues to be enmeshed in the homunculus problem. If we say that consciousness is simply a place in the brain where the perceptual information that has already been processed is now displayed on some sort of "readout screen," then we are in effect doing no more than positing a homunculus, which does not explain why the homunculus is any more conscious than any other physical part of the cause-and-effect sequence of perceptual processing.

In our view, by contrast, consciousness is not merely a final receiving of input, but is closely associated with the initial act of *sending* something—an action command, which then when inhibited forms action imagery, and then leads to an understanding of the action affordances of the environment through an *anticipation* of many *possible* inputs, while quickly refining and increasingly tuning itself to the perceptual environment. If this were not the case, then there is no final step in the receiving of information that could account for how the information becomes conscious.

Many criticisms of the self-organizational approach center on the idea that it requires calling in an ad hoc sort of "emergency metaphysician." That is, it seems to imply that an "emergent" entity, the self-organizing system, has causal powers not reducible to those of its constituents, which in turn seems to require some mysterious metaphysical properties; thus an "emergency metaphysician" seems needed to perform dubious patchwork operations around causal, ontological, and scientific problems. Our aim is to provide a coherent and non-dualistic theoretical grounding for the action-centered approach, rooted in the interdisciplinary fields of philosophy, psychology, and the neurosciences—an approach that is capable of linking phenomenally experienced processes with scientific accounts by means of a self-organizational action theory, and at the same time solving the main problems usually taken to be devastating for such accounts.

The classic example of the charge of metaphysical "mysterianism" against self-organizational and action-centered views is that they might seem to imply that physical systems will fail to be "causally closed" (Kim 1992, 1993, 1998). We shall show that self-organizational theory does not contradict causal closure at the level of molecules and aggregates of molecules in the nervous system. Notwithstanding the possibility of some causal indeterminacy at the quantum level, each step in a molar-level reaction involving large aggregates of subatomic particles can be taken as causally necessary and sufficient for the next step, but only on the condition that *certain background conditions are assumed* (Mackie 1974). For example, flipping a switch causes a light to come on, but only assuming that certain background conditions are in place—a good bulb, a complete circuit, and so forth. On our account, the organismic system as a whole can monitor and adjust these background conditions as required to render a given molecular-level event causally efficacious for the outcomes needed to achieve the system's overall objective, which is to keep acting in its own definitive pattern. Such a pattern will make use of very complex interrelations of homeostatic feedback loops, shunt mechanisms, overcausation, and "seeking" activities to achieve the needed regulation of the causal conditions governing its own components. As we shall argue, a system of this kind can develop ways to achieve enough intentional understanding of environmental action affordances to interpret disruptions of its self-organizational patterns as indicative of some aspect of an overall relation to the environment. This in turn can allow conscious representations of the environment.

The causal structure of self-organizing systems, in fact, can help to clear up some of the confusion about the way conscious organisms respond to causal stimuli. Throughout most of the twentieth century, the stimulus-response paradigm and its first cousin, the information processing paradigm, served the main purpose of a cause-effect analysis in psychology. The stimulus was supposed to be essentially the cause of the response, given the previous state of the organism (including the results of its conditioning history), and there was no room for a distinction between action and mere reaction, or a complicated network of mere reactions. Emotion theorists typically spoke of perceptual objects as the "causes" of emotional responses (for example, Ben Ze'ev 2000, Rolls 1999, LeDoux 1996, and many others). Consciousness was thought of as the *final step* in a chain of causes and effects, the final response to a stimulus, with information-processing going on in the intervening steps.

This paradigm led to epiphenomenalism, the idea that consciousness is a mere causal side effect of the mechanisms of its own components. According to that view, consciousness has no causal power, for example when we decide to move our bodies. Instead, according to epiphenomenalism, when we feel that we are deciding to move the body, what is really happening is that the micro-level cause-and-effect processes are causing the body to move, and at the same time causing us to have the feeling that we have decided to move the body. Our decision to act does not cause us to act, but is only a causal spin-off of the mechanism that causes us to act.

Epiphenomenalism actually created two types of problems for the theory of mind and consciousness: first, because consciousness was considered to be a mere side effect of the real causal processes, which were at the "physical" level, there was a tendency to assume that consciousness itself had no causal power. Since all physical events *do* have causal power, this implied that consciousness is not physical. So this distinction between consciousness and its "physical" causes unintentionally carries over the legacy of mind-body dualism. Most modern-day epiphenomenalists would cringe at the charge of dualism, yet the notion that mind has no causal power renders it non-physical, since physical processes do have causal power.

The second type of epiphenomenalist problem is not as egregious, but it still leads to some of the same confusing conclusions. Some epiphenomenalists do not go so far as to think of consciousness as causally powerless, and thus unable to be equivalent with any physical process (here again, physical processes do have causal power, so if consciousness is physical, then it must have causal power). But these more sophisticated epiphenomenalists do think of consciousness as a superficial overlay of the "real" causal powers, which are presumed to be at the level of the micro-constituents of the system. There is therefore still a tendency to *reduce* the causal powers of consciousness to those of its micro-constituents—the neurons, synapses, and so forth. And even this less egregious type of epiphenomenalism still precludes taking seriously the notion that a larger process might *seek out and use* the micro-constituents needed to keep the process going in its motivated patterns. Instead, epiphenomenalism of either type implies that the overall pattern is simply caused by the activities of its micro-constituents along with the inputs to the system.

But if consciousness itself is a mere epiphenomenon, and is formed by the larger pattern of interrelations of its elements, then to reduce the causal powers of that larger pattern to those of its elements is also in essence tantamount to removing causal power from the larger pattern—its power to appropriate its own elements, for example. This in turn would eliminate the most important causal powers of consciousness. Ultimately, it seems to require that we must think of conscious choice as an "illusion"—a view specifically advocated by Daniel Wegner (2003) and endorsed by Daniel Dennett (2003). Even sophisticated epiphenomenalism, then, seems to lead to the view that consciousness is passively buffeted about by its micro-constituents and not in control of its own action. That is one of the main reasons motivating us to develop an approach to consciousness that can make a coherent distinction between action and reaction, and then show how consciousness results directly and indirectly from the organism's ability to act on its environment, not by overtly acting, but precisely by inhibiting actions to form action imagery.

3. The Plan of This Book

In order to have a viable action-centered account of consciousness and the mind, we believe the first thing that needs to be done is to lay out a coherent definition of just what action, as opposed to reaction, consists of. Even when we read dynamical systems theory in its most technical elaborations (and we promise *not* to become very technical about it in this book!) we still come away with questions about the causal power of the process over its components. Does action mean that the organism can use its components rather than being used by them? And if not, then what difference is there between action and reaction, as found for example in a thermostat or any other feedback mechanism? Certainly not all feedback mechanisms result in consciousness, and merely increasing the complexity of the feedback mechanism does not seem to lead to any level of consciousness. So what kind of action is it that action-centered theorists are championing as the all-important foundation of consciousness? And how does action in this sense account for the existence of consciousness any better than a passive receiving model?

To answer this question, we begin in Chapter 1 by breaking down the hard problem of consciousness into its constituents—the various aspects of the problem of consciousness that seem to make it so intractable and puzzling. We then show that the breakdown of the problem can point the way to a theory that simultaneously resolves each of the aspects of the problem without exacerbating the others. This, we argue, is what is needed to address what Chalmers famously calls the "hard problem of consciousness." There are actually two hard problems in Chalmers's work. One of these two versions of the hard problem is important, and it calls our attention to why so many explanations of consciousness are found wanting. The initial insight was that empirically based causal theories alone are not enough to explain the mystery of consciousness, and this we shall agree with. As Levine (1986) puts it, purely empirical explanations always leave an "explanatory gap" that does not explain why the resulting process should have the property of being conscious.

The other version of the hard problem—the one that purports to suggest a dualistic ontological status for consciousness—actually illegitimately extends Chalmers's initially important insight to an invalid dualistic conclusion. In our view, Chalmers misuses his initial insight by arguing that consciousness cannot be an essentially physical phenomenon. The argument is that if consciousness were physical, then it should be impossible to imagine beings who are physically just like us, and yet lack consciousness. In our view, this is like arguing that, because we can imagine Clark Kent as not being Superman, it follows that Kent cannot be the same as Superman.

On the contrary, we argue that the complex of actions that leads to consciousness is essentially a physical process—although one that is free to act "on its own," free to initiate its own action. Moreover, "what it's like" to perform another person's actions is not fully accessible to purely empirical methods of investigation (as Chalmers rightly points out). People have a kind of access to their own conscious activities that is not available to others, in the same way that a dancer can't perform another dancer's actions. And this means that full access to the felt quality of a person's consciousness requires not only empirical knowledge, but also the addition of phenomenology and philosophical theory of mind.

In this connection, Chapter 1 will also include a discussion of the mixture of epistemological methods needed to address a question as complex and mysterious as the problem of consciousness. How did Western science and philosophy muddle themselves into a situation that seems to preclude any understanding of the ontological status of consciousness, almost by definition? How did the "hard problem of consciousness" get to be so hard in the first place? To understand how the theory of mind got itself into this strange predicament, it is helpful to explore a little of not only the history of modern philosophy, but also the currently hostile relationship between different epistemological approaches—especially the largely antithetical encampments of phenomenology and humanistic psychology on the one hand and scientific empiricism/analytic philosophy on the other.

Then in Chapter 2 we approach the all-important problem of action *versus* reaction. It is necessary to lay this groundwork if we are going to argue that consciousness has its roots in the capacity for action. Our strategy is to distinguish between action at the "macro" level, or overt bodily movements, and action at the "micro" level, which consists of self-organization at a sub-personal and physiological level, in which the organism as a whole can appropriate and constantly reorganize its own parts rather than being a mere puppet of them. We show in this chapter how conscious and mental processes are grounded in "action" in the broader sense of self-iniated bodily movement: the embodied action of the entire living organism functioning at a "macro" level in relation to its environment. Many self-organizational theories focus only on action at the "micro" level (for example, Freeman 1978; Kauffman 1993), while other action-centered approaches attempt to understand cognition in terms of macro-level action of the whole body (for example, Clark 1997; Noë and O'Reagan 2001). In our view, a workable mind-body theory must be grounded in "action" in both senses, integrated with each other. We believe the key to this integration is to take account of the role of action imagery, which involves frontal inhibition of action commands in the brain, and thus allows us to see cognition mainly as a brain process not requiring overt action of the whole organism, but implicitly grounded in first-person, sensorimotor imagery of such action.

Chapter 3 spells out our view of representation. As we have already noted, a theory grounded in action *imagery* rather than mere action will require a strong role for representation. We reject old theories of representation as neural groups or isomorphic patterns in the brain, in favor of the concept of representing the environment by forming action images, which in turn are grounded in motor imagery. Representations of objects, then, are built up from representations of the actions they could afford. We discuss the controversial status of representation, and argue for an approach that views representations as traces of sensorimotor experience that are only *potential* representations unless activated in a particular context for use by the subject, or agent. We further show how the same action-representational activity that underlies intentionality can ground the subjective-objective distinction—the concept of the external world. We attempt to show, not only how external objects are understood in terms of the agency of the subject, but also how the basic subjective/objective distinction can be understood by a subject in terms of her own conscious experience of goal-directed action. The general purpose of this chapter is to form a connection between the unique phenomenology of consciousness and the representational functions of the brain.

Chapter 4 then takes on the difficult problem of distinguishing between action and mere reaction in the "micro" sense. If this distinction is to hold up at the "macro" level, then macro-action in turn must be built up from "micro" action, and this is what gives it its freedom. The theoretical groundwork for this view of "micro" action can be found in the recently developing theory of self-organization. That is, action in a "micro" sense can be elucidated in the sense of a dynamical system that can replace its own constituents to maintain a stable pattern of activity, rather than simply being a causal byproduct of the behavior of constituent parts. We then turn to the apparently intrinsically mysterious nature of conscious experience itself, discussed in the previous chapter. We discuss these apparent paradoxes as "emergent" phenomena in the sense that they can be understood from the perspective of an account worked out in terms of the ontology of processes and their lower-order constituents. Our goal here is to show that apparent paradoxes or contradictions in experience can be robust but still objectively comprehensible, and that an enactive model of consciousness can best handle not only the "aboutness" of intentional mental states, but also the unique puzzles of phenomenal consciousness.

Chapter 5 shows how the causal structure of self-organizing systems makes room for mental causation. Importantly, we address this problem by refusing to sidestep the issue of causal closure at the level of the micro-constituents of brain processes. The regular principles of inorganic chemistry are not found to be violated in the organic processes in the nervous system, and therefore we cannot say that dynamical systems somehow supersede or suspend those principles. Yet at the same time, the dynamical system is not merely an epiphenomenon of its individual components. It has the power to appropriate, rearrange, and replace its own components on an as-needed basis. Working out this problem requires taking some causal issues seriously and working them out carefully and systematically.

In Chapter 6, we attempt an initial phenomenological characterization of conscious experience, one that will allow its distinguishable aspects to be associated with specific psychological functions, which can then be explained in terms of known brain processes. According to Levine's "explanatory gap" argument, as we mentioned earlier, given any physical explanation of consciousness, the "what it's like" aspect of consciousness does not seem strictly deducible from the physical explanation. It seems conceivable that all the elements in the explanation could occur, but *in the absence of* consciousness. To resolve this dilemma, we propose a biological-process-oriented physiological-phenomenological characterization of consciousness that can address the main "paradoxical" qualities we discussed above, which are so difficult to hook up with the empirical realm. Our goal in Chapter 6 is to identify those features of consciousness that will most facilitate a coherent explanation. We argue that, of all those features, the one providing the best access to a coherent, objective, and scientific account of consciousness is the experience of *agency*. Even after we have seen the physiological bases of the other features, we can include them in a single comprehensive view only by beginning with agency.

In Chapter 7, we pursue this theme of agency as the best avenue to a theory of consciousness. We discuss the recently popular theory of embodied cognition, sometimes called the "enactive" theory of conscious intentionality (Varela et al. 1991/1993). We provide extensive evidence and arguments to show that intentionality, or the "aboutness" relation between mental states and their objects, is rooted in our capacity for simple, goal-directed actions, and we explain how this result comes about. Our account entails a strong role for action representations in consciousness and intentional mental activity. Chapter 7 also argues that an action model, rather than the traditional perceptual model of consciousness, allows some of the entrenched philosophical puzzles to be resolved—for example, Jackson's "knowledge argument" and the problem of mental causation.

In the remainder of the book, now that the general enactive approach has been laid out, we examine in more detail the role of imagery in consciousness, and the brain mechanisms subserving it. In Chapter 8 we argue that a correct understanding of the sort of imagery at work in conscious activity explains introspection and its limits. In this chapter we are particularly interested in the earlier phenomenologists such as Merleau-Ponty, and ways in which his work anticipated our current conclusions.

Chapter 9 shows how efferent activity in the brain is central to making conscious imagery possible, by contrast to the nonconscious, primarily *afferent* processing emphasized by traditional accounts of imagery. It then becomes obvious how the action images discussed in earlier chapters fit into the larger picture. This chapter begins with a discussion of recent work by Humphrey (2000) that is highly relevant to the ideas in this book, leading us into an examination of scientific work on efferent brain processes and their role in conscious imagery. This role of efferent processes is much more vital than has been traditionally realized.

Finally, in Chapter 10, we offer a concluding summation of the general problem of connecting physiology with phenomenology. Here we look again at Merleau-Ponty, as well as other earlier phenomenological philosophers and psychologists who can be seen as precursors to the views described here, leading up to more recent phenomenological accounts such as Shaun Gallagher's. We draw attention to the close correspondence between these phenomenological accounts of mentality and what is actually found in recent work on brain mechanisms. We end on a hopeful note, suggesting that the theoretical framework offered by the understanding of emotionally motivated self-organizing processes can bring mind and body back together again.

1

The Devil's Pact (Or, Why the Hard Problem Is Now So Hard)

Part of the goal in giving a coherent account of consciousness and a comprehensive solution to the mind-body problem is to fit both *phenomenological* and *empirical* investigation into a consistent picture. Conversely, if subjective and objective approaches cannot be reconciled, then questions will remain unanswered as to the viability of *either* approach, since each will remain unsatisfactory according to the other's apparently legitimate minimal criteria for acceptance.

The splitting off of the subjective experience of persons from what can be empirically observed about the brain and behavior has always raised serious epistemological questions for psychology and the other mind sciences. Does the study and treatment of the psyche require different scientific and epistemological methods from the ones used for physical mechanisms and for the human body, which medical science treats as a physical system explainable in terms of the same familiar chemistry and physics that are used for other mechanisms?

After all, physical mechanisms in the brain can be redirected by the intervention of other physical mechanisms, such as drugs or surgery. The use of drugs to treat symptoms previously understood from a subjective, social, or psychodynamic viewpoint is becoming increasingly the treatment of choice, and physical explanations of the psyche are now the rule rather than the exception. Has psychology as a field of study thus worked its way out of a job?

There are implicitly two different questions here, but they form a circle with each other: What is the subject matter of psychology, and what are its methods of knowing about that subject matter? Many would answer the second question first, insisting that third-person empirical investigation is the only reliable kind, since we have all witnessed the impressive results of such methods in the physical sciences. But to begin with a purely third-person empiricism leads some to restrict the domain of knowledge to what can be studied with third-person methods—"the physical." This leads in turn to an artificial bifurcation: instead of one phenomenon, whose different aspects are knowable by different methods, we end up with different "entities," the mind and the body, which then seem irreconcilable. And since only "the physical" is *really* real, the psyche must be either a metaphysical ghost, or a mere epiphenomenon devoid of any explanatory or causal relevance.

1. How Psychology Lost Its Psyche

To a great extent, this situation can be traced to a more treacherous time in academia than our own—the early 1600s, when Bruno had just been burned at the stake for his scientific heresies, Galileo was forced to recant under threat of execution, and Descartes made his resulting deal with the Devil. For we all know that in the 1600s the Pope bore the ultimate responsibility for burning philosophers and scientists at the stake, and it was with the Pope that Descartes made his deal. The deal was this: I'll see to it that the scientists (the "natural philosophers") keep their hands off everything that pertains to the non-physical realm—God, the soul, and the like—if you'll let me pursue my scientific and mathematical studies unencumbered by religious or philosophical dogmas, and if you will implicitly guarantee not to burn me at the stake. In return for that guarantee, I'll ensure that none of my findings about the physical realm will be in conflict with anything you believe about the non-physical realm. I'll keep a strict separation between the two. More than vestiges of the same agreement survive today, between medical doctors and ministers. Doctors take care of the physical body, and allow other professionals to take care of the soul, provided, that is, that the other professionals adhere to their tacit agreement to stay off the turf of the doctors.

Later, scientists became more fully aware of how much they had to thank Descartes for. With the dramatic success of empirical methods, they realized that the "physical realm" includes precisely everything that can be studied by means of those methods. And thanks to still more recent philosophers, happy to be supported in their role of "handmaid to the sciences" (Danto 1968), empiricist criteria were developed for meaning itself (Ayer 1946; Hempel 1965). That which cannot be studied empirically, by means of repeatable, operationalizable, quantifiable, third-person data, is not only beyond the scope of and irrelevant to scientific knowledge, but in fact is "literally meaningless" (Ayer 1946).

Thus, for all practical purposes, only the physical is real, and only third-person methods can study it, because the physical is *defined* as whatever third-person methods can study. At the same time, scientists can hold out some vague hope that their own immortal souls are safe from the existential problems of finitude, since the division of labor prevents them from having to think too much about such issues.

By contrast to this Devil's pact in which everything is off limits except for the empirical, many thinkers since the time of Aristotle and earlier have recognized not one, but three general ways of knowing: subjective reflection or introspection; empirical observation; and logical inference and conceptualization (Giorgi 1971). The goal was to create the most *coherent* possible worldview, *reconciling* the demands of all three methods. It was also recognized that the subjective is the primary of these three, that empirical observation *is,* in large part, a subjective experience; observation entails an experience of sensory input on the part of an observer—a subject, hence subjective. The empirical always begins with this subjective component, which we then try to make more reliable through hypothetico-deductive reasoning, careful scientific controls, and rigorous logical reasoning (Husserl 1913). The twentieth century, however, has linked empirical methods with the physical, which in turn is defined as the real, so that the results of phenomenological reflection seem correspondingly unreal (Churchland 1989).

The problem here is similar to the problem encountered by Medieval "causal theories of perception." During that period, theorists like Aquinas explained perception as a causal chain leading from the perceived physical object, through the eye, to various brain circuits, finally resulting in the creation of a "phantasm" in the brain. The "phantasm" was thought of as a little picture of the object in the head, and this was supposed to account for our *consciousness* of the perceived object (Sellars 1978). But of course a picture *per se* is not conscious. If someone were to implant your favorite painting in your head, what is there about its being *located in your head* that would make the painting have more *consciousness* than it would have if it were, say, hanging in your attic?

This led to the first fully articulated "homunculus" problem: there needed to be a little person inside the head who looks at the little picture inside the head, and the same question arose as to how the picture of the picture, inside the head of the little person inside the head, became a perceptual *consciousness* of the picture, resulting in a still smaller homunculus inside the head of the original homunculus. As we suggested earlier about passive-receiving models in general, this use of the "phantasm"—the tiny, isomorphically-encoded replication of the external object—to explain consciousness leads to an infinite regress of homunculus-within-homunculus-within-homunculus.

Since that time, neuroscience has made great strides. In the Medieval brain, perceptual data were thought to be processed in the front of the brain, projecting the phantasm so that the homunculus in the back of the brain could be conscious of it. Contemporary neuroscientists are well aware, of course, that the situation is just the reverse: The perceptual data are processed in the *back* of the brain, in the occipital lobe (for visual data), and projected onto a phantasm in the parietal lobe, resulting in a conscious registering of it by the homunculus, which we now know resides in the frontal and parietal lobes—not, as the unsophisticated Medievals thought, in the *back* of the brain, and not, as Descartes thought, in the pineal gland.

But of course we are attempting to be facetious here. Regardless of whether the homunculus resides in the front of the brain or the back, the problem remains that empirical ways of knowing alone are inadequate to explain how a physical picture of the object, even if embedded in the brain, becomes a *consciousness* of the object. If only the physical can be seen through third-person knowing, then no matter how efficiently we explain the physical, what Chalmers (1995) calls the "hard problem of consciousness" still has not been addressed: What explains *how it is* that some physical mechanisms are accompanied by consciousness, whereas others are not? No set of empirical observations by themselves can answer this question, because empirical observations alone can explain only the physical mechanisms themselves, not how it is that they are conscious, let alone help us understand what the conscious processes feel like and how to deal with them if we are the ones to feel them.

We shall argue, however, that a combination of empirical and phenomenological investigation *can* show how a physical process can achieve consciousness. The key is to understand what some physical systems have that is missing in mere information processing machines: the ability to act as opposed to only reacting, which is a property of certain types of complex self-organizing systems discussed in this book.

Why does it matter whether we can understand conscious processes on their own terms, rather than only understanding their physical mechanisms? Of course, if someone complains of a severe pain, we can understand the experience in physical terms and provide medical relief; but the reason we have some idea what the painful condition must "be like" for the patient is that we compare it to our own previous *subjective* experiences of pain. So to understand the full nature of the state of consciousness, and what we should do about it, we need some sort of first-person perspective.

It makes a difference whether pain is conscious or not. Unconscious pain exists, of course, and has real behavioral consequences; but doctors also understand that it is humane to use anaesthetics to prevent pain from being conscious, even in cases where unconscious pain may still be present. Moreover, a pain, especially if it is emotional pain, may often be present because it is telling us something about the *meaning* of our experiences, and to warn us to take certain actions so that we can live better—perhaps even to help us learn what it *means* to live better. If we confine ourselves purely to third-person epistemology, we risk missing out on this kind of understanding of the intentional meaning of conscious processes.

But to reconcile empirical with phenomenological descriptions in psychology requires an *ontological* picture that can square consciousness with the physical without eliminating the very subjectivity that defines it. The twentieth century failed to do this because, like the Medieval theory of the phantasm, it attempted to construe consciousness as a "response" to "stimuli," or in some other way as the final step in a causal chain, which itself has no causal power. That is, we tried to model consciousness after inorganic cause and effect mechanisms, in which the efficient cause is a combination of the stimulus with discrete chemical reactions in the nervous system, as in Freud's famous electric eels. By understanding how an electrical impulse in a dead eel's nervous system could make the eel twitch, Freud hoped to explain everything about the nervous system in terms of electro-chemical reactions. We have now gone a long way in that direction. But ultimately, this model failed to distinguish between conscious and nonconscious information processing, leading to eliminative materialism (Churchland 1989).

To fit consciousness into the picture, we must not only get beyond the empiricist criteria for meaning; we must also get beyond the contemporary version of the Medieval causal theory of the "phantasm"— the stimulus-response and information-processing paradigms. Rather than thinking of consciousness as the final effect in a causal chain leading from some physical object or collection of such, we must find another way to think of consciousness. If consciousness is not the final effect of a causal sequence, then another alternative would be to think of it as an active, self-organizing process. In other words, it may be that we can escape the problem of the homunculus if we give up Descartes's fundamental notion that nothing in nature does anything unless pushed or pulled by some other physical mechanism. That seems to require a big leap, but it is one that we think contemporary self-organization theory can allow.

In the case of perception, for example, suppose the actions needed for consciousness are *prior to* rather than subsequent to the corresponding impressions of our senses. For instance, suppose consciousness of inputs is associated with the *anticipation* rather than the *receiving* of these inputs—and suppose sensations must be created by conscious or preconscious processes (processes that contain many of the crucial ingredients of consciousness) rather than the other way around, because we begin by imagining how we might act on anticipated possible inputs in order to gear up our sensory systems for registering them and paying attention to them. Then we would not need the homunculus to see the phantasm. Consciousness could be a special type of physical activity of the organism, but not one whose understanding can be exhausted by explanations of the disparate causal mechanisms that serve as its micro-level substrates. For example, if we destroy neural connectivities in the brain, the organism tends to find ways to construct alternative connections that can get essentially the same job done, as in stroke recovery, or as when an out-of-practice musician begins to practice again. This would distinguish conscious activity from a mere causal consequence of an input, and thus could get us away from the perception-then-phantasm paradigm.

If organisms are self-organizing in a motivated way, then they will *seek out* rather than passively receive information, and consciousness will be comprehensible as the result of the organism's knowing how to seek out and act upon elements of its environment rather than only react to it with transformed isomorphic neural patterns. Naturally, sensory input is important to the process as well, but its role is much smaller than is usually assumed. We intend to show in later chapters that consciousness is much more associated with the preliminary gearing up to seek out environmental action affordances than it is with the subsequent receiving of inputs.

This view might also entail a different understanding of "the physical," more resembling Whitehead's than Descartes's—one in which patterns of activity can appropriate and replace their own needed physical substrates rather than being mechanically caused by those substrates—a model of the physical that, fortunately, some recent biologists and biochemists such as Monod (1971) and Kauffman (1993) are now offering us. "Dynamical systems," as they are called, are modeled more after biology than inorganic mechanical functions. What is different about biological systems is that they are self-organizing—they actively appropriate and replace the physical components needed to maintain the continuity of the overall process or pattern of activity. If the pattern is not well subserved by one physical cause and effect mechanism, the organism finds another one that will work better.

Why does this fit consciousness into the picture better than a mechanical, inorganic model? Because self-organization allows a *purpose-directed* element into the picture, without contradicting normal physical and chemical principles. And this in turn allows the organism's activities to be directed toward purposes that are *emotionally* important for the organism's total functioning. This introduction of the affective, emotional, and motivational dimension into all conscious functions (by learning how emotion directs the active functioning of the perceptual and information processing systems) would allow us to distinguish between conscious and nonconscious information processing (Ellis and Newton 1998a). The organism must motivatedly "look for" X, or something related to X, if it is to *consciously* see X (as opposed to nonconsciously registering the information), and this "looking for" in itself can generate conscious imagery with or without any proximal perceptual input (Damasio 1994; Posner and Rothbart 1992). Thus all consciousness requires a motivational and affective activity of the organism (Bernstein et al. 2000; Ellis and Newton 2000).

This philosophical point correlates with the *empirical* fact that, without emotional brain areas such as amygdala and anterior cingulate directing attention and corticothalamic loops, no amount of *afferent* brain activity can result in consciousness (Aurell 1984; Mack and Rock 1998; see also Ellis and Newton 1998b). Afferent signals are signals that flow inward from the periphery to the central nervous system; and within the central nervous system, we can also speak of "afferent" pathways that continue spreading the activation in a subsequent processing stream. For example, when perceptual input affects the optic nerve, it is then transmitted to the thalamus and the occipital lobe, where it is fed forward through several layers of perceptual cortex that further organize it into information about the lines, angles, and colors that the input represents. (More on the details of afferent processes within the brain later.) It is now clear that these afferent signals alone cannot generate consciousness, no matter how complicated their transmission becomes. What is needed, in addition, is that the organism sends *efferent* signals, initiating actions toward its environment. These signals produce action imagery, which can then serve as a foundation for the organism's understanding the action affordances of its environment. This action imagery can occur even if the efferent action commands are inhibited by means of frontal brain processes.

If consciousness is a type of activity requiring motivation, and if it is an activity of the whole organism and must be actively executed in order to become a phenomenal experience, then introspective or phenomenological information would again have a role in psychology, integrated rather than competing with physical/empirical information. When we direct attention to our *own* experience, we have access to it in a way that no empirical observer can have, because our "view" is from a unique perspective—that of the one who is *executing* the self-organizing motivational processes required for any subjectivity (a distinction already suggested in Newton 1996). This special access not only gives direct insight into the felt nature of consciousness, but can even enable us to understand our own emotions more immediately and vividly than any outside observer could do. How this special access occurs will be explained in detail in later chapters, especially Chapter Eight.

As a preliminary example, suppose we initially think that we are angry with someone for insulting us. We can, as Gendlin (1962/1997) has suggested, refer directly to a bodily felt sense of the situation and realize that the insulting person's behavior is only a *trigger* for feelings about many other things. We then can imagine how our total organism would feel different if those other issues were resolved, and thus determine whether those issues could be interpreted in a way more resembling what the feeling is *really* about (Gendlin 1962/1997, 1992). To a person with access *only* to empirical observation (and not also with *subjective* access to past experiences with which the empirical observations can be correlated), this holistic perspective on the organism's active self-organizing emotional directedness might be overlooked, because feeling an emotion requires executing a bodily activity ourselves, not simply observing it from the outside. The pure empiricist's tendency is to see the triggering event (for example, the insulting person's behavior) as the cause and the intentional object of the emotional "response" (as in LeDoux 1996). It is a short step from this notion of emotion as a passive response, to a view of its intentional meaning that is overly narrow and thus misleading, because it fails to correlate experience with the full range of complex external events that the emotion is "about" (see Ellis 1986, 2005).

The fact that phenomenological reflection can yield such information directly, with all the associated phenomenal features, is by no means inconsistent with empirical methods. A coherent theory of consciousness consistent with all the relevant empirical facts, including those that support a theory of self-organization, *entails* that there should be such information that is not available from an external observer's standpoint.

The overall empirical story requires that one must be able to *execute* the holistic organismic motivations that create a state of consciousness in order to know that state subjectively. We therefore need a coherent psychology that integrates the empirical and phenomenological ways of knowing rather than setting them at odds against each other in an "us versus them" competition within the discipline.

Descartes's dualism was not only a political deal to keep off the turf of the theologians and priests. It was also motivated by the sheer fact that consciousness *is,* after all, a very mysterious phenomenon. The paradoxical and ineffable features of consciousness probably played a major role in getting Descartes to genuinely believe that consciousness could not be physical. We must therefore turn now to one of the most crucial parts of our overall argument. If we can break down the mystery of consciousness into a series of component paradoxes, we can then get an idea how to resolve each of those paradoxes in a way that doesn't exacerbate the others, as has happened throughout history. The remainder of the book will then attempt to resolve just that dilemma.

2. Why Is Consciousness So Intractable?

Alan Watts (1966) observed that most philosophers can be divided into two categories: "gooey" and "prickly." The gooey philosophers entertain thoughts of deep existential and emotional significance, and are willing to respect intuitively appealing, subjectivistic accounts of experience. The prickly philosophers insist on rigorous logical proof or strict empirical verification based on an exact application of scrupulous scientific methods such as the hypothetico-deductive method.

Consciousness is a paradigm example of a problem that exacerbates this division. The conscious mind is both difficult to incorporate into an image of the physical world viewed scientifically, and also difficult to define in a way that captures its phenomenal feel as well as its causal properties. As a result, most theories narrow their focus either to the phenomenal feel or to the causal properties.

Theories that focus on the phenomenal feel tend to be phenomenological, and encounter great difficulty explaining why brain events correlate so systematically with the conscious ones. The ways we experience free will, time, the power of the mind over the body, the apparent objectivity of primary and secondary properties of objects, and many other such phenomenological data are difficult to reconcile with scientific accounts of how the brain and nervous system work.

On the other hand, theories that focus on these latter problems do not explain how it is that the physical world can give rise to such a mysterious phenomenon as consciousness. No amount of causal explanation, as Chalmers (1995) points out, can ever completely explain consciousness, because we can still ask why the physical workings of the brain (including its information-processing outcomes) have the property of consciousness, rather than just another physical event in a chain of physical causes. Physical causes can explain only physical effects. This is the essential reason for Chalmers's "hard problem" of consciousness.

The same problem extends to the attempt to *define* consciousness. In order to study something scientifically, we have to define it "operationally," and this means that we have to define it in such a way that we can objectively *observe and measure* it. But to define consciousness in this way is already to make it into a third-person, physical, and empirically observable phenomenon, which means that the phenomenal feel aspect has been excluded. But it is the phenomenal feel aspect that constitutes the most interesting and difficult part of the problem. To leave out this aspect is to confine oneself to the "easy problems" of consciousness, and ignore the hard one.

On the other hand, if we give a first-person account of consciousness, we run into a seemingly insurmountable difficulty. If we carefully describe the subjective elements of consciousness—the emotional, imagistic, and logical aspects of "what it's like" to think and be aware—then the danger is that we cannot equate any of these first-person descriptions with particular physical correlates. For example, we must not simplistically reduce images to brain events that process and retain information, because then we cannot explain why these same brain events could not occur *without* conscious imagery, why they are not merely a neural pattern physically isomorphic to that which is imaged. The problem here is that a neural representation is not necessarily the same thing as an experienced image. A tiny photograph of a family member, implanted in the brain, would not be expected to give us a conscious image of that person.

Analytic philosophers have tried to equate "representations" with brain processes that are *isomorphic to* the imaged events that they represent. A photograph is a representation in this sense, yet presumably lacks consciousness. So by explaining how an isomorphic "representation" can occur in the brain is not the same thing as explaining how there can be "representation" in the sense of a consciously experienced mental image.

Here again, we have confronted only the easy problem of representation, not the hard one. We have explained how the brain can make an isomorphic replica, but not how it can be conscious of that replica. If we pretend that the solution to the easy problem already *is* a solution to the hard one, then we have equivocated the term "representation," so that by explaining representation in one sense (the sense defined in third-person terms), we can pretend that we have also explained it in its other sense (the sense defined in terms of first-person phenomenological experience). In other words, we have begged the question. The real problem is to understand why the representations in our brains can also have the additional property of being "like something" for a subject.

Our approach to this problem is to begin by looking at the particular first-person properties of consciousness that make it mysterious or ineffable. We take those properties to be the important ones for purposes of solving the mind-body problem because, by definition, they are the most difficult to incorporate into physical explanations. We can then trace each of these mysterious properties of consciousness to a particular aspect of the mind-body problem. Finally, we plan to show that the action-centered, self-organizational account is the most coherent theory capable of linking the phenomenological and physiological elements of each problem in a way that does not beg the question or equivocate terms like "representation," "image," "thinking," "wanting" or "feeling," as seems so widely unavoidable for previous theories.

Let's begin by considering the main aspects of phenomenal consciousness that make its subjective dimension so mysterious:

1. Consciousness seems *teleological*—oriented toward goals and purposes—but in the physical universe, we have been taught that goals and purposes are only illusions created by cause-and-effect mechanisms, such as natural selection. At bottom, reality is a series of purposeless events, which only appear purposeful from the human point of view. But this is mysterious precisely because we *experience* the purposefulness of our own activities.

    This mysterious "purposeful" property of consciousness gives rise to two philosophical problems: How can there be such a thing as purpose in the natural universe? And what is the purpose of consciousness itself? That is, if unconscious computations could solve the same problems for an organism as conscious ones, then what purpose did it serve for nature to make them *conscious* in some organisms?

2. The conscious experience of *representation* is mysterious and even paradoxical, as we have already hinted. Representations of objects seem to exist "in our minds," yet the object in our mind is often represented to us as if it were "out there in the world," even when it is the mental image of something not present in perception. Many cognitive theorists now say that, since analytic philosophers have failed to define the third-person concept of representation in an adequate way, we should abandon it altogether. The definitions have failed, they say, because it is always possible that a brain event isomorphic to some worldly event could be *caused by* the worldly event, yet not be a representation in any non-trivially "mental" sense.

But our subjective consciousness still does present us with representations, and this experience is not merely an artifact of philosophical confusion. People who have never heard of philosophy experience representations—mental images of states of affairs that are not currently occurring. Even the phantom limb illusion of the amputee is a representation of a non-existent state of affairs. So this subjective experience of representation remains a mysterious fundamental property of consciousness, and cannot be explained away as the result of reading too many modern philosophy books or textbooks on the science of vision. And this means that there is still a real philosophical problem of explaining how mental representations can occur, as opposed to merely physical representations like photographs.

3. Consciousness seems to present itself as if it were *non-physical*, since it is subjective rather than objective. That is, since we cannot *directly* observe another person's consciousness, yet physical things normally *are* objectively observable, there is a mystery as to what kind of thing it could be that is objectively non-observable. It is true that we can speculate as to what others' consciousness might be like, and make some educated guesses based on our own past experience. But it appears that we cannot directly observe what consciousness "is like" in the way that we observe physical phenomena. The more we think about it, the more we realize that a subjective event *in principle* is not objectively observable in the way that physical ones are.

To be sure, if we already assume that certain behaviors are signs of consciousness in an organism, then we can infer that cats and dogs, for example, are conscious. But their consciousness itself does not seem to be an observable feature by means of empirical knowledge alone: we must first know what consciousness is like *subjectively*, from *our own* point of view, before we can attribute consciousness to another being. This knowledge, in turn, is not based on empirical observation, but rather on subjective experience. So the paradox is that consciousness itself does not appear to us through objective observation, as do most physical phenomena, but only through subjective experience. And this in turn makes consciousness *seem* like an ethereal, invisible kind of being—again, very unlike most physical phenomena.

Does this mean that consciousness is non-physical? The problem with that view is not merely that science in principle does not leave room for non-physical events. The problem is that we *already know* enough about the brain to know that conscious events depend on brain events. Brain lesions result in changes in the patterns of the person's consciousness. Even military physicians in the earliest times could easily observe that head injuries lead to specific mental and emotional impairments. No great neurological sophistication was needed to make these observations.

So we seem stuck: neither a physical nor a non-physical explanation will do. Consciousness cannot be non-physical, yet if it were physical, then it should be empirically observable.

Correlatively, we are stuck with two intractable philosophical problems.

(i) The "problem of other minds" arises from the question: How can we understand what it is like to be another person if we cannot base such an understanding on empirical observation?

(ii) A related but even more difficult problem is posed by the "knowledge argument," as Jackson (1986) has called it. That is, if consciousness were equivalent with any collection of brain events, then complete knowledge of the brain should be tantamount to complete knowledge of what the corresponding subjective consciousness "is like." Yet it seems obvious that no amount of knowledge of another's brain, all by itself and without being supplemented by knowledge that is subjective in nature (such as what it's like to see in color, or be angry) *could possibly* reveal what the other's consciousness is like.

4. Another perplexing aspect of consciousness, interrelated with all three of the foregoing ones, is that consciousness seems as if it could be *"epiphenomenal."* That is, if consciousness itself cannot

be *a priori* equated with physical brain events, for the reasons just mentioned in item 3, then it seems imaginable that all the physical events *could* conceivably occur just the way they do *without* being accompanied by any consciousness. It has often been argued (for example, Chalmers 1995) that, if it is even conceivable that X could occur without Y and vice versa, then X and Y cannot be literally equivalent with each other. But, says Chalmers, it *is* at least *conceivable* that the brain could function in the ways it does without consciousness. As Levine (1986) argues, the fact that we are conscious is not logically deducible from the fact that we have such-and-such brain functions. If consciousness were strictly equivalent with any physical brain process, then it ought to be strictly *logically deducible* from it. And we cannot deduce from any purely physical description that the thing described must be conscious. There is an "explanatory gap" here, making it seem that consciousness is something extra, beyond the physical description. Consciousness thus seems like a "ghostly" extra layer of reality superimposed onto the physical layer. Moreover, since all causation is physical, this also makes it seem that consciousness can have no real *causal* power, and that the experience that our minds can move our bodies is merely an illusion, as Dennett (2003) and Wegner (2003) have specifically argued.

This apparent "epiphenomenality" of experienced consciousness gives rise to two other philosophical problems:

(i) What is the *causal role* of consciousness, and indeed how can consciousness even have *any* causal role? Philosophers have puzzled over this "problem of mental causation" at least since the time of Descartes.

(ii) If consciousness could be a mere epiphenomenon, and not part of the physical scheme of causes and effects, it would then seem that we can imagine *"zombies"*—creatures that process information and behave in just the way we do, but lack consciousness. If we can imagine such creatures, says Chalmers (1995), then they must be logically possible. But if it is possible that there could be creatures that are just like us physically, but lacking in consciousness, then again it seems that consciousness cannot *possibly* be physical. Yet we do observe, here again, that consciousness depends on brain functioning, which is physical. So again, the notion that consciousness could possibly be epiphenomenal (lacking in causal power and thus non-physical) seems not to fit this fact of observed interrelation with the physical realm. How can something that is not physical interrelate with the physical? Physics says that an object with a mass of zero can cause zero motion. This problem, in various forms, is also as old as Descartes.

In sum, all these problems—the explanatory gap, the problem of the causal power of consciousness, and the zombie problem—stem ultimately from the apparent epiphenomenality of consciousness, the subjective impression that consciousness is a causal spinoff of its physical underpinning and thus gives the impression of being an extra type of entity beyond the physical.

5. The subjective experience of *time and space* also seems out of kilter with our knowledge of objective time and space in several ways. In objective time, it is believed that time is a mathematically describable dimension, not necessarily homogeneous (as Poincaré and Einstein point out), but at least divisible into infinitesimal, non-overlapping points. Yet in experienced *subjective* time, each "now" seems to be a *segment* rather than a point, and thus seems to include a slight bit of the past and the future—not in the way that we remember things that are in the past or anticipate the future, but as if they were actually part of the present experience. When we hear a musical tone, the fact that the tone has duration seems to be part of our immediate present experience, not a unity that we *construct* by combining a remembered, just-past sound with a sound that we now experience as if in an infinitesimal point in time. James called this mysterious facet of time-experience the "specious present," and Husserl describes it well in his *Phenomenology of Internal Time-consciousness*. It seems that if consciousness is an event that takes time to occur, then no experience of an exact present moment should even be possible, yet we experience time as if it were divided into present moments, and as if we were temporally "located" at such a "now," with the past only in memory and the future only in vague anticipations of various future possibilities.

The Changizi (2008) experiment mentioned earlier illustrates this strange aspect of phenomenal time. Recall that when a light was flashed along the trajectory of a moving object, the subjects saw the object as being slightly *ahead* of the light, rather than at the exact same location as the light (which was its actual location). In a sense, the subjects were experiencing a tiny slice of the *future* (in which the object was anticipated to be next) *as if* it were part of the present.

Consciousness is similarly mysterious with regard to *space*. Anything that is spatially located should be objectively observable, but as noted earlier, consciousness is not objectively observable, and this would seem to imply that it is not localizable. Yet we experience ourselves as the locus of our consciousness, and we feel as if we see the world from a spatial point of view, located in a particular place. The world seems "out there" compared with where our consciousness is located, "in here." Yet the properties that our minds create, such as color and the pitch and timbre of sounds—which scientists have long known to be constructions of the mind, not objective properties of objects independent of the mind—seem in our experience to be "out there" at the surface of the object or filling objective space. So there seems to be a paradoxical confusion between what is going on "out there" and what is going on "in here," and this confusion seems inseparable from our everyday experience. Moreover, it is difficult to see how consciousness itself can even be the *kind* of thing in principle that can occupy a particular physical location since, as we have seen, it is difficult to exhaust the complete qualitative feel of consciousness by equating it with a physical, empirically observable object. The paradoxical nature of space seems analogous to the paradoxical nature of time when it comes to their relation to *experienced* temporality and spatiality.

Both these problems together give rise to the problem of *"indexicals"* in philosophy. Suppose we could give a completely adequate description of the physical universe. There is apparently nothing about this description that would locate "me" here in *this* person's consciousness, rather than there in *that* person's consciousness. That is, the universe would still be exactly the same objectively if I were occupying George Bush's consciousness or Bill Clinton's consciousness. The physical description would be exactly the same in either case. So it would appear that no physical description can capture the fact that I am this person rather than that other person, having this point of view in time and space rather than some other point of view. That is why Woody Allen's famous quip, "My only regret is that I'm not someone else," seems to have meaning. How would the physical universe be any different if Woody were Bill Clinton and Bill Clinton were him? And yet it *seems* that it would make a great deal of difference in some indefinable way. It seems important that I am *this* person rather than *that* one.

We have listed five mysterious features of consciousness that give rise to serious philosophical problems about consciousness and the mind-body relation.

1. *Teleology* (in an apparently non-teleological physical universe)
2. *Representation* (unaccountable for in objective terms, and entailing a mysterious contradiction between "in-hereness" and "out-thereness")
3. *Apparent non-physicality* (due to empirical unobservability, leading to the "knowledge argument")
4. *Apparent epiphenomenality* (leading to the problem of mental causation and the "zombie" problem)
5. *Spatiotemporal paradoxes* (problems of the "specious present" and the apparent localizability/non-localizability of consciousness, as well as the "problem of indexicals," and involving their own special "in here"/"out there" contradictions)

These five philosophical problems need to be bridged in order to satisfy the epistemological demands of both phenomenology and empiricism—to reconcile Watts' "gooey" and "prickly" philosophers.

In this preliminary preview, it is easiest to see how to unravel the problems in reverse order. The paradox of *temporality* (part of problem 5), is resolved when we see why consciousness seems both to *precede* the impact of an object on our senses ("looking for," anticipatory paying of attention) and yet to *follow from* their impact ("looking at," receiving information). Similarly, the paradox of *spatiality* (also part of problem 5) is resolved when we see why objects of consciousness appear both "out there" and "in here," due to our having to act on them (with the action originating "in here"). Resolving these paradoxes of temporality and spatiality leads to a resolution of a third paradox—that of *causality* (discussed in problem 4 above): we seem to cause our own experience of the world, yet the world seems to cause our experience of it. These paradoxes of temporality, spatiality and causality are the three overarching paradoxes emphasized by Kant in the *Critique of Pure Reason*, and we devote a separate chapter (Chapter 6) to resolving them.

Once these paradoxes are fully resolved, then problems 1, 2, and 3 above can be tackled. That is, the *teleology* of consciousness (problem 1) is explained by its essentially active as opposed to reactive character, which can be accounted for in terms of self-organizing systems. The problem of *representation* (problem 2) is resolved when we take account of the role of action imagery in representation. And the *seeming incompatibility of consciousness with physicalism* (problem 3) is accounted for by its dynamical character. The overall process is not simply reducible to the activities of its components, yet it is still a physical process. We shall devote a special chapter (Chapter 5) to explaining the causal structure of self-organizing processes, which in our view allows them to act rather than merely to react in complicated ways.

This entire unraveling process depends on two main elements. The first element, as already mentioned, is to use the idea of self-organization to ground a distinction between mere reaction on the one hand, and on the other hand action in a non-trivial sense. This concept of action can then be used to elaborate an action-based theory of consciousness, in which the difference between conscious and non-conscious information processing hinges on the distinction between acting *upon* the environment, and merely receiving signals *from* it.

The second element of our solution, discussed in the next section, is what we call the "Clark Kent-Superman principle." Essentially, the point of this principle is to be cautious in reaching ontological conclusions from epistemological assumptions. For example, we may believe that, since we can imagine consciousness without a body, this means that consciousness cannot be equivalent with any bodily process. But this would be like saying that we can imagine Kent as not being Superman, thus Kent cannot be the same entity as Superman.

We have already hinted at the advantages of an action-based approach for solving many of the most perplexing mind-body problems. For example, the apparent conflict between physicalism and the non-observability of another's consciousness from an empirical standpoint becomes much less paradoxical when we realize that to experience a conscious state is to *enact* something rather than to *receive some information*. Obviously, only the subject of any experience can *enact* that experience, so in order to directly "observe" this person's consciousness, we would have to literally be in the place where the person is, and in fact would have to *be* that person, in order to *enact* the person's conscious states so as to know what they are like. In the remainder of the book, we plan to show how an emotionally motivated self-organizational system can provide coherent resolutions to all the other problems we have just discussed.

3. The Clark Kent–Superman Principle

In addition to working out a coherent action-centered theory of consciousness, a second element of our solution is what we call the "Clark Kent-Superman principle." The point of this principle is to avoid confusing epistemological problems with ontological ones. Someone might say, for example, that we can imagine Clark Kent as *not* being Superman. And this means (they might argue) that a complete physical explanation of Kent would not prove that he is Superman. But if the physical explanation of Kent does not prove that he is Superman, then whatever properties do make him Superman must be non-physical properties. Such an argument would confuse epistemology with ontology— it would confuse our knowledge as to whether Kent is Superman with the actual reality as to whether he is Superman. The premise that we can "imagine Kent as not being Superman" is ambiguous: if we imagine *everything* about Kent, this includes imagining the fact that he is Superman.

In our view, the famous "zombie argument" makes this very mistake. It argues that we can imagine beings with physical properties just like ours, but lacking in consciousness. This is similar to claiming that we could imagine Clark Kent as not being Superman, and that therefore Kent cannot actually *be* equivalent to Superman.

Suppose the reality is that Kent *is* Superman. Then the fact that our knowledge of Kent allows us to imagine him as not being Superman does not refute the fact that he is Superman. It only means that our knowledge of Kent is limited. On the other hand, suppose the reality is that Kent is *not* Superman. Then no amount of knowledge about Kent would tell us everything we need to know about Superman. The important thing to notice is that our incomplete knowledge about Kent will not yield complete knowledge about Superman in either case. So we cannot settle the question as to whether Kent is Superman by checking to see whether our knowledge of Kent yields complete knowledge of Superman. *Our knowledge of Kent is limited to begin with,* and may not include just those facts about him that entail that he is equivalent with Superman. That is, we cannot reach ontological conclusions based on mere epistemology.

Similarly, Chalmers argues that we can imagine "zombies" exactly identical to ourselves in all their physical properties, but without consciousness, and he therefore thinks that whatever makes us conscious must not be physical. That is, whatever makes us conscious must be something the zombies lack; and since the zombies have all of our *physical* properties, then the extra ingredient they would need in order to be conscious must be non-physical.

But by arguing in this way, Chalmers is already tacitly assuming that consciousness is *not* physical. That is, if consciousness *were* physical, then it would be impossible to imagine beings with our exact physical makeup without imagining them as being conscious. To claim that we can imagine this is similar to claiming that we can imagine Clark Kent as not being Superman. Of course, if our knowledge of Kent is limited, we may *believe* that we can imagine all of his properties without imagining Superman. But this belief will be false, because we have assumed that the set of all the properties of Kent does not include the set of all the properties of Superman. In other words, we have already assumed *a priori* that "Kent" is not equivalent with "Superman," in order to imagine ourselves imagining all of Kent's properties without imagining Superman.

For the same reasons, the Clark Kent–Superman principle also applies to the "knowledge argument." Someone might argue that Kent cannot be Superman simply because, if the two were identical, then complete *knowledge* of Kent should yield complete knowledge of Superman. But even the most complete knowledge of Kent as such does not reveal whether he is Superman; therefore Kent cannot be equivalent to Superman. This would be analogous to Jackson's "knowledge argument" which we discussed earlier—the argument that Mary cannot know "what it's like" to experience her subject's consciousness even if she has complete knowledge of all its physical correlates. But here again, if Kent *is* Superman (or analogously, if Mary's subject's brain functioning *is* the subject's consciousness), then knowing *everything* about Kent (or about the subject's brain) *will* entail knowledge of Superman (or the subject's consciousness). The problem is that *empirical* knowledge does not tell us everything there is to know about Kent: it does not tell us "what it is like" to be Kent. There are different ways of knowing. So when we are careful not to confuse epistemology with ontology—and thus not to confuse ontological categories like "physical" with epistemological categories like "empirically observable from an objective and external point of view," then the "knowledge argument" is also transformed into a more manageable one. The problem becomes a matter of understanding why empirical knowledge about someone does not add up to knowing "what it's like" to be the person. As we have hinted, the action theory of consciousness can address this problem in a manageable way, because there is no supposition that complete empirical knowledge of a person would enable us literally to perform that person's actions. And to know what a subject's consciousness is like would require *performing* the actions that, according to our theory, are equivalent to the person's consciousness.

Also, the Clark Kent–Superman principle highlights a general problem for any attempt to argue from imaginability to possibility. For example, suppose someone argues that we can imagine the functioning body without consciousness or vice versa, so therefore none of the body's functions can be equivalent with consciousness. The problem is that we may not be in a position to know what it is that we have imagined. How would one "imagine a being with our exact physical make-up"? Is every neuron and every synapse to be visually imaged at the same time? That would be beyond human capacity. If it is argued, on the other hand, that the imaginer need not imagine every molecule of someone's physical make-up, but instead needs only a generic image in very broad strokes, then to claim on this basis that the physical makeup could exist without consciousness indeed begs the question. It would be like claiming that imagining a few general facts about Superman does not entail that he is identical with Clark Kent. But here again, if we were to form an image of *all* the facts about Superman, some of these facts *would* entail that he is Kent. Similarly, to know that the physical properties of beings like us can exist *without consciousness* would require *ruling out* all the combinations or interactions of neural events that could possibly entail consciousness; this in turn would require the superhuman imaginative powers described above. And if it could be done, then whether the result would show that we can imagine all these physical facts in the absence of consciousness just depends on whether some of the physical facts *are* equivalent with consciousness or not.

There is still another difficulty for this kind of "imaginability" argument. As the subject and agent of my own actions, I have certain phenomenal experiences. It is quite possible that in order to have these experiences, I must be experiencing at least some of the mechanisms producing the experience *with a different vantagepoint* and therefore *with different phenomenal properties* from those that would be available to any objective (external) observer. For example, conscious perceptual experience seems to involve the illusion that external objects are being directly experienced as unities of all their properties—that red is simply pasted to the surface of objects rather than created by a complicated series of processes in the nervous system. We know that distinct brain areas process distinct aspects of perceived objects, unifying these only after much initial processing. But in order to imagine what the subjective experience is normally like, we need to ignore or forget this complicated series of processing steps in order to experience the object as intrinsically unified, and as perceived directly with no intervening steps. In ordinary experience, objects are perceived this way, and we have no idea of how it might alter the experience if having the experience required imagining all those intervening steps. It is as if we were to try to imagine how it might alter the phenomenal feel of an emotionally moving movie to watch it on a screen that shows us the whole studio, with the technicians and all the machinery taking up most of the visual field, and the actors only a small part of it.

The main reason for all these difficulties, in our view, is that to know "what it's like" to be person X requires that one *execute the actions* that constitute the subjective consciousness that X experiences; and it is not possible to execute X's actions unless one is in the place where X is, occupying X's body, and doing all the things that X is doing. Externally observing the actions is not the same as doing the actions, so it should not be surprising that observing a person's brain events does not yield knowledge of what the person's consciousness is like. It is also far from obvious that having such third-person knowledge would provide the ability to put one's own brain into the state that one knows about empirically. I can know all about many physical processes without having the ability to produce these processes intentionally in myself.

We do not want to sound overly facile in this kind of statement. The problem posed by the "knowledge argument" is still a very difficult problem, because it is still hard to see why having complete empirical knowledge should *not* enable us to at least *imagine* actually executing the other's actions, which in turn should be expected to allow us to at least *imagine* what the other's consciousness is like. To understand this situation requires a fuller picture of the way self-organizing processes work. But it cannot merely be argued *a priori* that consciousness cannot be "explained physically" due to the knowledge argument, the explanatory gap argument, or the seeming epiphenomenality of consciousness.

The truth is that there are very different meanings of the word "explanation." When Chalmers argues that consciousness cannot be "explained" physically, we can take him in several different ways. He could mean simply a *causal* explanation, and of course it is a truism that a mere causal explanation of what goes on in the brain cannot tell us whether consciousness is physical. That requires an "explanation" in a larger sense—in the sense of a theory that may be accepted or rejected based on philosophical reasoning with respect to a variety of considerations: Which theory best accounts for the problem of mental causation? Which one accounts for the knowledge argument, the explanatory gap argument, and all the other philosophical problems just listed above, better than competing theories? In our view, this requires looking at all the mysterious elements of consciousness and its correlations with the physical, and accepting the theory that most coherently accounts for *all* the facts and logical problems, all at the same time.

We shall argue that a self-organizational and action-centered approach does account for all these problems in a coherent way. Perhaps someday someone will propose a more coherent solution; if so, then it will still be true that that new, more-coherent solution is the best "explanation" of consciousness. So it would still be misleading to argue that consciousness is not "explainable" on physical grounds. That depends on what is meant by "explain." What is required for purposes of full explanation is not merely a physical description of a cause-and-effect sequence, but also a philosophical choice as to which mind-body theory is the most coherent one, all things considered. Such a coherent theory—a self-organizational, action-based theory—is what we shall attempt to elaborate, in relation to all the interrelated problems and paradoxes, in the remainder of this book.

In our discussion we must therefore also avoid two common problems. First, there is a temptation for philosophers to try to solve, by purely conceptual methods, problems that cannot be solved except through empirical investigation. The work of some contemporary phenomenologists might typify this mistake, although Merleau-Ponty (1964) warned against it:

> Husserl was, therefore, well aware of the danger of self-deception in proceeding by 'eidetic intuition' . . . I can never be sure that my vision of an essence is anything more than a prejudice rooted in language—if it does not enable me to hold together all the facts which are known and which may be brought into relation with it. Failing this, it may not be an essence at all but only a prejudice. (75)

Another example of this type of mistake, from traditional analytic philosophy, concerns the nature of pain, and the question of whether it is essentially unpleasant. Research into pain mechanisms in the brain is essential for sorting out the issues, and attempts to settle the question simply by trying to "imagine having a pain without minding it" can become question-begging. Once, the concept of unconscious pain seemed self-contradictory; now we know, because of advances in techniques of anesthesia, that the valuational and motivating aspects of pain can exist without consciousness of the pain (Damasio 1999; Dennett

1991). A subject's hand is instinctively jerked away from a hot burner even under certain types of anaesthesias. One set of nociceptors transmits the valenced and motivating character of the pain while a separate set transmits the consciously hurting quality of it. Subjects under certain kinds of anaesthesias report that they are aware of the pain, but that it "doesn't hurt" (Newton 1989a).

A contrary but equally dangerous tendency is the temptation for non-philosophers interested in consciousness to use *only* the methods of empirical science for problems that cannot be solved except with the help of extensive conceptual analysis. An example is the claim put forth several times in the past two decades (for example, Crick and Koch 1992) that consciousness has been located in the firing of some specific neural groups, in specific patterns. But even if researchers agree that consciousness always accompanies such firing, it is not clear that they are all using the term "consciousness" in the same way. Without either a clear definition of consciousness or an unequivocal, reproducible set of empirical examples of it, empirical data are meaningless. Even if the term "consciousness" is well defined, moreover, the relation between it and the accompanying brain states needs conceptual clarification. The question as to why a particular combination of observable events is accompanied by consciousness requires a conceptual understanding not exhausted by the explanation of the component events considered separately. Thus consciousness cannot be fully explained by the purely empirical observations by themselves.

That is why the study of consciousness inevitably must be interdisciplinary. And in our view, this means also that the adequacy of a resulting theory must be tested by its coherence. Some theories may look good, if we ignore one or another of the interconnected problems, such as the problem of mental causation, the knowledge argument, or the hard problem. An adequate theory will need to draw from diverse areas of investigation, and search for a theory that is able to integrate them all with one coherent solution and without internal contradiction.

2

Action at the Macro Level: An Action-based Theory of Intentionality

The suggestion that conscious experience can be tied to self-organizing brain mechanisms is not a magical formula for resolving the problems of mind and body. Not all self-organizing systems "act" in a rich enough sense to ground consciousness and intentionality. We must examine the way the brain forms and uses action *imagery* in order to develop a coherent account of the kind of action that we humans and other higher animals can execute that makes us different from other dynamical systems. It is action at this "macro" level that will enable a shift from a perceptual model of consciousness to an action model. In this chapter, we discuss the difference, and argue for the advantages of the latter. This task will prepare us for a resolution of the mind-body problem in all its aspects, including the "explanatory gap." Such a resolution is worked out in more detail later in the book.

During the past decade, new "embodied" approaches to consciousness and intentionality have begun to replace the computational model that had been entrenched since the 1970s. So much has been written about that model and its limitations that we will not review them here except summarily. Instead, in this chapter we look, first from a distance and then up close, at the action model that is now replacing the computational one. The long view will allow a reorientation toward the organism as a whole, letting us see both cognitive and noncognitive activity as a product of enactive self-organizing mechanisms rather than as reactions to the environment. The closer view will select certain cognitive systems that are crucial for understanding conscious experience as itself an activity of organisms.

The term *embodiment* is frequently used by proponents of this new approach, and we shall do so here, speaking, for example, about *embodied cognition*. To say that cognition is embodied is to say 1. that certain types of bodily actions—purposeful motor activities—are themselves cognitive acts, or at least continuous with purely cognitive acts; and 2. that all cognitive activity, conscious and unconscious, is built on a framework of those same structures that enable the organism to act upon and interact with its environment. This means, most importantly, that the traditional distinction between pure reason on the one hand, and the emotionally motivated, physically acting body on the other, disappears. The advantages of this fact alone for understanding intelligent cognition will prove to be quite substantial.

Theories of embodied cognition are not merely theories that simply seek to extend the domain of cognition beyond the subject's body and into the environment. An example of this kind of approach can be seen in parts of Andy Clark's *Being There* (1997), in which he argues that one's knowledge should be understood to extend out into one's environment, residing in the tools and structures humans have devised to cope with the world. It is possible to hold this view—to which Clark refers as the organism's "embeddedness" in its environment—with or without a thoroughgoingly enactivist theory of consciousness and cognition. In the type of self-organizational action approach we want to develop, "embodied" cognition refers to the view that all cognition is at root derivative from self-initiated bodily action, whether in the form of overt limb movements, or in the covert activity of brain structures that underlie such movements. In his more recent work, Clark does seem to take this additional step (for example, see Clark 2002).

Many cognitive psychologists and philosophers support versions of this general theory of embodiment—Gallagher and Marcel (1999), Gallagher and Jeannerod (2002), Glenberg (1996), Humphrey (2000), Hurley (1998), Thelen et al. (2001), and Sheets-Johnstone (1998), in addition to Clark in some of his work. For some of these writers, representations of actions play a central role; others are uncomfortable with the notion of mental representation and attempt to account for cognitive activity using dynamical systems that can function without them. We hold that an explanation of consciousness entails an explicit role for mental representations. We understand the difficulties with the notion, and attempt to explain and to resolve them in this chapter.

This chapter focuses on only one aspect of the functioning of the self-organizing human organism: its conscious, intentional behavior. The other, more fundamental aspect is the unconscious self-organizing activity promoting homeostasis at all levels. Understanding this more fundamental aspect requires looking at neuroscientific accounts of motivational systems that activate the organism to seek means to correct imbalances, and thus orient it toward available environmental objects that will satisfy its need to maintain a continuing pattern of activity at a preferred level of complexity and energy. An enactive theory of embodied cognition views the organism as "acting" on many levels, some conscious and some not. The type of "action" that concerns us in this chapter is a specialized kind of action: intentional, goal-directed behavior directed toward some perceived object, which could be a part of the subject's own body. This kind of action is a further extension of the more limited sense in which organisms are "active" as opposed to merely reactive, involving the way motivating activity beginning in brain stem regions creates unconscious *readiness for* intentional action by means of neurotransmitter activation and inhibition. The more limited kind of "activity" is presupposed by the more elaborate, intentional, and goal-directed action with which we are concerned in this chapter.

1. An Outline of the Action Theory of Intentionality

The basic premise of the theory is that an organism's self-generated, purposive actions are, at the very simplest level, "proto-intentional"—that is, they already show the roots of intentionality in the traditional philosophical sense because they are "about" something: environmental action-affordances. The desire to suck, even if unconscious, intends a potentially suckable object. We want to argue that when actions in this most primitive yet non-trivial sense become *repeatable* in a controlled fashion by an organism such as a human infant, they are then intentional in the fullest traditional sense of the word. "Intentionality" is a term of art in philosophy. It refers to the ability of a thing—a mental state, a sentence in natural language—to have a meaning that points to something other than itself, or to be "about" some other thing. Intentionality is one of the properties of mentality traditionally viewed as essential and unique, and as one of the mental properties most in need of philosophical explanation.

A second thesis we hope to establish is that activated representations of these planned action sequences ("motor images" as Jeannerod calls them), along with imagery of the full range of sensorimotor, proprioceptive, and emotional experience normally accompanying them, are the scaffolding that supports all cognition, both conscious and unconscious. The result can be called a theory of "embodied cognition." The most vivid contrast between this theory and traditional ones that focus on "reason" as a distinct and separate human ability is that there is no such clean break: "reasoning" is completely continuous with other kinds of bodily activity. It is important here to emphasize that we are referring to motor and other image schemata as "representations" *only* when activated for purposes of action planning and execution in a particular context. When dormant, memory traces of such sequences are potential representations, but since they are available for use in a variety of different contexts and for different purposes, they cannot be said actually to "represent" anything when the context and purpose are undetermined. They do not, for example, automatically represent the inputs that *cause* them. This issue will be discussed in more detail later in this chapter.

If we wish to allow for the possibility of non-conscious mental processes, an action model must show that not only *consciousness*, but also *intentionality in general* (even when it occurs on an unconscious or preconscious basis) must be grounded in planned action sequences. Action sequences, as distinct from reflexive motor movements, have goals that involve some aspect of the environment. We can say that in performing a planned action whose goal shapes the action, the agent *understands* the action (see Newton 1996). This sense of understanding could also be called "proto-intentionality"; it may not be fully conscious and it may be preconceptual, but it contains the essential building blocks for more sophisticated and complex cognitive states. There is a recognized object, there is a goal (for example, grasping the object), and there is an available and familiar means for achieving the goal in the basic motor movements. Thus we can say that, at this primitive level, action and object are both "understood" in a way that can give rise to higher types of cognition.

This primitive basis forms the ground of the understanding of all features of the environment. Understanding an object or a state of affairs is rooted in our ability or inability to use the object for a variety of purposes—we see the object in terms of the opportunities it offers for us to interact with it. This awareness of the action affordances of objects may be conscious, or it may be preconscious—capable of being brought to full consciousness but for various reasons not so; if it is sedimented from previous conscious intentional activities, it will likely be preconscious, as with Donoghue's monkeys discussed in our introduction, who were trained to move a computer cursor by implicitly (not explicitly) forming motor imagery of their hands moving the joysticks.

In fact, we will *usually* be currently unconscious of the action affordances of objects, because most of the relevant action commands, even prior to being cortically inhibited on the specific occasion, were already habituated long ago as a result of the extensive practice and learning that grounded the action/object-affordance associations in the history of our past experience. For example, we understand a ball as something that could be grasped in a certain way and thrown with a certain effort and force; we understand it as something that, if propelled toward us, would have to be ducked, and if sitting on the ground, would have to be stepped over. Most of these affordances of the object are not explicitly and consciously imagined on any given occasion, but all of this imagery, sedimented from numerous past experiences of performing such actions relative to similar balls, goes into our current understanding of what a ball is, and what this particular ball seems to be.

Thus the present account is not intended to describe mental states that the reader can check by introspective access. The large chunks of matter in your environment are normally not all objects of current conscious awareness and comprehension; but your awareness of them, when it occurs, is an awareness determined by their affordances for actions related to your interests.

The action model aims to isolate the element of *mentality*, which apparently is possessed by conscious beings (and possibly by intentionally-acting but non-conscious animals), but is lacked by computers and robots; this element we call "understanding." It refers to the sense in which the English-speaking human in Searle's Chinese Room argument (Searle 1981) may not "understand" Chinese. In Searle's example, the Chinese Room is a computer-like room into which Chinese words are fed, and a person in the room, who does not speak Chinese, is able to follow a set of instructions that allow the correct English translations to be fed out of the room. Even after performing these mechanical operations, which appropriately respond to the Chinese characters, there is an important sense in which the person still does not *understand* Chinese—and this is the kind of "understanding" that computers and robots lack. The issue that the notions of "intentionality" and "mentality" are meant to capture is: What is it that computers are *missing* by not *"understanding"* what they are doing in the way that conscious beings sometimes presumably do?

The above claim should be qualified, however. We have argued that a computer program that carries out an "action" by using an action schema for initiating and controlling the action, and that incorporates a mechanism for evaluating whether or not the goal has been reached, has a version of the kind of "proto-intentionality" or primitive understanding that also underlies human activity. This level of understanding never advances, but it does contain enough of the essential components of human understanding to be useful in analysis. One important point that has been made about this issue (Boden 1982; Newton 1996) is that while the computer in Searle's Chinese Room case can in no sense be said to understand Chinese, there is an analogical sense in which it could be said to "understand" the simple tasks it does perform. But the crucial difference is that it cannot *use* these tasks *in the service of organismic self-organization.* In terms of the basic distinction between action and mere reaction, the components of the computer merely react. Thus such a non-self-organizing computer does not have even the basic components needed for consciousness and for mentality in the sense we are using.

To show that action planning is the foundation of all understanding of objects, we can begin by formulating a minimally sufficient condition for "understanding an *action.*" In other words, what are the minimal requirements such that, if they are met, we can say that we "understand" an action, in the sense emphasized in the previous discussions? Newton (1996) formulated such a condition in this way: "One understands a simple action if one is able to imagine performing the action, with an image rich enough to serve as a guide in actual performance" (71). While it is true that other conditions may also characterize action-understanding, the one just mentioned is a *minimally* sufficient condition, meaning that it does not include any superfluous elements which are not inherently required for action-understanding.

From action understanding, we can then proceed in a similar mode of reasoning to *object* understanding: S has an understanding of a perceived object O if S is able to imagine incorporating O into the performance of a token of action-type A that is already understood, with an image sufficiently rich to serve as a guide in actual performance. The "understanding" of actions and objects that we can develop from this beginning is precisely the kind of understanding that conscious beings possess and that computers or robots are missing.

How can more general understanding of object-types be based on the understanding of basic actions as they would occur in relation to concrete objects? The key to this question hinges on the notion that, when we *anticipate how we might act* in relation to an object or situation (in the sense of goal-directed action), we execute the rudiments of a *subjunctive conceptualization.* As Ellis (1995) suggested, to *anticipate* that "If I throw a ball at something (under appropriate circumstances), it *will* knock it over," is very similar (linguistically, neurophysiologically, and phenomenologically) to believing that "If I *were* to throw a ball, it *would* knock something over." Thus anticipations of the future ground our understanding of subjunctives.

Even abstract concepts, such as logical and mathematical relations, can be understood in terms of the same basic action schemas; here we are in accord with other writers (for example, Mark Johnson, 1987, and Andy Clark, 1997) who see all cognition as shaped by our "embodiment" in this sense. How can abstract reasoning (such as logic and mathematics) make use of bodily action abilities? Sensorimotor imagery—conscious or semiconscious activated memory traces of the experiences of performing basic actions—functions not only in action contemplation and planning but also in the mental manipulation of objects in abstract reasoning. Abstract thought builds on basic action schemas: bodies interacting with objects in space (for example, Huttenlocher 1968; Kitcher 1985). To those claiming to lack such imagery, it can be argued that such images are not necessarily fully conscious, and brain imaging studies are now becoming available that may be able to decide such matters (for instance, Donoghue's monkey-brain inplants). Also, when people are identified as "lacking imagery," what is usually meant is *visual* imagery. Even if a person suffers from akinetic mutism—a condition in which the patient is conscious but unable to speak or move—the person can at least imagine reaching out and grasping a coffee cup (Damasio 1999).

The key to this foundation of understanding is the process of *action-planning*. In the next section, we review some neuroscientific evidence for this point—for example, the finding discussed by Ito (1993) and by Damasio (1999) that the brain mechanisms underlying abstract thought are extremely similar to those underlying action-planning in the context of body movement, both anatomically and dynamically. For now, the point is that we can build from the initial conceptualization of "understanding" to specific implications not only of action and its neurophysiology, but also *mental imagery, language, emotion,* and the *interrelations* of the areas just mentioned from a neuroscientific standpoint, resulting in an approach to each of these areas that can be incorporated into a coherent account of now-available information about the brain and its behavior. It might be helpful to say a few words about how the action model has implications for each of these areas separately:

a. Imagery

Notice that the minimally sufficient condition for action-understanding involves *imagery*. But here we must be careful to address the concerns of Wittgensteinians and others who do not believe that *visual* or *auditory* or any other *sensory* imagery is present in all mental contents of which we can be conscious. The key to answering this type of objection is that we must expand our notion of "mental images" to include anything we can *imagine*, as opposed to limiting it to what can be imaged in the traditional "five senses" (Newton 1982, 1996). That's to say, there are proprioceptive, emotional and sensorimotor images, and these images play a role in cognition that is importantly different from the role of visual or auditory images. Just as a visual image means imagining what it would be like to *see* something, so a sensorimotor image means imagining what it would be like to *do* something; an emotional image means imagining what it would be like to *feel* a certain way, and so on.

The role of imagery in action planning therefore becomes correspondingly more prominent, since part of the action-planning process involves forming (not necessarily a visual or auditory image, but) a sensory *and/or* proprioceptive *and/or* sensorimotor image of oneself performing the action in the way planned. In understanding the Charleston, we imagine what it would be like, or feel like, for our bodies to execute the Charleston. In understanding the difference between a soft carpet and a concrete driveway, we imagine what it might be like to crawl on them or run our hand across them.

We can thus develop an account of the physiological underpinnings of mental imagery that shows why the consciousness of an image involves much more than the traditionally understood stimulation of the "sensory areas" in the cortex (for instance, the occipital area and area V4 for visual images, and the like). It has been known for some time that all these areas can be stimulated, yet the subject can still fail to be consciously aware of the perceptual object, resulting in a correspondingly less complete *processing of the information* than would result from consciousness of the object (Aurell 1989; Bernstein et al. 2000; Faw 2003; Posner and Rothbart 1992, 2000). As we have already suggested, it is known that *other* areas of the brain must be active before any perceptual consciousness can result—especially limbic emotional areas and anterior areas such as the anterior cingulate and the "motor area." These areas must be active in order for perceptual *consciousness* and its correspondingly enriched processing to occur (Coles et al. 1990; Damasio 1999; Faw 2003). What does this activity add to the earlier visual processing? *Understanding* the perceptual object means that we imagine what it would be like to use or deal with the object in the context of purposeful action, which involves the *emotions* and a process of *actively directing attention,* as well as activation of areas of the brain that correspond to motor activity (so that we are also imagining how we might act in relation to the object). Thus understanding can be understood, physiologically and phenomenally, as a sort of imaginary and truncated process of purposeful action-planning, which involves an emotional component as the organism's motivation for the imagined action.

b. Language

Part of the importance of the point that imagery is as broad as the entire range of human experience is that it shows the way language and logic use can be grounded in "imagery." It is often argued by those who belittle the role of imagery that, when we use most everyday concepts, many of which have abstract meanings (for example, the concept "president"), we do not imagine the way the White House, the Oval Office, or any particular president would *look, sound, smell,* or are otherwise sensed—nor does our normal usage of "president" *refer* to any of these specific images; the meaning of the term is much more abstract than can be captured in any sensory *image.* There must therefore be (so runs the traditional argument) a substrate for logical operations in the brain that is completely independent of any mental images; thus neurophysiological work on imagery cannot contribute to the understanding of abstract thought and linguistic usage.

But the expansion of "imagery" to include proprioceptive and sensorimotor images in the context of action planning completely disarms this argument. It has often been observed that one way to define the meaning of words is "ostensively"—that is, by listing possible sensory observations that, if performed, would reveal whether the type of object being defined is present or not. For example, temperature can be defined in terms of an observable thermometer reading or indirectly observable speeding up of the movement of molecules. Economic growth can be defined in terms of indirectly observable GNP or in terms of average real income, which is also indirectly observable—it is observable ultimately through sensory experiences.

Can more complicated abstractions, such as the concept "president," be defined and, more importantly, *cognized in everyday usage,* in this way? We could imagine a list of potentially observable conditions that would determine whether any given person is a "president"—that there had been an election in which a majority cast votes for this person; that other persons are willing to obey the orders of this person, or are required by law to do so; and so forth. Of course, we may not actually image any of these processes, or the White House, or the Oval Office, each time we use the word; but we do feel confident that we *could* imagine them, and this involves a minimal amount of firing of the neural nets involved in the execution of some of the sensorimotor and proprioceptive *imageries* relevant to executing an ostensive definition of the concept. If abstract terms are in principle definable in such "ostensive" terms, either directly or indirectly (that is, in terms which are definable in terms which themselves are ostensively definable), then when we understand the meaning of an abstract term, a key part of what we are doing is feeling confident (at a marginally conscious level) that, if we wanted to, we *could* imagine what it would be like to execute the operations involved in making the observations necessary for the fulfillment of the ostensive conditions that define what it is for someone to be a president. When we think of George W. Bush as president, we minimally recall that he commanded armies, that the Supreme Court ruled that officials should stop counting votes, and other such imagery; more important, we feel confident that we could continue listing many more sensory facts that support the statement that Bush was president, if we needed to. This feeling of confidence supports our feeling that we know what the term "president" means.

Natural language words are then used as tools in the context of action planning schemas, where the words are also understood as *objects* in terms of the kinds of action planning schemas relevant to object understanding. Language is a tool for achieving our aims in relation to the environment. These aims usually involve other people—fellow language-users—but can also involve keeping track of elements in private thought processes. The embodiment approach differs from the computational one in this important respect: the primary purpose of language is not to refer to and state truths about what is observed in the environment, as one would assume from the philosophical literature during the past thirty or forty years. Fodor, for example, was for many years concerned with problems such as failure of reference, a problem arising from the theory that understanding the meaning of a term is initially caused by learning the term in the presence of its referent. On the embodiment approach, language is indeed useful for referring to objects in the environment, but the primary focus is pragmatic, not semantic (Dascal 1987). A word or phrase is used to call to mind a feeling that *if we were* to elaborate our "felt sense" of the word (Gendlin 1992b), we would find ourselves imaging a rich array of action affordances.

c. Emotion

Emotion and motivation are key elements in the necessary underpinnings of any purposeful action planning. By "motivation" we mean the unconscious drives, needs and desires that activate organisms; by "emotion" we mean representations of how we are doing in dealing with one or several motivations during activity that is responsive to them. Emotions are not merely motivations with consciousness added; an emotion represents features of the organism's bodily states (including those which attempt to initiate action) and they represent these bodily states relative to features of the environment that are salient for specific actions. Emotion thus plays a dynamic role in terms of these features of the body and the environment that motivation does not play. Motivation is a holistic state; it is not yet "pinned down" to a specific purpose, with specific objects. Consciousness is, in large part, motivation that has become emotion. But we can still say that conscious emotion motivates (drives) action, and in a specific and detailed way that unconscious motivation could not. Motivation, we might say, is a *central function of organisms*, and emotion is one of the more sophisticated forms that it can take (see Ellis 2005).

If intentional actions must be motivated by emotional brain areas, then so must all other conscious processes. Consciousness involves a directing of attention (Mack and Rock 1998; Posner and Rothbart 1992, 1998). Understanding the mechanisms of selective attention and inattention is fundamental to understanding patterns of human neurosis, differing worldviews, and the meaning of actions and belief systems at the level of underlying emotional motivations for action and information processing. It is because we are living organisms with the needs and desires of organisms that we process information in the way that we do, and it is this element that most of all distinguishes our way of processing information from those of computers and robots. The analogue of motivation in computers and robots is the built-in choice mechanisms of their programs. There is, apparently, still no analogue of emotion in computers, even though they may be cleverly contrived to imitate emotional behaviors.

In the action model, no information enters consciousness unless we are motivated to direct attention to it, in the sense that emotions as general as curiosity and restlessness must be counted among the emotional processes that motivate us to attend to the environment. Curiosity and restlessness are produced by the brain's "seeking system" (Panksepp 1998), which motivates exploration in general. When information from an object first stimulates our senses, it then passes through the *thalamus* before being routed simultaneously to 1. the midbrain and PAG areas, deep in the subcortex, which begin to gear up the organism for action potentially relevant to the general type of environmental affordance that is as yet only vaguely anticipated; 2. the relevant *"primary sensory area"* in the brain, where the data can be interpreted in a more fine-grained way; and 3. the *frontal cortex* and other anterior brain regions, which begin formulating questions about the relevance of the object to the organism's action-planning goals (Bachmann 2000; Ellis 1995b, 2005). The sensory information therefore has already been screened by the midbrain and other emotional areas for its value to the organism, before the decision is made whether to pay attention to the object, and before the traditionally-understood "sensory areas" of the brain even get their hands on it.

Thus emotion and motivation play an independent and determinative role in the processing of information; they do not merely react to information that has already been processed. Information is not fully processed in the first place unless early selection motivates us to do so (although there is also some *later* selection from among the data that have been early-selected for processing—more on this point later). Understanding the neural substrates of this process can make the results of phenomenological reflection commensurate with those of cognitive neuroscience, when the latter is understood primarily in terms of the human organism and its brain rather than only in terms of digital computers.

2. Correlates of Cognition and Consciousness in the Brain's Action Circuits

Intentional actions require motivation. Even covert attention shifts depend on the interests of the organism (Changizi et al. 2008; Mack and Rock 1998; Summerfield et al. 2006); limbic structures such as the amygdala, the hippocampus, and the hypothalamus influence voluntary attention mechanisms in the anterior cingulate (Bernstein et al. 2000; Posner and Rothbart 2000). Actions that are *imagined but not performed*, as we have already seen, are both activated and inhibited by means of the frontal lobes and motor cortex; inhibition, controlled in large part by the hypothalamus, allows action images to be consciously experienced (Jeannerod 1997; Stippich 2002) along with the emotional values associated with the actions.

The combination of the embodied-action approach with recent work on emotion is therefore powerful, allowing the formation of a global theory of brain function in which dynamic interactions among brain areas and brain events can be mapped at many levels of organization. An important prediction of the approach is that brain mechanisms once thought devoted to motor activity are also active in emotional and cognitive activities (see Ellis 2005).

A key example is the cerebellum, which was traditionally associated with learned motor skills such as riding a bicycle. Recent research (for example, Schmahmann 1997, Schmahmann et al. 2001) shows that the cerebellum is not only a coordinator of motor actions, but also of reasoning (Ito 1993; Ito, et al., 1998; Courchesne 1991), tool use (Imamizu et al. 2000) and, most recently discovered, the cerebellum is a coordinator of emotional with cognitive states (Anderson 1998; Anderson et al. 1999; Lauterbach 1996; Loeber et al. 1999). If reasoning and other cognitive activities make use of motor schemas, this is exactly what one would expect. The cerebellum appears to be not just an organ for the coordination of actual motor activities, but also for coordinating the output of both cortical and subcortical structures involved in affect laden cognitive activity at all levels. Neurophysiological studies have focused increasingly on the cerebellum's role in cognition. Cognition is empirically studied more easily than consciousness, but by looking at the cerebellum's role in cognition, we can see quite easily why it would be important for consciousness as well, notwithstanding the fact that animal studies which amputate the cerebellar cortex seem to leave everyday conscious activities intact (Rawson 1932). Part of the grounding of the action theory of consciousness therefore involves noting the brain systems that include the cerebellum in the coordination of both cognition and consciousness.

a. Cognition

There are two ways to look at the theoretical implications of the new findings for the role of the cerebellum in cognition. One is to say that, whereas we used to think that the cerebellum was geared primarily toward executing action routines, we now realize that the cerebellum has multiple functions that are not essentially interrelated. The other way is to say that the integral role of the cerebellum in cognition shows that cognition essentially *involves* implicit action routines. A hint that this may be the case can quickly be seen if we combine Damasio's (1994, 1999) notion that cognition involves imagery with Jeannerod's (1994, 1997) observation that action imagery involves the inhibition of actual efferent action commands in the brain, and Merleau-Ponty's (1941, 1942) suggestion that the intentional representation of any object involves imagining how we could act in relation to the object. As Merleau-Ponty says, knowing involves "know-how."

TIMING OF BRAIN EVENTS DURING PERCEPTION OF NOVEL STIMULUS

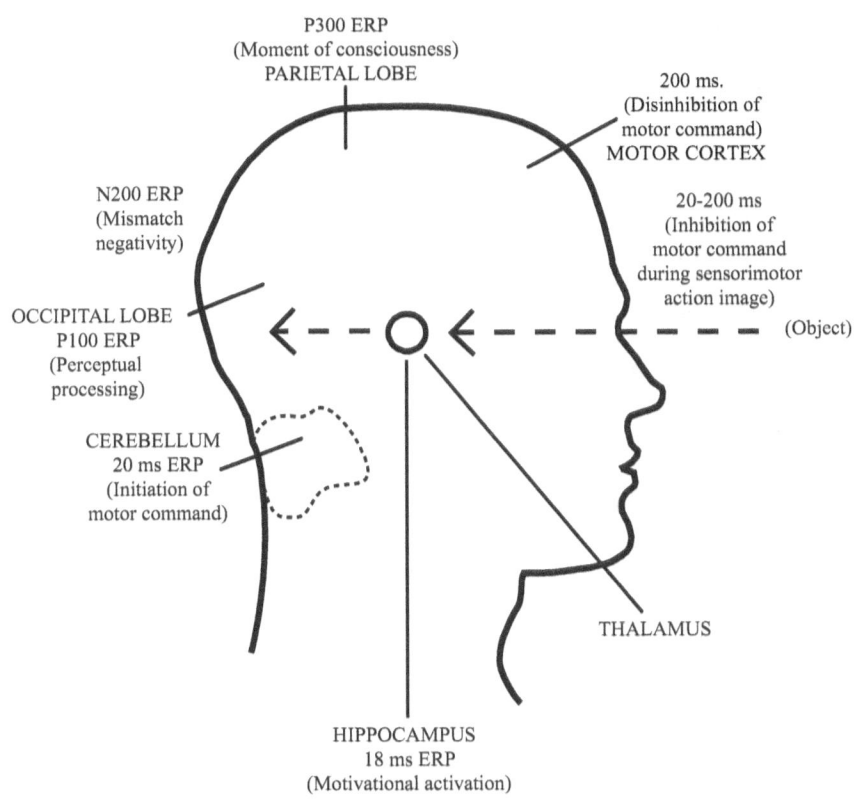

If we combine the new data about the cerebellum with what is already known about other brain areas, we can construct a clearer picture of the role of the cerebellum in all cognitive processes, including thinking, perception, emotion, and learning. Based on these considerations, a better understanding of the role of cerebellar functioning in our intentional representations of the world begins to emerge. We can construct a five-step model of the patterns of neural activation that must be present in order for the brain to execute the transformations involved in the information processing needed for intentional representation.

1. Brainstem-hypothalamic loops can sense a homeostatic imbalance for the organism.

2. They then activate neurotransmitter pathways in the interest of general arousal, and begin sending efferent signals to alert the brain that action is needed. This includes looping with the cerebellum (see Haines et al. 1997), because the cerebellum can activate highly *specific* action sequences based on past learning. The cerebellar-brainstem loops then send efferent action commands as far as the motor cortex, mediated by the cerebellum's loops with the thalamus and hypothalamus.

3. These action commands are *inhibited* by frontal processes, as Jeannerod (1997) points out; the result of this inhibition is

4. *Action imagery.* When the action imagery is fully informed by specific action commands of environmental stimuli, the resulting "object understanding" (Newton, 1996) becomes an *intentional image schema,* which vaguely represents categories of possible objects, *but only in terms of their action affordances*.

5. When the action imagery and the action-affordance image schemata resonate with the primary and secondary sensory areas (for example, in the occipital or temporal lobes), either because the latter has been triggered by perceptual input, *or* because the image schemata are so powerful that *they* activate the occipital or temporal areas on an efferent basis, the result is vivid *perceptual* imagery or actual perceptual consciousness. The point at which *resonance* is achieved between these two separate brain processes (one primarily efferent and anterior, reflecting action affordances; the other primarily afferent and posterior, reflecting received perceptual data) is the point at which a parietal P300 electrical potential can be observed using EEG measures during perceptual experiments in which an un-anticipated object is presented. The P300 registers the resonating between anterior and posterior cortical regions that correlates with consciousness of the perceptual object. During the milliseconds leading up to this resonance, the perceptual data were being processed, and the action commands were being orchestrated, but until those two processes achieved resonance, there was no *consciousness* of the perceptual object (see for instance Aurell 1989).

Essentially, then, instead of generating efferent commands to take some action *in general,* what the cerebellum does is to generate more *specific* action commands by initiating the thalamo-cerebellar and hypothalamo-cerebellar loops that Haines et al. (1997) discuss, and also hippocampal-cerebellar loops (Haines et al. 1997; see also Woodruff-Pak 1997), so that the action that is commanded (and which then gets inhibited in the motor cortex to form action imagery) is a *highly specific* action, rather than just an efferent command to perform "some action or other."

It has long been known that adult pigeons with ablated cerebellums still have adequate vision (Rawson 1932). But Held and Heine (1952) show that kittens without cerebellar development (deprived of movement by being strapped to carts pulled by other cats) end up as "functionally blind" adult cats. The answer to this paradox is that, as Gallese and Goldman (1998) show, the premotor cortex can encode much of the past cerebellar learning by means of premotor "canonical neurons." So if the cerebellum is lost or damaged in adulthood, the basic capacity for motor imagery crucial to consciousness of visual objects remains possible. Also, the Rawson results must be tempered by such findings as the Clarke (1974) study showing that decerebrated pigeons to some extent can respond visually via the cerebellum alone.

Also, it is important to note that in eyelid conditioning experiments the cerebellum responds *within 20 ms.* of the delivery of the airpuff (Woodruff-Pak 1997). This shows that in effect there is a very *early* event related potential (ERP), along with the early hippocampal ERP that Coles (1990) reports finding *as early as 18 ms.* after presentation of a novel stimulus. Both these ERPs occur long before the perceptual processing occurs in the "perceptual areas" of the cortex—the occipital 100P and the 200N "mismatch negativity" potential (at 100 and 200 ms. respectively). These very early cerebellar and hippocampal ERPs probably reflect early activation of the hippocampal-cerebellar loops that Haine et al. (1997) report, along with cerebellar-PAG loops. After chemical *neurotransmitters* have alerted the brain that action needs to be taken, the subsequent *electrical* nervous impulses are ways of elaborating what *specific* action is needed. This is a monumental computational task, so it makes sense that the cerebellum, which has its own separate cortex and comprises fifty percent of the brain's neurons, must be recruited for it.

In some instances, brainstem motivationally-initiated neurotransmitters tell us to take action, but without the electrical circuits being able to give us a clear indication of what *specific* action is needed. That is, the emotional areas have aroused our felt need for action, but the cerebellum cannot yet decide *which* action routines to begin activating. This is when we consciously feel ourselves in the grips of powerful, disturbing emotions like anger, fear, grief, or anxiety. As soon as we start taking the needed action, the anger, fear, and so forth, feels less cataclysmic, because we are not just getting the neurotransmitter rush in its purity, but rather as tempered by the fact that some of our attention is taken up with the specificity of the action commands. The cerebellum's role is primarily to make the action commands *specific* enough so that we can "understand the objects" of cognitive, perceptual or emotional states. When the neurotransmitters are delivered to the various brain parts, the expectation is that specific action commands will be not far behind, so to receive the neurotransmitter activity *without* the specific action commands can be emotionally disturbing. Here again, the specificity of the action commands depends on the cerebellum. And the cerebellum, even though it is in the back of the head, actually has its own separate *cortex* for the purpose of calculating and fine-tuning the relevant action routines.

When the action command is conveyed from the subcortex through the cerebellum's complex action circuits, it then loops with the thalamus and hypothalamus to interact with the motor cortex in the frontal brain regions. As we saw from the monkey studies cited earlier, the activity in the Supplementary Motor Area is exactly the same for an imagined action as for an actual one (see Stippich 2002). The difference is that in the sensorimotor cortex the action command is inhibited when we only *imagine* the action without overtly performing it. For an excellent and readable overview of the different roles played by the Supplementary Motor Area and the sensorimotor cortex in this process, see the web-based tutorial provided by the Canadian Institute of Neurosciences, Mental Health, and Addiction (2006), referenced in our citation list. A good overview of the entire process of the "microgenesis" of perception during the 300 or so milliseconds required for the process to unfoled, can be found in Bachmann (2000).

What emerges is a picture of action imagery in which the action command begins with *efferent* brain signals, signals that originate deep in the subcortex and are directed outward toward the motor cortex, and from there are transmitted through the parietal body map to the body parts involved in the movement. Because action imagery is used to consciously perceive what is there, our theory posits that all of this efferent activity is presupposed before the *afferent* signals being received from the sensory organs to the brain's sensory areas can become conscious. This explains why, in the Mack and Rock "inattentional blindness" studies, the subjects are *unconscious* of the presented object until they pay attention to it. On our view, the difference attention makes is that the brain must gear itself up to actively imagine how it could interact with the object being seen. And this means that an *efferent* system of brain signals must be activated by the self-organizing system itself, as motivated by its own purposes at the moment. In the Mack and Rock studies, the main motivation is to decide which arm of a cross is longer, and this is the attentional preoccupation that prevents the discriminative stimulus from being consciously seen. In general, the main motivation in perceptual experiments is simply to do whatever is necessary to obey the commands of the experimenter.

An intriguing example of the way efferent activity (which usually indicates the sending of an action command, even if the action is inhibited) seems to lead to consciousness is the case of subjects who have lost a limb, yet continue to experience a "phantom limb," and sometimes feel that they can perceive the phantom limb moving. Neurologists who have studied the phantom limb phenomenon believe it is likely that efferent commands directed toward the non-existent limb play a predominant role in creating the illusion that the limb is there. In such cases, even in spite of the lack of the corresponding *afferent* feedback, the subject still feels as if the limb were actually there. Many researchers believe that the sense of the phantom limb movement occurs because the movement has been imagined by means of sending the *efferent* signals *toward* the limb. Staub et al. (2006, 2141), in a neurological study of phantom limb movement, state that "A preserved sense of agency provided by intact premotor processes translating intention into action may lead to the vivid feeling of movement in a paralyzed limb, similar to kinesthetic illusions in amputees. The interruption of thalamic afferences may explain the persistence and stability of the phantom by preventing any correction of the mismatch between expected and effective movement." According to a study by Katz (1992, 811), "The results suggest that the presence of a phantom limb, whether painful or painless, is related to the sympathetic-efferent outflow of cutaneous vasoconstrictor fibres in the stump and stump neuromas." According to Reilly et al. (2006, 2211), "Our data suggest that the experience of phantom hand movement involves the activation of hand motor commands. We propose that preserved hand movement representations re-target the stump muscles to express themselves and that when these representations are voluntarily accessible they can instruct the remaining muscles to move in such a way as if the limb is still there."

It should be acknowledged that the entire field of phantom limb experiences remains controversial. Some maintain that efferent processes alone can cause the phantom limb experience (Katz 1992; Levine 2007; Staub et al. 2006), without much in the way of afferent feedback. Others (for example Gandevial 2006; Ramachandran and Blakeslee 1998) believe that phantom limb experience and phantom limb pain (if not phantom limb *movement)* may result from afferent feedback from pathways that grow into the now-defunct part of the parietal lobe. Also, the explanation of phantom limb *movement* may be very different from the explanation of phantom limb *pain*. The pain *per se* may result from the fact that no afferent feedback is received to cause corollary discharge of the electrical potential built up in the efferent system; or it may be caused by afferent feedback that is mismatched to the efferent commands. But clearly, efferent processes play an important if not determinative role in either case. Ramachandran, even though he believes that afferent processes play a role in phantom limb pain, still emphasizes that the pain involves a mismatch between efferent signals and afferent feedback. This is the basis of one of his treatment methods for phantom limb pain. The pain can be reduced by artificially supplying some afferent feedback—for example, by having the subject "move" the missing phantom limb simultaneously with the remaining real one, and rigging mirrors so that the subject can "see" the limb moving, and thus receive afferent feedback through the visual system that is a better match for the efferent signals being sent through the motor system. Ramachandran believes that this procedure reduces the imbalance between the efferent action command and the afferent feedback from it.

What the phantom limb experience means for our purposes—especially the experience of phantom limb *movement*—is that efferent processes can play a crucial role in creating our conscious experiences. The phantom limb movement studies even suggest that, at least in some cases, we may sometimes consciously experience things by means of *only* efferent processes. We shall not argue this stronger claim here, because it is sufficient for our purposes to note that efferent processes are a necessary and important part of any conscious experience. Just by trying to move a phantom limb, the subject may consciously feel as if the limb were there.

It is also important for our purposes to note that in the case of phantom limb movement consciousness can occur not because the subject *actually does* move anything, but because the subject is *imagining* moving. This *imagining* of self-movement is subserved by brain processes similar to those in *actual* movement, all the way up to the point where the process may be interrupted, either by a deliberate inhibition by the frontal cortex, or a severing or sedating of nerves in the efferent pathway. So here again, movement is by no means necessary for consciousness, as paralyzed patients show, but efferent processes that gear us up to *imagine* moving are an important part of understanding the action affordances of objects, and therefore play a role in our consciousness of them.

b. Attention and Consciousness

Ito (1993), Schahmann (1997), and others have shown that the cerebellum plays a coordinating and synchronizing role in the brain. If so, then this role must be an important determinant of the structure of conscious as opposed to non-conscious processing, because conscious processing is a whole-brain activity of a self-organizing system, and cannot result merely from passive stimulation. This is clear from the fact that occipital activity alone does not yield perceptual consciousness (Aurell 1989; Posner and Rothbart 1998; the perceptual studies by Mack and Rock 1998 also entail this conclusion although Mack and Rock do not discuss the neurophysiology involved). Moreover, the fact that cerebellar activity is very similar in abstract thought, physical movement, and the mere imagination of physical movement (Ito 1993; Schmahmann 1997), shows that the cerebellum plays an important role in the most sophisticated intellectual operations (an inference followed through by Schmahmann 2002), and that intellectual understanding is accomplished as an extension of the manipulation of action affordances (Newton 1996; Varela et al. 1991/1993). In addition, as noted above, recent research increasingly indicates an important role for the cerebellum in the most sophisticated mental operations, including learning, conditioning, and abstract thought.

It has been known for some time (for example see Asimov 1965) that conscious wakefulness results not from the activity of one particular brain region, but from the synchronization of wave patterns in diverse regions, especially between the thalamus and the cortex. Since the cerebellum controls widely distributed synchronizations, this means that the *timing* work of the cerebellum is crucial for the difference between sleep and wakefulness—and the implications of this fact for understanding the physiological correlates of consciousness are obvious. A fact less often mentioned but equally important is that coordination between the hippocampus and other subcortical regions, and the effect of this coordinated activity on the extended reticular thalamic activating system—which in effect "tunes" the thalamus to select for incoming stimuli that have emotionally important action affordances—is necessary for *consciousness of perception* as well. Occipital processing alone (in the traditional cortical "perceptual areas"), as we have seen repeatedly, *is not conscious*. Before we are conscious of a visual stimulus, subcortical and limbic brain areas must be activated, as well as more anterior areas such as the anterior cingulate, and this activation must take place in response to a motivational-emotional evaluation; since all of this activity involves synchronization of wave patterns in different brain areas, the cerebellum also plays a part here, because the cerebellum is involved in coordinating the timing of diverse brain processes throughout the cortex and subcortex. In short, if all consciousness begins with action affordances, or Damasio's (1999) "as if body loop," then the cerebellum—the brain area most important for coordinating bodily actions—must be pivotal for understanding consciousness.

As we have already seen, the hippocampus shows an event related potential (ERP) within 18 ms. of presentation of a novel perceptual stimulus (Coles et al. 1990)—indicating subcortical activation involving wave synchronization phenomena, and thus implying cerebellar involvement as well—whereas the first *occipital* (that is, "perceptual area") ERP does not begin until around 100 ms. and is not fully developed until about 250 ms. So the anterior and subcortical activation is not a *response* to an *occipital stimulus*; on the contrary, this activation must *already* have taken place before perceptual consciousness is possible. And the extended reticular thalamic activating system (sometimes equated with the "limbic system," but here we mean to emphasize its selective gating function) is guided by *emotional subcortical* purposes involving *action affordances*. This guidance by motivational purposes therefore is what *determines* whether any given perceptual input will even register in consciousness, that is, will be attended to.

When a visual stimulus is unexpected, from the time occipital processing is complete to the time when all the other brain processes needed for perceptual consciousness are activated, there is a time *delay* of about one quarter-second (Aurell 1989; McHugh and Bahill 1985; Srebro 1985)—much too long to be accounted for simply by the speed of spreading activation. At the rate neural signals travel, the activation should spread about *ten feet* in that amount of time! So we cannot simply say that the activation takes a quarter-second to spread from the occipital to the immediately adjacent parietal area. Instead, the quarter-second delay must result from the time needed for the emotional areas to activate the anterior cingulate, frontal and parietal areas to "look for" important categories of objects which the thalamus, in response to hippocampal and cerebellar tuning, has *already* alerted the organism may have relevant action affordances. This "looking for" activity has already begun the forming of preconscious proprioceptive and sensorimotor imagery associated with possible action affordances *prior to* any occipital activity having any effect on our perceptual consciousness (since at this point the impulse has not yet "traveled" from the occipital to the parietal and more frontal areas). Bernstein et al. (2000) provide ample evidence that a looping between the anterior cingulate and the frontal eye fields is necessary for the voluntary direction of visual attention, while Mack and Rock (1998) have shown that the attentional act is a necessary condition that must precede any state of perceptual consciousness. Haines et al. (1997) show that the cerebellum coordinates the timing of these limbic-frontal loops, which actually can now be viewed as limbic-frontal-cerebellar loops.

Even in *involuntary* attention, and even in rare cases where the prefrontal cortex has been completely removed, the limbic system still selectively gates incoming stimuli in accordance with general motivational purposes of the organism. Attention is gated via subcortical control of neurotransmitters and by the achievement of various kinds of resonance between such activity and the intact posterior cortical activity (Damasio 1994; Watt 1998, 2000; Faw, 2000, 2003). This allows *consciousness* rather than mere "blindsight" (*unconscious* perceptual knowledge) to result. Moreover, a person with no cingulate would be in a persistent vegetative state (Damasio 1999), so even involuntary attention would be impossible without it. Thus the model of the mind as a passive *receiver* of causal work done by stimulus *inputs* places the cart before the horse.

This way of looking at the neurophysiological substrates of perception reverses a traditional way of thinking of the causal ordering of brain events where perception was thought to drive emotion, which in turn was assumed to drive action (Goleman 1994, 18 succinctly reviews this traditional model). The findings cited above show that just the reverse is the case. The organism must first be geared up to look for data that are important for its purposes, the most fundamental of which involve action and thus are tied to cerebellar functions. This subcortical tuning, with the help of earlier cerebellum learning, activates the frontal and limbic regions to begin "looking for" important categories of items, in effect forming preconscious image schemas associated with those items, prior to presentation of the stimulus. If the presented stimulus then resonates with this self-generated activity, a more vivid image of the object is formed in consciousness, and one that is felt as the image of an emotionally salient present perceptual object rather than as a mere mental image (Aurell, 1984, 1989; Summerfield et al. 2006).

For example, as we track the movement of a soccer ball, our expectation as to where we should look for the ball is at each moment motivated by categories of utility combined with the retention of the ball's previous location. When the ball suddenly turns up where we are not looking for it, we then take at least a fourth of a second to find the ball again, by which time the opposing player may well have outmaneuvered us. The motivation to attend precedes perceptual processing. The object catches our attention because it presents a meaningful affordance for the overall motivated pattern of activity of the organism, which is already ongoing.

Since this activity is self-organizing, it must be holistically coordinated, and here again the evidence suggests that earlier cerebellum learning is crucial for the synchronizations needed for this purpose. In some instances, the emotional motivations not only pre-exist the presentation of the stimulus, but are also activated in a primitive, pre-perceptual way by the stimulus itself, through direct contact with the emotional brain prior to perceptual processing. In other words, our emotions are activated more quickly than we can even process any perceptual knowledge of what we have seen.

Because perception is motivated by categories of utility, and because the frontal and parietal areas must be activated by lower, emotional brain areas (PAG, anterior cingulate, hypothalamus, hippocampus, and amygdala), we first tend to see *schemas* or *Gestalts* in accordance with abstract concepts, not the *specific details* of what is there. Wertz (1987) points out that we see the sinister nature of a smile without noticing the details that tell us it is sinister. As Merleau-Ponty says, we notice the disorder in a room without noticing that a particular crooked picture frame is what makes it look disorderly (Merleau-Ponty, 1942, 173).

These considerations entail that consciousness cannot occur in nonliving information-processing beings, such as digital computers. It occurs only when activated by an enactive, self-organizing system that represents its *purposes* as a result of the self-organizational aim of the organism to maintain a total homeostatic balance at a suitable level of energy and complexity. Emotion, then, which includes represented motivational purpose, is essential for consciousness.

But at the same time, motivational purpose obviously is not a *sufficient* condition for consciousness. Plants and very low animal species have organismic purposes, and are self-organizing, but have little if any consciousness. Consciousness must therefore occur only when motivation is combined with something else—representation of how the motivation can connect with specific organismic outcome conditions in a specific environment of affordances. When representation occurs, not as a passive reaction, but as an activity of the directed organism, then consciousness can occur.

Emotional agnosias, or the inability to feel our own emotions (sometimes called "alexithymia"), can occur when patients cannot represent what their emotions are "about." They cannot form imagery that is appropriate to consciousness of their emotions (see Ellis 2008). This does not mean that they do not have *motivations,* the basis for emotions. We become emotionally conscious by forming representations in response to our motivations. And even when we are unconscious of any motivation, it is still present, and therefore still drives the representational processes in which we do engage—for example, as in tracking soccer balls and having our attention pulled by sinister smiles and crooked picture frames. Even pure curiosity is an emotion that motivates us to explore our environment and represent what is there (Panksepp 1998; Ellis 2005). We may be unaware of the fact that emotions drive these perceptual and imaginative processes, but the above data indicate that they are so driven nonetheless.

Representation is therefore the ingredient that must be added to *self-organizational motivation* in order to allow consciousness to occur. But as we acknowledged earlier, representation is a controversial concept in the cognitive sciences. In the next chapter, we explain our view of representation in some detail, and in a way that is very different from traditional notions of how representation occurs.

3

Action Imagery and Representation of the External World

We are proposing here that emotionally motivated self-organization is necessary but not sufficient to account for intentionality and consciousness. An equally necessary ingredient, we have argued, is representation, which consolidates the "aboutness" relation between motivations and the external situations that afford the motivated actions.

Many recent embodiment and enactive theories, as mentioned earlier, prefer to eschew the concept of representation altogether (for example, Hutto 2005; Thelen et al. 2001) because the past half-century or more of linguistic philosophers and computationally modeled theories have so badly botched the definition of what a "representation" should consist of. In our view, we cannot dispense with the notion of representation, but instead must set about to give an action-based account of how it works, to replace the outmoded account derived from linguistic philosophy and the interrelated computer metaphor. In everyday experience, mental imagery and abstract thought play the practical role of representation, and this representational capacity is important for our ability to act in the world and to form conscious thoughts about it. Accordingly, we devote this chapter to working out a thoroughgoing, action-based concept of representation.

1. Mental Representation

Because of the controversy surrounding the meaning, the role, and indeed even the existence of "representation," we devote this section to clarifying the sense in which we believe representation is an indispensable element of intentional consciousness. The notion of "representation" has been used in a variety of different senses that often are not distinguished from each other. Damasio's theory that consciousness always involves "imagery" is consistent with our account, but runs into objections from those who are suspicious of the notion of "representation" because of increasing evidence that the brain does not store physical configurations, or even configurations of neural activity, that are isomorphic to a "represented" object.

One can develop limited but useful theories of embodied cognition without mental representation. Thelen et al. (2001) deny it a role in embodied cognition. While we believe that this denial is mistaken, it is a sign of the value of the embodiment approach that it lends itself to use by representationalists and nonrepresentationalists alike. It is theoretically robust and intuitively plausible, to such an extent that it can be twisted in a variety of ways without incoherence. Theories of embodied cognition, nevertheless, need an account of mental representation if they are to explain the full repertoire of human behavior: infant conceptual learning as well as skill learning; the source of the traditional "folk psychology" concepts of belief and desire; and cognitive skills such as natural language and abstract reasoning, as well as phenomenal consciousness.

The current theory of embodied cognition emerges from two predecessors: computationalism and phenomenology, both essentially including mental representations. Embodiment theory is indebted to the phenomenological tradition: much of its language is that of Husserl, Merleau-Ponty, and Sartre. But the embodiment theories also evolved out of computationalism, which defined the problems that contemporary embodiment theory seeks to solve. Computationalism sought a theory that 1. could in principle be implemented in a computer, and 2. could be applied to brain mechanisms. Traditional phenomenology had a different goal: exploring the phenomenal field to develop a science of consciousness with its own terminology and laws. The insights developed in this effort have shaped theories of embodied cognition, but those theories share the aims of computationalism just as much as those of phenomenology: to develop a science of cognition continuous with biological science, that can be modeled in dynamical systems theories.

Throughout this transition, the concept of intentional mental representations has survived from its original definition (as "ideas") by Brentano, through the abstract symbol-systems of computationalism, to most of the contemporary embodiment theories, including those that reject either the existence or the importance of "representations" defined in this tradition. Brentano's account of the relevant kind of intentionality is "direction upon something": we think of something by having it "present to consciousness" (Brentano, 1960). He did not use the term "representation," but his "ideas" are supposed to represent or "present" what thoughts are "about." These ideas are objects of judgments (propositional attitudes) and mental states like desire.

Fodor tells us that Brentano's "ideas" are *symbols*. Fodor summarizes his own Representational Theory of Mind as follows:

(a) Propositional attitude states are relational.

(b) Among the relata are mental representations (often called "Ideas" in the older literature).

(c) Mental representations are symbols: they have both formal and semantic properties.

(d) Mental representations have their causal roles in virtue of their formal properties.

(e) Propositional attitudes inherit their semantic properties from those of the mental representations that function as their objects. (Fodor 1975: 27)

Fodor's representations are like the symbol-strings manipulated by computer programs; hence the "computational theory of mind."

This problematic notion of mental representations has not been replaced by one more appropriate to an embodiment theory. In what follows, we would like first to show what is wrong with this traditional kind of account of representation, and then suggest a better account that avoids these problems. Representations are still viewed by most as static, semi-permanent symbol strings, usually as neural groups linked together by past experience (via mechanisms like Hebbian synapses, which are literally groups of neurons arranged in a certain way in the brain, representing external objects). These "representations" are supposed to trigger each other in response to appropriate input. Such neural groups, like symbol-strings in computers or the words of natural language, *carry content in themselves*—either actually, with "intrinsic intentionality" (Haugeland, 1985), or potentially, waiting to be employed by a user (Dennett 1987). Either way, the neural groups themselves literally *are* the representations, and it is they that bear the intentional content of a thought. It is true that Dennett, along with Millikan (1984), holds that the *user determines* the content of the representation. But for them content is fixed by evolution: it is that which the representational mechanisms have evolved as their "proper function." Spontaneous creation of novel intentional content, central to human cognition, is not explained.

This notion of representation is common in neuroscience as well as in cognitive psychology and philosophy of mind. It is compatible with the view that representations are groups of neurons linked together and available for cognition. The representational neurons are causal intermediaries between stimulus and response, in most views: they are caused by external events that stimulate sensory mechanisms or by interoception of internal events (as with motor representations), and in turn they play a causal role in behavior, providing patterns that guide action planning and execution.

How is the content of these representations determined? On most accounts, it is the external *causes* of the patterns that are represented. Thus, in the visual cortex, various neural patterns are said to "represent" external visual objects in different ways, depending on what features trigger them: early ones may represent, for example, stimulus location; later ones represent familiar objects. Bodily input also forms representations (which may also be innate): "body maps" in locations like the parietal cortex "represent" aspects of the body for action preparation and maintenance of physical well-being. Content is also determined by what the representations cause: a motor pattern that causes a particular action is said to "represent" that action (Jeannerod 1997).

a. Problems with Traditional Theories

There is enormous difficulty in giving an account of the content of representations conceived of as static, enduring neural groups. For example, misrepresentation: if patterns represent their causes, how could an activated pattern *mis*represent its cause? Problems of this kind lead some researchers, such as Thelen, to reject talk of representations altogether:

> [R]ecently . . . the range of internal events considered to be representations has expanded. In this newer view, any dynamic internal event that is causally related to behavior is a representation. This is fine by us. . . . But notice such a move takes all meaning from the term: a hurting knee becomes a representation of the fall that gave rise to it. It hardly seems worthwhile to ask whether a theory posits representations or not. (Thelen et al. 2001)

Thelen is right that indiscriminately labeling any causal component of a perception-behavior sequence is pointless. She is also right to reject representations as symbols that stand for what is represented, and are distinct from the user's cognitive processes. But there is an essential role for mental representations nevertheless. In what follows, we discuss two problems with viewing representations as fixed neural structures. We then explore the notion of representation as a mental *activity*. The term "mental activity" is significant here: it is not synonymous with "mental state"; it refers to an intentional action, similar to motor action except for being covert, and controlled by the same brain structures as those involved in overt activity (the cerebellum, the motor and premotor cortex). In this sense, thinking is acting.

The first problem is that embodiment theories work primarily as metaphorical extensions of our concepts of bodily activity, and there is no suitable bodily analog for representations as fixed neural patterns. This makes modeling difficult. Bodily activity is driven by needs of the organism and is aimed at environmental features that satisfy them. These environmental features, in most recent embodiment theories, are given in the perception of the environment directly as "affordances"—they have no prior "objective" meaningful content for the embodied subject, but instead acquire content only *through* this interaction.

So the problem is this: If we were to think of cognition as an extension of this activity, while positing *stored neural patterns* as possessing meaningful content, then we would need two distinct theories of content. One theory would explain how content is created by the emotionally driven activities of an organism seeking to satisfy its needs through the environment. This theory would show how, just as we can ask about any behaving animal what it is "trying to do," so we can ask about a person who forms sensory imagery in the course of planning an action or solving a problem what she "means by" the imagery. Say her imagery is a memory of the ocean. We cannot say that her imagery "means" the ocean; it has been activated in order to play a role in her current cognitive activity—for example, deciding whether to rent a summer cottage on Lake Michigan. Now the memory traces have entirely new content: they represent future possibilities carrying emotional and other features foreign to the original memories.

The other theory would explain how neural traces have content "intrinsically," even when inactive. Below we examine the problems with this type of theory. Even without these problems, however, it seems unparsimonious for a general theory of cognition to require two quite different types of representation.

Still another problem with the traditional concept of representation concerns difficulties with accounts of content in stored neural patterns. The difficulties apply also to linguistic content, because these neural patterns are seen as language-like. Causal theories are notorious for problems in explaining misrepresentation (Bickhard, 1993, 2000). They give, moreover, no account of creativity, whereby structures with fixed content acquire novel uses, an essential feature of human cognition. And, as Thelen et al. (2001) argue, solving such problems in terms of causation results in a vacuous account: anything involved in a causal system becomes a "representation."

b. Toward a More Adequate Theory

Given the above problems, we suggest seeking an account of mental representation in which content arises only *during cognitive activity*. If we reserve the notion of "mental content" for *active* components of representational behavior, and treat *stored* patterns neutrally as traces of brain events, then these problems from philosophy of language disappear. If what gives a symbol its content is the *way it is used,* then focus on the use. Representations arise when we actively represent. Content is provided by the *context and goal* of the representational activity; it is not ready-packaged in pre-existing neural patterns.

The idea that representation arises in goal-directed action is far from novel. Polanyi, for example, writes:

> We may say in general that by acquiring a skill, whether muscular or intellectual, we achieve an understanding which we cannot put into words and which is continuous with the inarticulate faculties of animals.
>
> What I understand in this manner has meaning for me, and it has this meaning in itself, and not as a sign has a meaning when denoting an object. I have called this earlier on an existential meaning. (Polanyi 1958, 90)

Performing a learned action is exercising one's understanding of the action: the action has meaning. One understands what one is trying to do, or what the action is for. In other words, the meaning of the action is the goal of the action, which one tacitly understands in intentionally performing the action. Performing the action *is itself* the activity of representing the goal as a goal, the desired outcome of the action. The goal is not represented *separately, as a detachable component.*

Merleau-Ponty rejects the idea of a "representation" as an independent component of a behavioral sequence: the action as a whole has "immanent meaning" in the unification of means and end. Unless the end and the means are internally related in the action, the action lacks meaning for the organism:

> [I]f . . . representative consciousness is only one of the forms of consciousness and if this latter is defined more generally by reference to an object . . .

> the felt movements will be linked together by a practical intention which animates them, which makes of them a directed melody; and it becomes impossible to distinguish the goal and the means as separable elements, impossible to treat human action as another solution to the problems which instinct resolves: if the problems were *the same,* the solutions would be identical. An analysis of the imminent meaning of action and its internal structure is substituted for an analysis of the goals of action and their means. (Merleau-Ponty 1942/1963, 173–74)

Working toward a goal is representing the goal *as* the aim of the means. Independent of the means, the goal would not be a goal; independent of the goal, the means would be meaningless.

Neural patterns *can be used* representationally in goal-directed actions. Jeannerod (1997), for example, argues persuasively that action imagery is recruited in a performance of the corresponding action type and plays a vital role. Action images *in use* represent the action that they facilitate, because they are sensorimotor images *of the unified performance,* in which means and ends are blended and derive their significance from each other. Again, by a "sensorimotor image," we do not mean a visual image of ourselves performing the action, but rather an imagining of what it would "be like" or "feel like" to perform the action. There is a huge difference between imagining what one would *look* like while swinging a bat, and what it would *feel* like to swing the bat. The "appearance" imagery actually gets in the way of performance, whereas the "feel-like" imagery facilitates it. So our concept of sensorimotor images is that such images are carried out, representing means and ends in a blended and mutually dependent way, but they do so *only when in use.* Otherwise they are merely *potential* images, *potential* representations of actions. And when they are actualized in a performance, they represent the action token that they are currently facilitating, not action types. We therefore propose the following definition for representations in action:

> R represents object O or state of affairs S if R plays the role of O or S in an imagined action, or imaginative rehearsal of an action, involving O or S (because of some appropriate isomorphism or other feature of correspondence between the way R can be used and the way O or S can be used).

R is any component of an action image that is in use when the action being imaged or rehearsed would have been an interaction with an actual or imagined external object or situation, but R is being used to play the role of the object or situation. The "isomorphism or other feature of correspondence" is indefinitely variable: any property of the image that would allow the interaction will serve. So, for example, musicians typically "mentally rehearse" their music by imagining themselves playing their instruments. The imagined act of fingering an instrument might represent the sound of the note to be played. Similarly, the sensorimotor image of myself reading the note "G" can "stand in" for the sensorimotor image of myself playing the G on an instrument. The reading of the note thus represents the action of playing the note, because the enactment of the sensorimotor imagery of reading the note bears a certain relationship to the act of playing the note, which in some habituated instances could involve both reading *and* playing the note. Moreover, when I read the note in the context of other notes, the brain's manipulation of the sensorimotor imagery is isomorphic in some ways to some of the imagery used to play the note in context. For instance, I go "up" to read from a G to an A, and the gearing up of my auditory cortex would prepare me to hear the note going "up" in pitch. Notice also that the isomorphism could still work even if lower notes on the staff were written higher. The jazz keyboardist Joe Zawinul constructed a special keyboard just for practice purposes, so that the notes that "sounded" lower were actually "higher" on the keyboard and vice versa. The purpose of the exercise was to expand his creativity, but he was still able to navigate the altered keyboard because there was still an isomorphism between the way the notes sounded and the actions he performed to play them.

If neural groups actually in use represent objects involved in the relevant actions, then the action image as a whole would logically be expected to represent the action as a whole. This relation can also be defined:

> Image I represents action token A if I plays the role of A in any mental imagination or mental rehearsal activity involving evaluating, planning, activating, controlling, or completing A. When quiescent, the capacity for I only potentially represents.

These definitions allow action images to represent actions they are currently facilitating, and also allow components of those images to represent components of the actions. They represent them in the classical sense of standing for them, or playing their functional roles, in a given mental imagining or rehearsing of an action. Representation is an *activity;* it is not an external relation between two static *objects.*

This action-based concept of representation is based on the discussion of representation in Newton (1996), and bears some superficial similarities to Rick Grush's (2004) "emulation theory," but with key differences. In Grush's approach, the action image emulates the goal state of the action we might actually perform, and thus the representation is engaging in a pattern of activity that emulates the external object or process that is an aspect of a goal state of the organism. Like Newton (1996), Lakoff (1987), and Johnson-Laird (1983), Grush holds that representation is based in human behavior and perception, and thus representation can be defined in terms of motor control systems. Grush's alternative to pure feed-forward or feed-back systems is one in which the final goal state is "emulated" by a mechanism allowing the system to perform its goal-directed actions in a type of "rehearsal" of the decisive final actions, for fine-tuning, without commitment to a final outcome. What is new about Grush's proposal is that his hypothesized mechanism for signal processing, the "Kalman filter," performs this function. The Kalman filter is a hypothetical brain system that pre-selects for perceptual contents relevant to actions that can use those contents as part of the goal state envisioned for an action. Thus we can say that, in using the Kalman filter, the motor system is "representing" its goal.

The main problems here are the same as in the traditional accounts of representation. We still have to ask how the subject can be *conscious* of the external object rather than having a mere isomorphic "copy" as a merely physical process in the brain—even if the process now being proposed is an activity rather than a neural group. The Kalman filter in Grush's account is not a representation, but a mechanism *allowing* representational activity by providing, among other things, appropriate *isomorphism* with the goal state. So, as in traditional accounts, isomorphism bears the brunt of establishing the relation of "aboutness." To be sure, we could say that the Kalman filter, *together with the motor control system that employs it,* constitutes a representation of the action in the static sense, but that would be inaccurate, because the combined system as a whole is related to the goal action only when employed in the *process* of preparing for the final action. If we want to call that system a representation, then representations are much too ephemeral to allow for one-to-one correspondences between the brain activity and the content of the representation. It is true that the goal of performing a long division task, for example, entails carrying the number, and so on, which is a motivated activity. But the process of "selection" that the Kalman filter performs is not by itself sufficient to pick out the cognitive content that is represented by the mathematical operations being performed.

It is much more useful, in our view, to take the motor control system as a whole as a basic example of representational *activity*, because this way of understanding representation will allow us to define it in a firm, noncircular manner. On our view, representation is the process of performing goal-directed activity in a manner that allows the activity to be rehearsed and optimized in advance of the realization of the goal. This goal-realization (whether planned or simply hypothesized) is what is represented by the activity.

Correlatively, we also still must ask how, on Grush's account, the subject can infer that the perceptual activity in question represents *this* object or *that* one. Suppose I want to play the note G. Many perceptual objects are relevant to performing this goal: the instrument, my fingers, the written music, the chair on which I must continue sitting in order to play the note, and so on. The Kalman filter selects all of those relevant objects to focus perceptual attention on, but how does it know which one the idea of "G" in my mind is representing? If the answer is that the brain activity represents the object that *caused* it, then we are again left with the problem that *any* causal process that causes an image would still seem to count as what the image "represents," even if the causal process has nothing to do with what the image is *about*. A scientist's probe in the brain tissues can elicit mental images (Bickle and Ellis 2005), but the scientist's probe certainly is not what is being represented by those images.

Our approach is completely different on this score. First of all, the reason the subject is *conscious* is because the anticipatory activity constituting the image is already self-organizationally enacted before there is any external object to be imitated or not imitated. What the representing image then "emulates" is not an external object, or even the goal state associated with an action one could take in relation to an external object. What the representing activity "stands in" for is an imaged object relative to which we could take a possible action; our *imagined action* relative to the *representing* image is *used by* the subject to "stand in" for the action we *could* imagine taking *toward the represented object*. A main difference from Grush's account, then, is that in our view an *action image* (the image of the action we could take relative to the representative image) stands in for *another action image* (the action that we could take toward that which is *being* represented). The action does not need to emulate the goal state.

For example, the artist, instead of presenting the viewer with a vase of flowers, allows the viewer to "rehearse" the *activity* of looking at a vase of flowers with a particular focus and affective response. Thus the artist and the viewer are both engaged in representational activity. To say that the painting *itself* represents a vase of flowers can be a short-hand way of referring to the process, but unless this process is understood as representation in the *active* sense, we will continue to wonder how one physical object can bear such a profound relationship to another physical object (a neural group or pattern of activity in the brain), with no visible connections and all by itself. On this point, we are in agreement with Grush.

Theories of embodied cognition cannot achieve their task simply by explaining intentional representation on the level of basic action performance. Complex cognitive behavior involves not only overt action, but also covert, abstract thought. How can abstract reasoning (for example, mathematics) make use of bodily action abilities? Many theorists argue that sensorimotor imagery functions not only in action planning but also in the mental manipulation of objects in abstract reasoning. Abstract thought builds on basic action schemas; it begins by imagining how our bodies could interact with other objects in space (for example Huttenlocher 1968; Newton 1996). As noted above, recent work on the cerebellum (Schmahmann, 1997) is an exciting confirmation of the theory of embodied cognition (Schmanhann et al., 2001).

It is vital to bear in mind that we must carefully define the term "image" here. Many people think of all images as visual, but there are excellent reasons to expand the term to include representations of *all* sensory, motor, proprioceptive and affective states. The mechanisms of visual imagery, which include many areas also involved in visual perception, are completely analogous to those involved in reactivated experience in other modalities. Motor images, for example, involve activity in the motor cortex similar to that present in actual motor behavior (Jeannerod 1997). In short, we can image anything we can experience.

If it is indeed possible to form images in any modality, then traditional objections to an imagistic view of cognition collapse. Pylyshyn, for example, argued that mental representation is propositional, because we can represent relations that cannot be captured pictorially:

> ... while two visual images of a chessboard may be pictorially identical, the mental representation of one might contain the relation between two chess pieces which could be described by the phrase "being attacked by" while the representation underlying the second image might not. (Pylyshyn 1973, 11)

Pylyshyn assumes that images are only visual. It is true that chess players constantly imagine alternative configurations of the board. But using the expanded notion of imagery, we can easily form an image of two chess pieces in the "attack" relation. One way is to evoke sensorimotor imagery of the possible moves of the pieces, combined with affective imagery of their hypothetical "emotional states": aggression in the one, fear or defensiveness in the other. This description is perfectly consistent with the language used by Pylyshyn to describe the relation: "being attacked by" is a relation inherently associated with negative emotions. Chess is an abstract game, but unless abstractions are grounded in concrete experiential states, they cannot be meaningful or useful to a player whose moves depend on actual conscious experiences of the abstractions.

2. Action Representations and the Concept of the External World

Most accounts of consciousness, whether or not they involve brain activity, raise but do not resolve the ultimate problem of solipsism. This problem haunted Nagel (1974b) in the following form: if we cannot know what it is like to be a bat, how can we know what it is like to be anything other than ourselves? And if we cannot know that, then what justifies the belief that we ourselves are not the sole reality? Thus we need one more element to complete our action-based theory of intentionality: an account of the way action affordances can lead to representations of the external world as such.

We bump into solid objects, it is true. But the bumping is experienced entirely in ourselves. We know how to verify that we have not "imagined" bumping into something: we can measure it with instruments, ask other people to observe it, and so on. But these methods are notoriously inadequate; we might be imagining the verification. Not only that, but there is a deeper problem: how can the question about the existence of an external world even arise for a conscious being? Jackendoff offers a casual answer: "That's what we are built to think! . . . Realism is a stance which we are built to adopt" (Jackendoff 1987, 428). We can't stop here, however. In a book about "understanding," we must explain *how* we understand *everything* in our world, and this includes the difference between ourselves and the rest of the world. We argue, first, that the semantic grounding of the concept of externality lies in our experience of error in planned action. Second, we show how, in the absence of error, action representations determine the structure of the external world for an agent.

In an earlier work, Newton (1989c) suggested that "a defining characteristic of our concept of external reality is *that in terms of which our beliefs can be false*" (Newton 1989c, 396, italics added). The ultimate "need" for the concept of an external world, in other words, is as a source of error.

The idea is as follows. Action inevitably involves error; it is because of the high probability of error that brain mechanisms such as "efference copy" exist. It must be possible to compare the intended action with the actual outcome of an effort, to decide whether or not to keep trying, and if so, what to change. Errors can be made on several levels. Most generally, one can distinguish between errors of action and of belief. Following Norman (1981), we can divide action errors into two types. First there are "planning errors" that result from mistakes in selecting the original action plan. An example would be picking up a hot pan without using a pot-holder, and thus burning one's hand. Second there are "production errors," which involve incorrectly activating an appropriate plan. Here an example would be getting into the car to drive to a new unfamiliar dentist, and absentmindedly driving to the old one instead. A simpler example is hitting one's thumb with a hammer instead of the intended nail.

Planning and production errors, both errors of action, are monitored and corrected by feedback; we recognize and correct our mistakes when the faulty results are compared with the original plan. (Recent work has suggested that some of this comparison takes place in the cerebellum; for example, see Schmahmann 1997; Schmahmann et al. 2001.) Errors of belief require more in the way of correction. Such an error involves an action plan that was both appropriate and carried out correctly; nevertheless, the outcome was different from the desired one. There is only one place to turn if one wishes to correct one's mistake and achieve the desired outcome: the belief upon which the original action plan was formulated.

Beliefs are the essential background without which intentions could not be formed. One must believe, or at least think it is probable, that one is capable of performing the action; and one must believe that a set of circumstances obtains that will provide for success. If one is wrong about the first belief, an action error of some sort will occur. If one is wrong about the second, then we are dealing directly with belief error as the immediate cause of a failure in attaining one's goal. For example, I set about cooking my dinner; I do so successfully, eat the meal, go to bed, and later discover that I am ill. What went wrong? I believed that the food was safe to eat, but in fact it was spoiled. Nothing was wrong with what I did; the problem lay with the world. The world was not the way I thought it was.

Failure of our efforts that cannot be traced to internal mistakes in our action plans and their execution must be accounted for somehow, and the only way is in the realm beyond our actions, beyond our direct control. We suggest that the simple experience of actions going wrong, when we have "done everything right," grounds the concept of the external world. Something exists outside of my own direct powers; I can interact with it, but it is something more than my own willed actions. If it were not for the experience of this kind of error, there would be no way out of solipsism. If all of my anticipations were fulfilled, then there would be no reason not to believe that the universe is identical with my will. It is in this way that the "external world" is understood by an agent as "the ultimate source of error." In the very notion of being external, this concept manifests itself: "I", the agent, control myself; what I cannot control is not a part of "me." And the only way for me to know that I cannot control it is to try to do so and fail.

Grounding the concept of the external world in the experience of error is not the most common move, but a look at the terms that are used to describe external reality justifies such an interpretation. The world has, or is, an "independent reality"; it is "objective"—it is not dependent upon our states of belief. It is "brute fact": not kind and yielding to our wishes. The most immediate and obvious manifestation of this essential property is that the world can surprise us and thwart us; it can defeat our will. We learn this through making errors, ones that are immune to our internal action control mechanisms. It is true that not every action runs up against an unyielding world; most of what we try to do is successful. It may be this fact that allows us to conceptualize the external world as being more or less the way it seems to us. But we know it is not always exactly as it seems to us, and this knowledge is what it is to have the concept of *objective, external* reality.

In these first few chapters we have taken a broad look at the enactive, or embodied, theory of intentionality. This examination was necessary as a preparation for the account of phenomenal consciousness as a process of self-organization. It will also be necessary as we proceed to bridge the gap between the "action" of self-organizing entities in general, and the intentional action of the type of self-organizing entities that can be conscious. But in order to incorporate intentionality into a general theory of the actions of which all self-organizing systems are capable, we first needed to show what sort of action grounds intentionality, and eventually, phenomenal consciousness. And in order to do that, it is also necessary to show how self-organization can enable action as opposed to mere reaction in the first place. That will be the subject of the next chapter: How do we get from action in the "micro" sense to action in the "macro" sense? That is, how can self-organization allow a genuinely "teleological" kind of causation, in which the whole organism, including its brain, can appropriate and reorganize its own micro-constituents rather than merely being pushed around by them? That, after all, is part of what it means to act rather than just react.

4

Do We Need an Emergency Metaphysician? Action versus Reaction at the Micro Level

1. Self-Organization, Self-Similarity, and Consciousness: An Organic Approach

The ability of dynamical systems such as living organisms to initiate and execute actions is one of their most distinguishing features, and is a key concept in understanding both behavior and mentality in beings like humans. In our view, this ability to act differs from mere reaction, no matter how complicated the latter may become. Action in the dynamical sense requires that a system can use, reorganize, and replace its own constituents to maintain a coherent overall pattern of activity. Our central proposal is that organisms that understand their environment in a literally mental sense do so by acting upon it, or imagining ways they could act upon it; and that the structure of this acting differs from mere reaction in more important ways than just how complicated its feedback loops and processing streams may become.

But as we have already suggested, "action" can be understood in at least two senses that are relevant for our purposes, action in both the "micro" and "macro" senses, and different theories have stressed either one or the other. Some think that consciousness can be understood as a function of the behavior of dynamical systems—that is, in terms of what we have called action at the "micro" level. Others focus on action at a more "macro" level, arguing that consciousness is enacted by means of bodily movements vis-à-vis the environment. We have already seen that both perspectives are necessary. The macro-level perspective depends crucially on the micro-level one, in order to have a coherent account of the difference between action and mere reaction. On the other hand, we cannot simply move straight from dynamical systems to consciousness without passing through the intermediate layer of action at the macro level. Without macro-level action, a dynamical systems account runs the risk of becoming merely another information processing account, and fails to show what makes some self-organizing systems conscious and genuinely intentional, while others are unconscious, and only superficially behave *as if* they were intentional (for example, nuts-and-bolts computers and robots).

Both levels of explanation are necessary for still another reason. An enactive account must not require that all consciousness depends on bodily actions in too literal a sense. Otherwise, people with total paralysis, such as patients with locked-in syndrome, would fail to be conscious. As we can already see from the previous chapters, not action, but rather action *imagery* is the key element of understanding all forms of consciousness and intentionality. Action imagery, in turn, is based on the *anticipation* of overt action. The anticipation of action, which is itself an action, even precedes perception. When a new, unexpected stimulus is presented, the cerebellum, whose main purpose is to coordinate action, is activated much more quickly than the primary perceptual areas (Haines et al. 1997; Woodruf-Pak 1997).

If we assume that action is motivated, then a very interesting conclusion is suggested by this early cerebellar activation, especially if we take note of the "inattentional blindness" phenomenon (Mack and Rock 1998), in which subjects whose attention is preoccupied fail to consciously see presented stimuli: The suggestion is that the motivation to direct attention is a *prerequisite* to consciously receiving information, not simply a *consequence* of it. That is, the early cerebellar activation, which precedes perceptual processing, is required in order to initiate action imagery with respect to which the data are evaluated, as part of the initial process of selectively directing our attention to them, and thus before we are perceptually conscious of them. We are arguing that the ineffable, phenomenally experienced aspects of subjective consciousness result more from the *motivation to act upon* the anticipated input than from the receiving and processing of inputs, with emphasis again on the dynamical structure of action by contrast to reaction. But if so, then we must also rethink the entire cognitive structure of the way sophisticated organisms process and use information.

Using self-organization as a framework for understanding the mind is far from novel (Bickhard 2000; Bunge 1979; Freeman 1987; Juarrero 1999; Kauffman 1993; Kelso 1995; MacCormac and Stamenov 1996; Monod 1971; Newton 2000, 2001; Prigogine 1996; Searle 2000; Thelen et al. 2001; Thelen and Smith 1994). But we believe that insufficient attention has been paid to the way macro-level action is built up step by step from the micro-level structure of the self-organizing system, at all levels of organization—including, in conscious and living organisms, the motivational and emotional aspects, which must be included in any model of higher levels. Every element of self-organizing processes at the lower physical levels is present at the higher levels as well, including goals, mechanisms for achieving the goals, and the motivations that drive the process. Consciousness cannot be understood without taking account of the way all these lower-level processes are appropriated and coordinated at the higher levels and the way the tendency toward "self-similarity"—that is, similarity in ascending levels of organizational paterns—expresses itself as each level organizes the next.

In particular, the role played by the motivational and action-initiating components in these processes is often neglected in the modeling of higher levels (such as chaos theory). Many readers are familiar with the geometric graphics yielded by fractal computer programs, in which self-similar patterns are nested, infinitely narrowing spaces, or in which vein-branching patterns in leaves are repeated in the tree as a whole. Similarly, the smaller shapes of beaches are repeated in the larger contours of the edges of continents (Mandelbrot 1983, 1999). But to move *directly* from chaos theory to an attempted explanation of consciousness presents the temptation to leave out crucial levels of organization needed for an adequate explanation, including a coherent assessment of the "micro"-action basis of motivation and emotion drives and organizes action tendencies in the sense of "macro"-action, and the way this in turn grounds cognition. As a result, the power of the concept of dynamical systems in understanding conscious levels of organization in the brain has not yet been fully exploited.

An important reason for considering motivation and emotion as indispensable to a self-organizational understanding of consciousness is that self-similarity in complex systems is multidimensional. In other words, any form of life has certain necessary features: a mechanism for state change, a system of goals (intermediate and final), a mechanism for detecting and evaluating successive states, and a source of motivating energy that drives the organizing process. This source of energy must be available to be harnessed by the organism and directed toward its self-organizational ends by means of its own internal mechanisms. The energy available to the system must conform to the needs of the system to maintain its structure across replacements of its material microcomponents. It must be able to drive the system toward states that answer these needs.

An obvious example in simple organisms is nourishment. If it is to survive, the organism needs food; but it must also "want" the food ("want to survive") if it is to make use of it and not passively die, as with marasmus deaths in infants who get too little emotional interaction with caretakers even though their physical subsistence needs are met (Spitz and Wolf 1946; Ellis 2005). This pivotal role of emotional processes in sustaining other mental functions of living beings suggests that the distinction between motivated action and mere reaction is key to the distinction between the intentional (or truly mental) and the non-intentional (which sometimes may superficially resemble the mental).

Note that we are not putting the cart before the horse here; nothing has been said about the origin of motivation. We are assuming that processes like natural selection and adaptation are necessary for the existence of motivated self-organizing systems in the first place. An unmotivated group of entities would soon cease to exist as a complex yet unified being if a great deal of effort is required to maintain its unity. A full appreciation of self-similarity in more complex structures requires identifying this motivating power on higher levels of organization as well as lower ones. In conscious beings, there is a conscious counterpart to the unconscious motivating drives of the lower system. This counterpart is emotion, which is always at least potentially conscious. We believe that without recognizing the full role of emotion in consciousness, we cannot understand either completely.

Motivation, which manifests itself consciously through emotion, is the driving force of self-organization in the conscious psyche. This motivational dimension of our information processing is what makes ours conscious (unlike digital computers or very simple animals). Emotion and motivation allow genuine action, as opposed to passive reaction, which in turn enables us to understand the world by acting upon it in the "macro" sense of overt bodily movement, or at least by imagining how we could act upon it (truncating the action circuits through inhibitory processes).

On this action theory of consciousness, the solution to the traditional mind-body problem—hinted at in certain obvious features of both cognition and phenomenal experience—is directly before us but "hidden in plain view." Julian Jaynes (1976/1990) points out that bodily metaphors are ubiquitous in discussions of mental states and entities: there is the "mind's eye"; there are mental acts upon mental objects; both mental states and physical objects are "experienced" by us in certain ways. The Platonic tradition taught that the mind is in some ways an invisible analogue to the body. This is close to the truth, but not in the way Plato intended, and thus can be fatally misleading. There are analogues to physical entities in mental states, but the reason is not that there are two semi-independent and parallel entities: mind and body. It is that the physical processes themselves are more dynamic than the linear, non-self-organizing perspective would lead us to believe. These dynamical processes can produce the mind by replicating some of their own features at higher levels of organization.

The need for a better understanding of part-whole relations, including the power of a self-organizing whole over its own parts, in both physical and mental manifestations, has been hinted at throughout the history of philosophy. The way the higher-level pattern maintains itself, by appropriating and replacing its own micro-components, offers resources to explain the phenomena of mental causation and other paradoxes of the mind-body problem without recourse to metaphysical dualism.

2. From Micro- to Macro-level Action

The principles of organization that produce living beings at lower levels are the same ones that produce mental states at higher ones. The ultimate source and nature of these self-organizational principles are still not fully understood, although they have been the subject of intense study in recent years (Anderson 2000; Bickhard 2000; Juarrero 1999; Kauffman 1993; Kelso 1995; Prigogene 1996). It is not necessary, however, to wait for the completion of a theoretical explanation to see the workings of these principles in biology. If we search in the right way, we will see the inevitability of the well-known phenomenology of conscious states in processes already discovered in the brain. The important thing is to keep in view *all* of the dimensions of the body's systems for maintaining itself, and this includes its motivational system. On the level of consciousness (and sometimes in preconscious states), the motivational aspect manifests itself as emotion. It will become increasingly obvious that, if we look at consciousness from the inside, as it were, seeing it as a larger-scale operation of self-organization that encompasses, appropriates, and often overrides that of its component parts, much of the mystery of the mind-body problem and the "hard problem" of consciousness (Chalmers 1995) will disappear.

In the quest to understand the mental properties of consciousness and intentionality (the property of being "about" something, or having a meaning), it has become conventional to note analogues to physical states by marking those physical states that bear superficial, functional similarities to mental states. Thus: conscious beings act to achieve goals that they understand and desire; purely physical systems "act" (they simply move) to reach end states that they only appear to understand and desire (for example, Searle 1981). We tend to speak of "as if" beliefs and desires in thermostats and computers, but we reserve the full-fledged intentional use of these concepts for living and/or conscious beings like humans. This practice has helped to obscure not only the origin, but also the composition of intentionality in these lower-order physical states. This result is ironic because conscious intentional states are built out of unconscious, proto-intentional ones; we cannot understand the former independently of the latter. A damaged brain, designed in part for communication, will in its more global organization co-opt areas in the right hemisphere to facilitate speech functions normally executed by the left brain. Similarly, the goal-oriented creature, when faced with a problem that its subordinate modular structures cannot solve separately, will organize these structures on a higher level, appropriating their motivational mechanisms to unify and drive the organism as a whole.

Consider another more commonsense example. You want to shift a huge rock. That job requires all your strength, which means all your component parts working together in relations optimal for the exertion of physical force. All parts of your body are harnessed to the task; you even clench your teeth, which in itself might make no direct contribution but it helps you to unify your effort. By contrast, cats have a more difficult time harnessing all their strength in one unified direction. We see that they want to push a heavy door open, and we know that they are muscular enough to have the physical strength to do it, but they lack the ability to harness all that strength in a unified effort. There are limits to the levels on which they can appropriate and organize their separate parts. Of course cats can do this in certain instinctive activities, such as leaping to a high ledge. But when the needed unification is not instinctual, they are less likely to find new ways to coordinate their subsystems to achieve it. Continuing in this vein, we can even see that groups of humans can self-organize for larger tasks, like building cities. But the emergence of collective intelligence in large groups composed of individual humans is not a subject of this book.

How is this appropriation effected? What mechanisms can unify the separate systems and sub-systems on a higher level? As hinted at earlier, we believe that *representation* is the primary method (Damasio 1994, 1999). By "representation," as already stressed, we do not mean an abstract symbolic event isomorphic to and caused by its referent, as traditionally postulated by theorists in philosophy of mind (for example, Fodor 1975, 1987). We also do not mean purely pictorial representation, as the term "imagery" traditionally implies. By representation we mean an activity in which we imaginatively simulate embodied sensorimotor actions toward a symbolizing element, where the isomorphism, as Merleau-Ponty (1942) suggested, is between the *actions* afforded by the symbol and those afforded by what the symbol represents. That which the symbol represents, on this view, is determined not by the stimulus that originally produced it, but by the imagined actions performed upon it.

Why make representation play such a pivotal role? Consciousness requires representation because it exists to help organisms *unify their efforts* so as to achieve goals that require long-range planning, and thus must be represented. Goals such as appeasement of hunger, whose satisfaction mechanisms are not built into the system, must be explicitly represented in such a way that the representations can activate higher-order goal-seeking activity. Just as a feeding mechanism recognizes when it has achieved a state of satiation, and when it has not, so a conscious organism requires a way of recognizing when it has achieved its more abstract goal. Lacking a hard-wired system for identifying, say, the state of having successfully completed one's PhD dissertation, we need to create a representation of that state, and then organize our multiple abilities to achieve it, and to recognize when it has been achieved. Mechanisms for mental representation are designed to make this behavior possible, through comparison processes.

On a lower level of organization, a desired bodily action is represented through the activity of the cerebellum looping with parietal "body mapping" (Damasio 2003; Haines et al. 1997) and the inhibitory functions of the motor and premotor cortex that lead to action imagery (Jeannerod 1994, 1997). Feedback from the completed action is compared to the original (retained via efference copy), errors are corrected, and the goal is deemed to be satisfied (Ito 2000). Longer-range goals, such as acquiring a Ph.D., are similarly represented, although in a more complicated way. Represented actual results are then compared with these anticipatory representations.

In this book, our goal can be represented in words rather simply: we aim at an organic account of consciousness, one that emphasizes its continuity with other activities of a living entity. In explaining any feature of a living thing, one can either view it as having developed adaptively out of other features, or one can view it as primarily a novelty, as in the case of a mutation. An example of the latter in the area of language would be Chomsky's (1965) theory, which views human language not as having evolved in earlier life forms but as originating fully-functional in human brains. While most contemporary theorists do not hold that human consciousness is a bolt from the blue, they do write as if it embodies a completely novel element not present in other biological systems. We believe that all features of consciousness are continuous with other biological attributes, and that contemporary neuroscience and psychology already possess the tools for understanding this development.

Specifically, we must show how a self-organizational dynamical systems approach can take account of the emotional purposes of the organism that initiate and structure the processing of all conscious information (Cytowic 1993; Pribram 1980; Watt 1998, 2000; Ellis 1986, 1995, 2000a, 2001a, b; Newton, 1996, 2000; Ellis and Newton 1998a, 2000a, b). Only then can a dynamical systems approach account for the difference between conscious and nonconscious processes in a way that accommodates both physiological and philosophical considerations more coherently than competing theories. One cannot simply skip directly from, for example, mathematical chaos equations to consciousness, because the result of such a move is always an accounting merely of physical processes, not an understanding of why they are conscious, or how the conscious ones are different from nonconscious ones. One must move slowly and methodically up the ladder from biological purposes (which are self-organizing) to motivation and emotion (with specialized brain circuitries adapted to handle certain kinds of organism-environment imbalances), to action planning, inhibited action which results in action imagery (Jeannerod 1997), object affordances for possible actions (Gibson 1986), and finally the intentional understanding that results in phenomenal consciousness. At the level of intentional understanding, clear philosophical concepts are indispensable.

Why should the inclusion of emotion in the understanding of consciousness make such a difference? Emotion is central because it is necessary for the kind of genuinely purposeful activity that can occur in the most complex beings; purpose in turn is what unites the unconscious and the conscious levels of brain activity. There is an important sense in which you are the self-same individual awake, asleep, or in a coma, and essential to this identity is that the purposes of your living organism are continuous from the unconscious to the conscious states. Of course there are purposes that exist only at the conscious level; there are also purposes that never become conscious. Additionally, various purposes in your mind and body can be at odds. But all of these purposes are nevertheless active in a single continuity. Higher levels of organization incorporate, or seek to incorporate, the lower levels into a single organismic goal, and resolving the problems of opposing purposes is the central general and continuing goal of complex organisms such as humans. The striving for unity of diverse brain systems for the accomplishment of a single organismic purpose is the reason we can become conscious; the complexity of our type of organism demands it. Consciously, we experience the striving for this kind of unity of function by means of emotion; the experience of emotion is the means by which we select, organize, guide, and evaluate our actions.

Bickle (2002) and also Bickle and Ellis (2005) discuss the fact that stimulation of only a few hundred brain cells can result in a phenomenal experience such as an apparent perception or memory. However, both are aware that, even if a conscious "brain in a vat" could be possible (as philosophers like Putnam 1996 have argued), a single "neuron in a thimble," in isolation from a living system, would not be conscious. Even in the context of localized microstimulation, it is necessary that the emotional brain initiate the release of neurotransmitters such as GABA, in order for waking consciousness or even dreaming sleep to be possible (Bickle 2005). The stimulation of a few localized cells leads to consciousness only in that larger context, which includes motivation and self-organizational functioning within a dynamical biological system.

Organization of the disparate reactions to the stimuli affecting a living entity is essential for an adequate response, in any organism that is not completely preprogrammed, like the famous wasp, which is unable to represent explicitly the ultimate goal of its action sequences, and so must begin at the beginning whenever it is interrupted (Gould and Gould 1994). Our type of organism has evolved to seek to make coherent the stimuli that impinge on it, so as to coordinate appropriate and efficient responses, and it has evolved diverse strategies to do this. Consciousness is one of them. If the goal of consciousness is unity of the organism's responses within emotionally grasped purposes of action, then a self-organizing approach to both the organism as a whole, and to consciousness in particular, seems appropriate. It is the nature of organisms to create unities of function by organizing themselves and their environments.

In order to build a theory of consciousness around self-organization, it is necessary to have a minimal characterization of the structure of self-organizing systems in general. Even such a preliminary definition of self-organization will already lead to an understanding of how different the causal structure of consciousness is from the traditional, passive-receiving model of perception, and from non-conscious information-processing machines.

a. What Is Self-Organization?

"Self-organization" refers to the ability of some "open" thermodynamic systems—that is, those which exchange energy and materials with their environment across organizational stability—to maintain their existence and function by means of internal mechanisms, not by external control. An example of external control would be a living body on "life-support," with vital functions maintained by external invasive technology. Without that intervention, the functions would cease. In contrast, living and healthy biological systems are self-organizing: in many of their systems and at many organizational levels, if one component fails to perform its vital function adequately, others can often step in and supply the necessary elements. Thus "self-organization" refers to a system's ability to re-organize its components and appropriate new elements as necessary for a continued pattern of functioning. (For detailed, technical discussions of this aspect of self-organization, see Kauffmann 1993.)

Self-organizing systems are goal-directed; the primary "purpose" of self-organization is self-maintenance, ensuring the continuity of the essential functions of the organism (including growth and reproduction) and preserving the integrity of the system against the invasion of its boundaries by external forces and loss of energy to the environment. A system is physically defined by its boundaries. A self-organizing system, even if it is "open" in the thermodynamic sense defined above, has boundaries that are permeable only under conditions normally controlled to a great extent by the organism itself. It functions somewhat independently of invasive external forces. To the extent that it does depend on its environment for continuity of function—and all systems do to some extent—it itself plays a role in selecting and co-opting those environmental contributions.

One example from recent research in biological sexual reproduction concerns the female egg awaiting fertilization in the fallopian tube. It was once thought that the egg was a passive recipient of one successful, active sperm. It is now known that it is the egg itself that makes its borders penetrable by a suitable sperm, through chemical evaluation of it before the sperm is allowed to pass through the egg's outer membrane (Swanson et al. 1998). In that sense, the egg is both self-maintaining and self-organizing—the latter because its own components partly determine whether or not it becomes fertilized.

While self-organization in biological systems has long been recognized, it has been studied as an intrinsically interesting natural process only in recent years (Monod 1971; Kauffman 1993). Self-organization has begun to look, to some researchers, like the key to the nature of life itself. Kauffman in particular is interested in how a non-self-organizing collection of entities can, with increasing complexity, become a self-organizing system.

The authors are aware that since ancient times explanations of human behavior have been modeled on the latest developments of technology and theoretical science, from push-pull mechanisms to parallel-processing computers and quantum mechanics. Thus self-organization might seem to be just another step in this process, doomed to be replaced sooner or later. Since, however, self-organization is largely applicable to *biological* mechanisms, not inanimate ones, we can afford to be somewhat optimistic.

b. How Does Self-Organization Apply to Conscious Organisms?

Every self-organizing system has "goals," which determine the particular adjustments it makes in its structure. For example, the egg has the "goal" of becoming fertilized by a healthy sperm; it therefore adjusts the permeability of its boundary in response to perceived criteria in candidate sperm. The sperm has a different goal: not that the egg be fertilized with the healthiest sperm, but instead that *it itself* be the sperm that fertilizes the egg (however, see also recent work suggesting that groups of sperm work together to advance the prospects of just one of their members—for example, Evans and Florman 2002). Because each sperm wants to be the selected one, rather than sharing the egg's goal of the *best* sperm being chosen, the egg must exercise control over its boundaries. Every self-organizing entity has its own goals which it cannot "assume" are identical with the goals of anything outside itself. Self-organization, in other words, could be seen as a form of distrust, or even paranoia, though that can go only so far; trust must be present as well. The egg cannot determine *all* relevant information about the sperm.

In the general research project currently investigating self-organization, we can distinguish two main types. One is the study of the mechanisms themselves—how, for example, a group of unrelated elements become a self-organizing system; or how many different mechanisms of self-organization exist or are possible (for example, Kauffman 1993; Kelso 1995). The other type is the attempt to understand how inclusive self-organization is in biological, and possibly other, systems (Juarrero 1999; Thelen et al. 2001). For example, could a computer be constructed to be self-organizing in the way a biological organism is? And, within biology, how much can the concept of self-organization explain? Can it explain, for example, consciousness? If we view consciousness on a self-organization model, would that help to resolve some of its mysteries, in the way this move has helped to resolve some mysteries of life processes in general?

It sounds plausible enough to say that consciousness is a vital function of organisms like humans, and thus also easy to say that, in some way or other, this function like others must be self-organizing. But the transition from life in general to consciousness is not smooth, because the mysteries of consciousness still appear, as they have for thousands of years, to be *of a different order* from other mysteries of life. They seem irreducible to *any* physical mechanism, whereas self-organization is a physical mechanism. We must still remember that, even if we could know everything about the physical mechanisms of consciousness, this would not seem to entail knowledge of what that conscious state "is like," unless we have prior subjective experience of it that is *not* based on such empirical-scientific observations (Jackson 1986). Thus a complete physical explanation of the neural substrates of consciousness still would not automatically explain why those particular neural mechanisms could not just as well occur *without* being accompanied by consciousness, even if the physical mechanism in question is a self-organizing one.

Nonetheless, many people believe that consciousness is a physical mechanism, regardless of how it may seem; and if so, then it might be that the concept of self-organization could be extended, alone or with other hypotheses, to cover consciousness as well. That is what we seek to do in this book. At the same time, we must ask ourselves this question: Extending the concept of self-organization from biology in general to consciousness seems *prima facie* just as difficult as crossing the mind-body gap by any other means has been. So what possible trick that hasn't already been tried could we use to illuminate consciousness in its full robust subjectivity using the objective methods of physical science?

Ironically, a clue to the answer can be found in the apparent novelty of the concept of self-organization as it is applied biologically. That application is exciting precisely because the concept invokes *teleology*, which we learned in the Twentieth Century to dismiss as an Aristotelian remnant contaminating scientific thinking. If we say that a bunch of molecules, cells, and bodily organs can organize themselves for a purpose, aren't we imputing human-like goals to a blind mechanistic process? The exciting answer turns out to be No. A nonconscious, non-human system can embody goals and organize itself with the purpose of achieving those goals, and do so in a way that appears "intelligent" and "planned." But then, once it has been accepted that a nonconscious biological system can be self-organizing in that sense, it is suddenly thought difficult to understand how consciousness, the original home of teleology as deliberate, purposeful planning, could be self-organizing in the *same sense*. We are never satisfied!

It *is* possible to view conscious mental processes as self-organizing in the same sense as purely biological ones. It can be done, moreover, without adding to the system any completely novel elements, such as the unanalyzable component of "consciousness," a distinct element in the universe as Chalmers would have it. Recognizing different levels of self-organization, and understanding the ways each level organizes its components to achieve the purposes appropriate for that level, entails recognizing properties that are "emergent" in a sense, but not in the sense of giving rise to a *new type of entity* unexplainable in terms of the old components. Acknowledging a more modest kind of emergence does not require rushing to visit our old friend the "emergency metaphysician," as it were. Emergent properties are nothing but the self-organization of the properties from the lower level, combined in such a way that they constitute a novelty *from the point of view of a particular observer—the subject*. This does not imply an ontological dualism (or pluralism) in which novel entities at one level of organization require completely different ontological constituents from those required for lower ones, and would exist in an objective sense in principle independent of intelligent observers. Instead, we argue that conscious phenomenology—that is, experience—is an emergent property, for the subject, of certain levels of organization of brain states, and that this level emerges in the process of those levels being *put to use* by its subject. Emergent properties are, in other words, the results of attempts by agents to combine components belonging to lower levels of organization into novel wholes for the purpose of achieving certain goals for that agent.

The goals of a conscious organism are novel, but not qualitatively so. They involve the attempt to achieve a desirable future state of being for the agent, which is continuous from the behavior of one-celled organisms to the most idealistic human aspirations. The further the desired state is from the current state of the organism, the higher the levels of organization needed to achieve it. In the development of forms of life, it seems to some humans that a great qualitative leap occurred between the mundane desires of lower animals and the ideals of human beings, and that this leap required the emergence of consciousness as a novel element in the universe. We think this view is incorrect. Consciousness is novel only in the sense that it is a new combination of elements all of which existed previously. Conscious agents combine their own mental states in novel ways, and the result to them is qualitatively unique; however, these unique qualitative states exist only *for them,* in the *execution of their own efforts,* and these efforts can be objectively understood from a scientific standpoint.

Consider an analogy. Sam wants to see if he can visualize an object that is red all over and green all over, at the same time. Now, we know that it is impossible for a normal person to have such a visual experience, because of the opponent-processing mechanism of color vision, and we are assuming that Sam is a normal person. Nevertheless, Sam doesn't understand the science of vision, and he believes that such a visual experience should be possible. So he searches his memory, and comes up with an image of a fall maple leaf, which has an unusual bronze-like appearance. The appearance is caused by a rapid alternation of red aspects and green aspects affecting Sam's visual system. Sam thinks that the bronze-like appearance is a simultaneous blend of red and green; in other words, he believes that he is observing a single, steady color, red-green, but in fact he is perceiving an alternation of red and green. The bronze-like appearance is not caused by a single stable color, but Sam thinks that it is. To him, his image is what it is like to see something at once red and green all over.

There is no such red-green object in the physical world, and there could not be, but in Sam's experience, such an object plays an important role. The image and other sensations and emotions produced by it become important functional components of Sam's consciousness. In an important sense, Sam is "deluded" in thinking that the bronze maple leaf that seems simultaneously red and green in his experience *matches a physical object in the world* that is simultaneously red and green, when in fact the object in the world is alternately red and green. Moreover, Sam's own perception actually produces the illusion of simultaneous red and green by alternating what it would do to produce red and to produce green, so rapidly that Sam is unaware of it. But at the same time, there does exist a novel element in his consciousness that plays a role in his psychology. An outside observer, moreover, can understand exactly what is going on with Sam—both why Sam believes he can see a simultaneously red-green object, and why what Sam is really doing is to alternately see the object as red and as green. But the scientific observer cannot fall under the same delusion as Sam, because the scientist's knowledge prevents taking the bronze-like appearance to be the appearance of a red-green object.

Sam has a special state of consciousness, the impression that something can be simultaneously red and green, and this impression plays a causal role in Sam's psychology. This state of consciousness is an emergent property, one that exists only in Sam. It emerged in the activity of attempting to combine actually incompatible elements into a single entity, and then treating that entity as if it also represented a physical reality. The entity doesn't represent reality in that way, but Sam's higher-order mental state of believing that he experiences it is itself a higher-order physical reality—an emergent property of Sam. It emerges out of simpler component features: his ability to see red, and his ability to see green, plus his attempt to unify those two abilities into one perception in order to achieve a unitary purpose.

We want to argue that consciousness itself is an "emergent" property in the same sense as the red-green physical object Sam thinks he sees, with the difference that consciousness itself is not the unique creation of an individual who is ignorant of something that is known by others. Instead, it is a built-in characteristic of human-like brains that, as they gain the ability to aspire to goals beyond the immediate, make use of combinatorial mechanisms that automatically blend "incompatible" elements, and as a result produce emergent properties common to all creatures with similar brains. Because all the other creatures with whom we communicate have the same impression of reality, as if the relevant perceptual qualities existed independently (or at least they act as if they have the same impression of reality), we do not think of such impressions as delusions. We accept them without question—until, that is, philosophers and scientists point out to us their inherent problems—that the red and green are alternating rather than simultaneous, and that perceived colors themselves are created by our own perceptual activities rather than embedded in the surfaces of physical objects, as they appear to be. We must remember that what Locke called the "secondary qualities" of objects such as colors result from the perceptual apparatus of the subject, and are not as they appear to be.

The key point is that emergent properties are created by combining pre-existing ones in novel unities that serve certain purposes for the organism. This notion of emergence suggests an answer to the question of how to bridge the gap between self-organizational mechanisms in unconscious biological processes, and consciousness. All self-organizational processes produce properties that are emergent *for the organism in question*. We might say that the process of self-organization is the process of emergence. In that case, the puzzle of consciousness becomes, not how a new property can emerge, but simply how does this emergent property result from the combination of others, and how does it differ from the lower level unities from which it is composed? The difference, we will argue, is not as dramatic as many think; it is, moreover, quite predictable from the components and the patterns of emergence at lower levels. It turns on three key notions: *emotion, action, and representation*. These notions have been central to traditional discussions of consciousness. Our aim is to show that if they are viewed as continuous with processes at lower levels of organization, in which analogues of them perform central functions, then consciousness will be seen as the natural and inevitable next step in organismic development. Let's consider how each of these levels of organization use the emotional level in particular to build a system that can incorporate all of them into a nested hierarchy of motivational demands arising from the various levels of self-organization that make up the whole dynamically stable organism.

c. Motivation and Emotion as Self-Organizing Phenomena

There is a primitive sense in which all self-organizing systems are "motivated," in that their organizing activity is goal-driven. The goal could be as simple as maintaining homeostasis in the presence of environmental perturbations, the way crystals do, but it can also involve growth and reproduction, as in living organisms. We can speak of motivation even in very primitive organisms; motivation is simply the tendencies manifested by the organism that distinguish it from its environment. A non-self-organizing entity, a simple collection of objects, has no such tendencies in itself. One could speak of entropy as its tendency, but entropy does not distinguish a collection of elements from other elements in its environment.

With the evolution of greater complexity, self-organizing beings develop new complex ways of organizing their tendencies, as well as the mechanisms that realize them. In animals like us, these tendencies are sometimes manifested as emotions. In line with normal usage of the terms, we regard emotion as a higher-level phenomenon than motivation. Emotion refers to an organism's attempt to balance the needs of the various motivational tendencies within its system in interaction with environmental factors.

This agenda also requires a system for monitoring the various motivations and some of their interrelations with each other, whether consciously or not. For example, when proprioception reveals a churning up of the stomach combined with increased heartbeat and adrenal secretion, a tensing of certain muscles and a constricting of certain systems of blood vessels, the result is a monitoring that tells the unified total system that there is an imbalance of the system. *Motivations* may express the needs of subsystems within the organism, but *emotions* are monitored at the level of the whole organism. Moreover, the monitoring of the system's imbalance may be automatically correlated with certain immediate action tendencies, because each of the subsystems giving rise to the relevant motivations is aimed toward acting in its preferred self-organizational pattern to begin with. That is, the aim of motivations is for the system to maintain patterns of activity, not just patterns of stasis; therefore, the aim of motivations and emotions is to facilitate patterns of action. So when the balance of the system's action tendencies is "off," there will be a corresponding automatic altering of the organism's action tendencies. If no further sophistication is achieved, such as an ability to inhibit action, the result may be a simple reflex action.

At a still more complex level, when the organism is able at least to attempt to represent what an emotion is "about" relative to its environment, even in a very primitive way, we can speak of "feelings," or conscious emotions. So, in line with traditional usage, we refer to motivation as a self-organizational tendency. Emotion is the sentient organism's attempt to balance all its self-organizational tendencies, which also requires a monitoring system for its motivations. And conscious emotion is the feeling of the body's emotions along with a representation of what the feelings are about. At each of these stages of sentient sophistication, there will be corresponding action tendencies, because motivation intends action in the first place. The pattern that the system is aiming to maintain is a pattern of activity, not stasis.

This progression, however, is not as clean as these abstractions might make it sound. First of all, when an organism evolves to the point of being sentient enough for its nervous system to be able to connect representations of "aboutness" to emotions within an action-planning process, it is also already sentient enough to monitor even some of its own simple motivations and interpret those by means of afferent feedback from proprioceptive pathways. We can even perceive (or "proprioceive") our own heartbeat in this way, if we pay careful attention, yet the heartbeat is not an emotion. But only an organism that has enough sentient sophistication to have emotion can perform such a function. That is, only an organism capable of emotion would have the facility to perceive its own heartbeat, even though the heartbeat itself is not an emotion.

Emotions therefore are only the tip of a much larger iceberg. In many animals, there is a complex system in the brainstem for generating neurotransmitters that activate various behaviors needed for growth, reproduction, or just maintaining homeostasis or allostasis in the face of environmental changes; we shall speak of the states produced by these neurotransmitters as motivational states. Because of our complexity, the motivational states can interfere with each other, creating a need for higher-level organization to determine priorities, compromises, or integrations of the conflicting goals. If the higher-order resolution necessarily requires prediction of and planning for the future, then the competing motivations become components of conscious planning activities, and become enacted representations by the organism who is their agent, along with representations of possible future states; only in this way can these alternatives be compared and the best ones selected.

The relationships among emotion, motivation, consciousness, and intentionality are complex. We should not think of emotions simply as "motivations made conscious," as if emotion merely made conscious what was already present motivationally. Consciousness should not be thought of as if a "spotlight" is now shining on the motivations, or as if some "internal eye" is observing them. A conscious emotion is a way for the organism to monitor how well it is doing in maintaining itself vis-à-vis various mixtures of motivations to which environmental conditions may be relevant. Therefore, unlike motivation simpliciter, emotion can *represent itself as salient* to a decision the organism must make; it is represented as a component of a future state of the organism, along with other sensory-motor representations of that and alternative states. The emotional representation takes a form that is appropriate to the other representations with which it is associated. The emotion can then itself serve as a motivator, precisely because it has played a role in a conscious representation of a possible future. This analysis of emotion represents the carefully thought-out consensus of both authors, but for more detailed discussion of these issues, see Ellis (2005).

d. Action and Reaction

One of the traditional concept-pairs that has been used to talk about the mind-body problem involves action *versus* reaction. We must carefully distinguish true *action* from mere activities that resemble actions but are really only passive reactions. The starting point for our way of distinguishing between conscious and non-conscious information processing is the observation that conscious and intentional beings can *act*; whereas unconscious automata only "act" (with quotation marks)—that is, they move or execute operations, but their executions lack intentionality and hence are not full-fledged *actions*. They do not mean anything by what they "do," or understand their own goals. We might say that a sluggish engine is "trying" to turn over, but it is not really *trying* in the way that *we* intentionally try to do things.

Part of our present task is to try to unify those two senses of "action." We suggested earlier that action in the full-fledged or "macro" sense depends on action in the "micro" sense. So the apparent bifurcation between acting and mere "acting" (acting in a sense that is analogous to, but not the same as self-initiated, purposeful action) is more superficial than has been thought. Conscious, intentional actions are continuous with the unconscious "actions" of a self-organizing being. Particularly in our discussions of phenomenal consciousness, and of mental representations, we adopt an approach similar in some ways to that of Alva Noë (1999; see also O'Regan and Noë 2000, Noë et al. 2001). He argues that consciousness is a form of activity of a subject; that the subject's phenomenal experience *is that subject's own activity*, rather than being the passive appreciation by a subjective "self" of qualitative properties of "an experience" taken as an object-like mental entity. His account is similar to one we have put forward (Ellis and Newton 1998a) in taking an enactive view of conscious phenomena, although we hold, with other critics, that this view alone is inadequate as a complete account of phenomenal consciousness (O'Regan and Noë 2000).

We discuss this view at length in later chapters. Here, it is important to note that part of the self-organization view entails that the "actions" of any self-organizing being and the actions of a conscious being are not so different as is usually supposed. Taking an enactive view of consciousness opens the way for a full-fledged theory of human mentality that emerges naturally from more fundamental processes of life. Later chapters will go into more detail with these specific processes, which need to be carefully clarified in order to have a viable concept of action. But first, we want to emphasize that it is crucial to understand the causal role of "dynamical systems" in relation to their own micro-constituents. The notion that action can be distinguished from mere reaction is an indispensable part of what is needed, not only to understand consciousness as an action-based phenomenon, but also to show how this account resolves aspects of the mind-body problem that were intractable for the traditional receptive model of consciousness with its supposed intervening "information processing" of inputs and outputs.

Accordingly, the next chapter addresses a difficult but necessary part of a self-organizational approach: showing how a system can act on its own, using its own micro-components rather than merely having its activity determined by the additive juxtaposition of the causal sequences in the micro-components themselves. In other words, how can the causal power of a system over its own parts be reconciled with Kim's "causal closure" at the micro-level?

5

Herding Neurons: The Causal Structure of Self-Organizing Systems

1. Action and the Mind-Body Problem

Throughout this book, we have been focusing on reasons why a self-organization theory of the kind to be explored here is capable of solving philosophical problems involving consciousness that are intractable from other approaches. Traditionally there have been several main types of conceptual problems that pull against each other in such a way that it seems virtually impossible to solve all of them at the same time. It is important, therefore, to show how a self-organizing theory can slice cleanly through these problems. In brief, there are three main stumbling blocks: First, there is the "explanatory gap" problem, also known as the "hard problem" of consciousness. According to Levine's (1983) "explanatory gap" argument, the relation of consciousness to the physical world is paradoxical because, given any physical explanation of consciousness, it is conceivable that all the elements in that explanation could occur, with the same *information processing* outcomes as in a conscious process, but *in the absence of* consciousness. For example, any digital computational process could occur *in the absence* of consciousness. This is essentially the same problem as the "hard problem" of consciousness put forward by Chalmers (1995): Even if we could show how consciousness regularly accompanies a certain pattern of physical events, we still would not have understood why just those patterns, and not others, should be accompanied by consciousness. That is, if conscious state X regularly correlates with physical process Y, explaining what causes Y to occur, by itself, does not explain why X correlates with Y. Those are two separate questions. The second of the two—explaining why X correlates with Y—is what Chalmers calls the hard problem.

A second obstacle is the problem, long emphasized by phenomenologists, that knowing about physical processes doesn't allow an observer to know "what it's like" to experience another person's conscious state—a point elaborated in Jackson's (1986) "knowledge argument."

And third, there is the problem of mental causation. If physical events at the micro-level were really sufficient to cause a subsequent action, then whether these micro-level events are organized in the form of a conscious choice or not should be causally irrelevant; the consequent should occur just as well with or without a conscious choice, but in many instances we can easily observe that our conscious choice to do an action does result in the action. Philosophers have puzzled over this paradox since the time of Descartes.

First consider the way a self-organizational approach with an appropriately prominent role for motivational processes could account for the explanatory gap problem. If we describe consciousness as a process in which possible action affordances are anticipated by an emotional interest in the environment, we can have hope of understanding how and why the human organism would entertain these emotionally interested anticipations, and how the anticipations result in representations of the world. We saw earlier that the Mack and Rock (1998) inattentional blindness studies show that subjects whose attention is preoccupied fail to consciously see objects that otherwise they could easily see. Mack and Rock conclude that attention is a *prerequisite* for perceptual consciousness rather than a *result* of it. The mechanisms of the direction of attention in turn are controlled by brain processes whose motivation is to achieve the purposes of the self-organizing organism. In this sense, the act of directing attention is motivated. Extrapolating from these kinds of observations, we can see that all conscious states require motivational components. This suggests the common-sense notion that the first concern of any conscious state is to discern the action affordances of the environment.

All consciousness, then, includes an imagining of how we might act relative to the world. Jeannerod (1997) has studied the neurophysiology of this kind of action imagery, and has shown that in order to imagine oneself doing action X, our brains (at the subcortical and cerebellar levels) must actually send the action command X to our efferent body-moving systems, and simultaneously *inhibit* the signal (at the level of the supplementary motor area). The upshot is that even perceptual consciousness involves understanding ways we could act relative to objects, and these action images in turn must be motivated. Conscious experience, then, by contrast to unconscious information processing, entails an emotionally interested anticipation of actual or possible sensory and proprioceptive input.

When conscious experience is characterized in this way, it begins to make sense that emotionally motivated agency could be what drives the anticipatory process and thus lends a feeling (or "what it's like") element to the subject's rehearsal of the action affordances of the world in terms of action imagery. At this point, we can make use of the recently popular theory of embodied cognition, which sometimes has also been called (with Varela et al. 1991/1993) an "enactive" theory of conscious intentionality. Intentionality, or the "aboutness" relation between mental states and their objects, is rooted in our capacity for simple, goal-directed actions.

Such an account entails a strong role for *action representations* in consciousness and intentional mental activity. We have argued for an approach that views representations as traces of sensorimotor experience that are only potential representations unless activated in a particular context for purpose-directed use by the subject, or agent. In principle, the same action-representation process that underlies intentionality can ground the subjective-objective distinction: in other words, it can ground the concept of the external world, by taking note of the errors or failures of action. The external world is what makes such error possible, since otherwise all actions would be equally affordable. So not only external objects can be understood in terms of the agency of the subject; the basic subjective-objective distinction itself can also be understood by a subject in terms of its own conscious experience of goal-directed action. That is, by attempting actions, we can note the ways in which objective conditions do *not* facilitate the subjectively intended actions. In this way, we can form a connection between the unique phenomenology of consciousness and the representational functions of the brain.

We have also seen how an enactive approach can also address the other two major philosophical puzzles—Jackson's "knowledge argument," and the problem of mental causation. These apparent paradoxes reflect emergent phenomena that can be understood from the perspective of a general account of emergence, including contexts other than mentality. With regard to the knowledge argument, it is obvious that an external observer cannot execute a subject's unique actions, because the self-organizational processes that give rise to that experience are unique to the subject. If the scientist Mary observes Jackson's brain, the "what it's like" dimension for her arises from her own body's motivations for observing it, not from Jackson's. Thus the conscious experience she ends up having is her own, not Jackson's. She cannot perform his actions.

The mental causation problem is also tractable for a self-organizational/emotion-centered approach. Emotions arise from a holistic level of aim-orientation. This holistic level is able to readjust the *background conditions* needed for any micro-process to be causally sufficient for a given outcome. If the same micro processes were to occur in a different pattern, they would not have the same outcomes. The larger pattern that provides the necessary context here is determined not only by the holistic concerns of the dynamical system to maintain itself; as Panksepp (1998) and Ellis (2005) suggest, the overall pattern must also fit with a certain preference for more complex basins of attraction over simpler ones. That is, the organism wants to maintain itself at a suitably high energy level and with a certain degree of organizational complexity.

In concrete terms, we can see simple examples of this self-organizational causal structure at work in the shunt mechanisms of biological energy cycles, in the plasticity of brain development, and in the body's ability to appropriate new cells to take over the function of destroyed cells—within certain limits, of course. So, in principle, the apparent paradoxes or contradictions in experience that are reflected in the traditional mind-body problems can be robust, but still objectively comprehensible, and an enactive model of consciousness can handle not only the "aboutness" of intentional mental states, but also the unique puzzles of phenomenal consciousness.

The self-organizational model also accounts for the notoriously intractable problem of defining what is meant by representation, when it is reformulated in the way we indicated earlier. We have spoken of representation in terms of the conscious organism's understanding of the action affordances of its environment. The concept of representation is controversial. Some dynamical systems theorists deny altogether that there *are* representations, while others assign them a limited role. Most theorists continue to think of imagistic representations as purely *visual*. We have taken pains to dispel this tendency.

We do not hold that representations are pictorial, or that they are displays inside the head that reflect what is going on outside. Like consciousness itself, we think of representation as an *activity,* one that incorporates all sensorimotor modalities. Representing is the method by which subjects think about and plan their future activities.

The most nagging problem with traditional accounts of representation is that they emphasize that the representing entity must be both isomorphic to and closely causally linked with the represented element. Neither isomorphism nor causation, of course, can make one thing represent another in a meaningful sense. As Thelen et al. (2001) point out, any dynamic internal event causally related to something external would then constitute a representation, which would be absurd.

But representation does take place—through a subject's use of it in context of embodied (organismically purposeful) action. Notice that this formulation allows for both conscious and preconscious representation. R represents object O if, because of some appropriate isomorphism, R plays the role of O in an imagined action involving O, either consciously or preconsciously (for example, in a "habituated" way, as with Donoghue's monkeys that we discussed earlier).

In sum, we have suggested so far that a self-organizing-process model of consciousness is especially promising because it makes possible the solution of problems that are intractable for other approaches. Among recent theories, we find many forms of epiphenomenalism, interactionism, and other closet dualisms that are incompatible with the causal sufficiency of neurophysiological processes. At the same time, many reductionist psychophysical identity theories seem incapable of making sense of other well-known problems such as Jackson's "knowledge argument." If consciousness is simply identical with its micro-constituents, then complete knowledge of the micro-constituents, which can be obtained empirically, should also include complete knowledge of consciousness, including its mysterious "what it's like" dimension; but apparently, it does not (Jackson 1986). One of the exciting aspects of a self-organizing process approach, when it is elaborated along the lines of dynamical systems, is that it can overcome these conceptual difficulties. Only a self-organizing process that *executes* its actions can know "what it is like" to execute them, because to know them *is* to execute them. An external observer only witnesses the actions, and the resulting knowledge is very different from knowing what it is like to execute them.

Thinking about the enactive-process approach to consciousness, and how it is different from linear computer thinking, requires clarifying several very difficult terms that were somewhat elusive for twentieth-century science and philosophy. Among the terms that need to be rethought are:

Living organisms must be distinguished from "merely mechanical" systems that process information and engage in feedback loops—such as thermostats—and also from systems that are self-organizing and do appropriate their own needed substratum, such as mineral crystals, yet are not living.

Self-organizing systems must be distinguished from systems that do show a tendency to maintain themselves across multiply-realizable replacements of their parts, yet obviously merely result from causal operations *on* them, and therefore merely react rather than act, remaining purely externally regulated rather than self-organizing—for example, a sophisticated robot that has been designed to replace its own parts when they quit working.

Emotion must be distinguished from a completely mechanical and non-conscious process in which things "want" outcomes only in the sense that they exhibit a *tendency* to behave in certain ways—for example, atoms "want" to achieve electrical neutrality by filling or emptying their outer electron shells, and this atomic "wanting" fits together with others to form nervous systems that "want" to reach electrolytic balance, and so on; yet there seems to be a difference between mere "wanting" in this sense, of which atoms are capable, and *emotions* which are capable of being consciously *felt* in the way that humans when awake or dreaming can consciously feel them. We want ultimately to show, however, how the latter develops from the former.

Purposeful intentions must be distinguished from mere *tendencies*, which of course all natural phenomena, even the simplest, exhibit, and which are merely descriptive of the principles of physics and inorganic chemistry. If living self-organizing processes are really to be distinguished from nonliving ones, we must understand how the overall process can be purpose-directed in a way that is compatible with linear causality, yet whose explanation is not completely exhausted by principles of linear causality applied at the micro-level of analysis.

If we really take these needed distinctions seriously, we realize that what is needed, at the bottom level of analysis, is a clear delineation of just how the causal structure of self-organizing systems is different from that of linear systems. Many discussions of self-organization attempt to gloss over this question. Does self-organization, after all, contradict the normally observed regular patterns of sufficient causation that seem to be applicable to chemical, and yes even biochemical processes? In our view, there is no contradiction between self-organization and the "causally closed" sequences of sufficient causation that occur at lower levels within the system. But we need to know for sure that there is indeed no conflict here, and this requires a careful analysis of how the two systems of causation, linear and self-organizing, actually occur simultaneously within the same system. To put it differently, we need to know how a self-organizing causal structure is built up from lower-level efficient causal sequences. The next and final section of this chapter, then, should be especially interesting for those who remain skeptical on the question of whether there is a real difference between action and mere reaction, and correlatively, whether there is really teleology in natural systems such as living organisms.

2. Why "Top-Down" Dynamical Causation Is Compatible with Causal Closure

It is absolutely crucial that self-organizational dynamical systems approaches to consciousness face up to the problem of causal closure in a direct and fully explanatory way. We cannot deny that the principles of inorganic chemistry still hold when in the context of organic chemistry reactions; and the principles of organic chemistry are not broken when in the context of larger biological systems, including the nervous systems of animals. John Bickle (1992, 2002, 2005, 2000) and also Bickle and Ellis (2005) have continued to demand that the notion of causal sufficiency at the micro-level not be sacrificed in order to make room for the plasticity of brain functioning, or the apparently "top-down" nature of mental causation, or even the distinction between organic and inorganic systems.

At the same time, we are in agreement with Mark Bickhard (1993, 2000) that there must be such a thing as top-down causation in complex dynamical systems. In this section, we take the bull by the horns, and present our reconciliation of these long-irreconcilable viewpoints, by showing how causal closure is maintained in a system in which, at the same time, the process has the power to select, appropriate, and reorganize its own micro-components. We believe that the way we have worked out this problem is highly consistent with the "interactivist" approach for which Bickhard has long argued, and which is grounded in self-organizational theory.

Many theories of dynamical systems begin at the level of indeterminate quantum activity (for example, Globus 2003). Since quantum behavior is indeterminate, it is chaotic, and causal analyses are not necessary in order to reach mathematical conclusions about which patterns of organization are more or less likely to obtain at the aggregate level where phenomena like consciousness occur. So dynamical systems theory, often called "chaos theory," can be developed without the need for mechanical causation at the smallest scale of physical processes.

On the other hand, it is also possible for a dynamical systems or chaos theorist to remain "agnostic" about whether quantum processes are causally indeterminate or not. At some point in the future, scientists may change their minds on whether quanta are really non-causal, but if so, the fruits of self-organizational theory would still survive, because it does not depend on either causality or non-causality at the smallest level.

Moreover, the problems and paradoxes about the causal role of consciousness and mind will remain, even if we jettison causal determinacy at the quantum level. The reason is that, as soon as we ascend above the quantum level, causal statements can still be made—as when we say that flipping a switch "caused" a light to come on—and these causal relations work the same as they would whether there is quantum indeterminacy at the quantum level or not. Even if there is quantum indeterminacy, we still have the observable patterns of relations that scientists have always found reliable. Ionization of neurons still "causes" an electrical signal to travel in the nervous system; a shortage of serotonin can still "cause" depression; and pushing against something with my hand can still "cause" it to move. If these causal relations must still be taken into account, then we still need to reconcile the apparent causal power of conscious and mental processes with the fact that purely *physical* processes are sufficient to account for the causation of the outcomes in question—speech behavior, the movement of body parts, and so forth.

Some cognitive theorists, such as Wegner (2003) and Dennett (2003) simply bite the bullet and grant that there is no such thing as conscious will, that when we think that a conscious choice leads to a movement of our bodies, this impression is only an illusion. On the contrary, they argue, the action command to move the body has already been sent before we experience ourselves as "deciding" to move, and this action command can be measured by means of a "readiness potential," which Libet (1999) showed is already measurable in the supplementary motor area of the brain *prior to* our supposed decision to move the limb.

This counterintuitive rejection of the causal power of consciousness is based on two fundamental mistakes. First, as Jeannerod's (1997) work on action imagery implies, the "readiness potential" does not correlate only with a final decision to execute an action command. It can also correlate with the process of *imagining ourselves performing* an action. Jeannerod shows that, *before* we can actually decide to do an action, we must first *imagine* the action about which we are deciding; but even imagining ourselves doing an action already requires that we send the corresponding action command to the supplementary motor area, where it is inhibited from feeding forward as far as the parietal lobes, from where it would then be transmitted, in the case of an overt action, to the body's extremities. In other words, as Ito (2000) had already suggested, some of the brain processes involved in imagining an action are very similar to the brain processes used to execute that same action. This point is explained in greater detail in Ellis (2005a, 2005b).

The second mistake of the Wegner-Dennett "illusory choice" model is that, if consciousness had no causal power, this would seem to imply that it would be a non-physical phenomenon, if we assume that all physical phenomena do have some causal powers or other. But to say that any conscious event is non-physical would require positing a metaphysical dualism, with all the attendant philosophical problems and contradictions entailed by such a view, as we preliminarily outlined in our introduction. We doubt whether Dennett or Wegner would want to endorse dualism, but it is entailed by their view of mental causation.

The problems connected with mental causation and the puzzles about how consciousness can fit into the causal processes of the brain remain real problems, and cannot be eliminated either by denying the reality of conscious choices, or by denying that there are causal processes in the brain. For our present purposes, then, it is not necessary either to advocate or to reject submolecular causal indeterminacy. Causal indeterminacy at the quantum level is neither necessary nor sufficient for a self-organizational understanding of consciousness, because what is needed is an understanding of how an overall process can have causal powers that are not reducible to a mere summation of the causal powers of its micro-constituents. If so, then we can say that such a process *acts* in a sense that is distinguishable from a complicated combination of mere reactions.

First, let's be clear on some definitions. When we say that flipping a switch causes a light to come on, we mean not only that if you flip the switch, the light will come on; we also mean that if you did not flip the switch (given the background conditions as they exist), the light would *not* come on. We are making a subjunctive statement about what would have happened under certain conditions if you had not flipped the switch.

Every causal relation presupposes background conditions. In order for flipping the switch to cause the light to come on, certain background conditions must be in place—a good bulb in the socket, the appropriate pattern of wiring, a power source, the principles of physics as they happen to be, and perhaps even a larger reference system in which gravitational and other forces may be different from what they would have been if the larger reference system had been organized differently. When we say that flipping the switch caused the light to come on, we do not mean that flipping the switch all by itself could have caused the outcome, without the presence of many background conditions.

When we make the statement that flipping the switch caused the light to come on, it makes no difference whether there is causal indeterminacy at the quantum level or not. What we mean when we make the statement is that, given the relevant background conditions as they existed, if you flipped the switch, the light would come on, and if you did not flip the switch, the light would not come on. That is, under the given background conditions, flipping the switch is *both necessary and sufficient* to ensure that the light would come on. To say that X causes Y is not to commit ourselves to any more than that. It does not necessarily require committing ourselves to any particular theory of physics or any particular theory about what the underlying mechanism of the cause-and-effect relationship might be.

At the organizational level at which brain processes and consciousness occur, we can make causal statements of this kind. The question for our purposes, then, is whether such a notion of causation leaves room for an overall pattern of activity to be genuinely active rather than merely reacting to the summed reactions of its own micro-constituents. Such a self-organizational system is what we mean by action as opposed to mere reaction in the "micro" sense. Once we have elucidated how there can be such a distinction in the "micro" sense, then we can use this concept of action to ground an account of action at the "macro" level—the level of willed limb movements, action imagery, and so forth.

It is not enough simply to assert that a dynamical system has the power to "constrain" lower-level causal sequences. What does "constrain" mean here? Is causal closure violated, or not? We cannot simply abandon the obvious fact that when **Na+** is added to **Cl-**, the result is **NaCl**, regardless of whether this reaction takes place in the context of a dynamical system such as the brain, or whether it takes place in any other context. So how can a dynamical system "constrain" this or any other micro-level causal sequence, without violating the elementary regularities in chemical and physical events that we have repeatedly observed to hold, whether inside or outside the brain?

In the face of this problem, then, how can an overall process or pattern of activity have the power to appropriate and replace its own micro-constituents, and to reorganize them as needed to maintain the stability of the pattern into the future? Is this causal power not simply an epiphenomenon of the way all the *micro-constituents themselves* react to micro-constituents in the environment, and to each other?

There are some instances in which what is causally necessary and sufficient for outcome O (given relevant background conditions BC) is *not* a particular set of micro-level events, P, but rather a relation, R, which might be multiply realizable by alternative sets of micro-level events. We could picture the situation this way:

$$\text{Given BCs,} \quad R \text{-------} > O$$
$$|$$
$$\{P1 \text{ or } P2 \text{ or } P3, \text{ etc.}\}$$

P1, P2, and P3 in this diagram refer to alternative sets of micro-level events, any one of which would be capable of fitting together to make the relational pattern R. Superficially, it appears from this diagram that neither P1 nor P2 nor P3 is necessary or sufficient for O, given the relevant BCs. Either P1 or P2 or P3 could serve as the micro-level realizers of the larger relational pattern, R. And if this is true, then it would seem that R is necessary and sufficient for O, and that either P1 or P2 or P3 could be used to subserve the pattern R, depending on the background conditions; in this case, we might think that O would be the result, regardless of which of them subserved the relational pattern R.

But we have to take account of two important caveats about this claim: first, R may *not* be multiply realizable once *all* the background conditions have been nailed down; at that point, there may be only *one* way R could be realized. That is, P1, if it occurs, must already have been caused by something, and the same for P2 and P3. Once those prior events have occurred, then whether P1 or P2 or P3 will serve as the micro-constituents for R has already been predetermined. And if so, then this would mean that, given BC in its *entirety*, R may *not* be multiply realizable, and therefore the micro-constituents of R *may* be necessary and sufficient (given BC) for O after all.

And the second caveat is that, even if R is multiply realizable, this is very different from saying that R itself was not caused to be the way it was by some *previous* micro-level events (Ps). In that case, everything may ultimately be caused at the level of the micro-constituents after all.

If self-organizational processes, which are relational ("R"s), really are to be capable of appropriating their own needed micro-constituents ("P"s)—and thus genuinely acting rather than only reacting—then what we need to show is this: there must be *some* processes (which we call "self-organizing" processes) in which not only is a multiply realizable relation R necessary and sufficient for O given the BCs, but also, in those same types of processes, R has the power to arrange the BCs in such a way that, if P1 is not able to subserve R given the BCs, then P2 will be able to subserve R given the BCs. We could picture this situation this way:

$$R \text{ - - - > BCs under which ... } \quad R \text{ - - - - - - - - - > } O$$
$$|$$
$$\{P1 \text{ or } P2 \text{ or } P3, \text{ etc.}\}$$

That is, R pre-arranges for the background conditions that would be needed to ensure that, whichever of P1 or P2 or P3 is available, one of them can be used to subserve the relational pattern R that is needed in order to ensure outcome O.

This is a logically possible type of process, because it is possible that the relation R, if it is maintained through time, could have been sufficient (at an earlier instant of R's realization) to cause the BCs to be arranged so as to facilitate the availability of some micro-level Ps which, given those BCs, would be necessary and sufficient to subserve R, and thus allow R to cause O. (Incidentally, in this case we could say that the Ps that actually obtain *also* cause the O, given those same BCs, even though some of the BCs in turn were already controlled by R itself). If this logically possible situation (a "self-organizing" situation) were to occur, then R would be a necessary and sufficient precursor of O even if no particular micro-level P were a necessary or sufficient precursor for O, because R (at an earlier moment of its realization) would have the power to rearrange the BCs so as to facilitate alternative Ps being able to subserve R, which then causes O in the future. We could then say that R is able to appropriate and organize many of the Ps that are needed to continue its own pattern into the future, rather than being only a result of the activities of its micro-constituents.

This same situation would occur even if some particular P were unavailable for the purpose of subserving R, provided that one of the alternative Ps were available; thus no particular P would be necessary for O. (Nor would any particular P be *sufficient* for O, because under different BCs, P would not have been able to subserve the relation R that is needed to cause O.) In this case, no particular set of Ps would be necessary or sufficient for O, but R (which would be multiply realizable by alternative sets of Ps given the BCs, which in turn are controlled by R at an earlier time) would be necessary and sufficient to ensure outcome O.

In this case, we would say that R is the necessary and sufficient cause of O given the relevant BCs, and that no particular P was necessary or sufficient for O until R put the relevant BCs in place that are needed in order for those Ps to be the ones that can realize R and thus can cause O.

From this point, two apparently contradictory viewpoints can be developed: Some people (the "micro-reductionists"—such as Bickle 2002) want to say that, even in the case just described, the Ps *are* necessary and sufficient for O once *all* the relevant BCs have been nailed down. That is,

Given BCs-1, R - - - - - > O   **Given BCs-2, R - - - - - > O**
             | |
         {P1}   {P2}

This picture shows that, as soon as *all* relevant BCs have been nailed down, causal closure demands that there is only *one* unique set of Ps that can subserve R, given those particular BCs. An alternative set of Ps subserving R would require an alternative set of BCs, because something in the past would have to have been different in order to cause a different set of Ps to subserve R.

In opposition to this viewpoint, others (the "multiple-realizationists"—such as Horgan 1992) want to say that only the R (which is realizable by alternative sets of Ps) is really necessary and sufficient for O given BC, because which BCs are in place has been determined at least in part by R itself.

The resolution of this antinomy is that, on the one hand, it is literally true that, once *all* of the BCs (including the ones that are under R's control) are in place, then the micro-level Ps that subserve R *are* necessary and sufficient for O. But it is also true that (in the logically possible type of case under consideration—the "self-organizing" situation) some of the BCs are under the control of R, and therefore there is no unique set of Ps that would be necessary and sufficient for O given all the BCs *other than the ones under the control of R*. This can be seen by looking again at the previous diagram but one:

R - - - > BCs, given which,   R - - - - - - - - > O
                                                  |
                              {P1 or P2 or P3, etc.}

In this diagram, we see that R is really in control of the BCs (at least in part), and therefore whatever effect the BCs have is actually an indirect effect of R itself (at least in part). Moreover, whether P1 or P2 or P3 is the set of micro-constituents capable of subserving R is determined by the BCs, which are (partly) determined by R itself. So neither P1 nor P2 nor P3 would be necessary or sufficient for O if it had not been for the previous impact of R itself. To the extent that R can control the BCs needed for a subsequent realization of R, R itself is the necessary and sufficient antecedent of O—not P1 or P2 or P3—because which of them can subserve R will be determined by the previous action of R itself. In this sense, R (in its earlier instantiation) is ultimately the necessary and sufficient condition for O given the BCs, if by the BCs we mean all the BCs that are not under the control of R itself.

So the crucial point is that (in the logically possible type of case under consideration, the "self-organizing" type of case) R is necessary and sufficient for O given all BCs other than those controlled by R itself, whereas no particular P is necessary and sufficient for O given all BCs other than those controlled by R itself.

The fact that some unique set of Ps are necessary and sufficient for O given *all* the BCs (including the ones under the control of R) guarantees causal closure. That is, for any event, there are necessary and sufficient micro-level causal antecedents, given *all* the relevant BCs needed for that causal relation to hold.

On the other hand, the multiple realizability of R in terms of Ps, plus the fact that R has already previously controlled the needed background conditions that determine whether P1 or P2 can subserve R (and thus cause O), shows that neither P1 nor P2 is necessary or sufficient for O, given all BCs *other than those controlled by R itself*. So this means that R is necessary and sufficient to determine O, given multiply realizable combinations of Ps, under some set of BCs that are under the control of R itself.

This resolves the antinomy between micro-reductionism and multiple-realizationism. Both are correct, depending on whether what we mean by BCs is "all BCs other than the ones controlled by R itself," or whether we mean "all the BCs *including* the ones controlled by R itself." The multiple-realizationists are correct to say that R is necessary and sufficient for O, whereas no particular set of Ps are—in the sense that whether a given set of Ps are or are not necessary and sufficient for O under the given BCs depends on R itself (at a previous moment of its instantiation). This, again, can be seen clearly from the above diagrams.

We are now in a position to distinguish actions in the "micro" sense of "action" from merely complicated combinations of reactions. Action that is more than a complicated system of reactions is made possible by certain kinds of patterns of activity—we call them "self-organizing processes"—that are capable of arranging and rearranging the background conditions needed to allow some available set of micro-constituents to be sufficient to subserve the continuation of the process into the future. The overall process in this type of situation has certain causal powers that are lacked by any particular combination of micro-constituents—which is to say that the overall process selects and organizes its own micro-constituents rather than only being determined by the way those micro-constituents would behave independent of the effects of the overall process. In technical terms, it is possible for a certain type of R (at a certain moment in its history) to control the background conditions needed for its own Ps to subserve that same R (at a later moment in its history); thus such an R is causally efficacious for O, even though no particular set of Ps would be causally efficacious for O unless R itself had previously set up the BCs needed for those Ps to cause O. Such an R is what we mean by a "self-organizing" R.

Notice that, if mental processes are self-organizing "R"s in this sense, then the problem of mental causation would be solved. The mind is able to self-organize the micro-constituents needed for its own pattern to continue, as well as to cause other outcomes such as the movement of the body, because the self-organizing process that the mind is can appropriate and replace micro-constituents on an as-needed basis. But at the same time, causal closure is assured, because the micro-constituents themselves, once all the background conditions are in place (including the ones already having been controlled by R at a previous time), each micro-constituent event can be explained by some combination of prior micro-constituents that, strictly speaking, were necessary and sufficient for that outcome under those given background conditions.

The question then remains whether this logically possible type of R *actually exists* anywhere in nature. And that is an empirical question. But clearly, we do find such Rs in the case of biological organisms. Here we find instances where, if the R had not previously arranged the needed background conditions for certain micro-level Ps to be causally efficacious for certain outcomes O, then those Ps would not have been efficacious for O. Instead, R itself, by continually arranging and rearranging the needed background conditions, is efficacious for O, with multiply-realizable sets of subserving Ps, given the fact that R has previously controlled the background conditions that would determine *which* Ps are needed to produce O under the relevant BCs (some of which, again, are controlled by R itself). This type of R can rearrange and replace its own subserving Ps, and in some instances (for example, in animals) it can rearrange some of its Ps in such a way as to facilitate going out and *searching* for some of the Ps needed to keep R going into the future.

This notion of action in the micro sense is a necessary but not sufficient condition for understanding consciousness and the mind-body problem. We first need a theory that can show how action in this sense makes possible action in the *macro* sense. Action in the macro sense enables not only sensing the action affordances of the environment, but also the process of "action imagery" that, we shall argue, is a basic building block for the mysterious phenomenon of subjective consciousness, with all the experienced ineffability that we discussed earlier.

How does intentional action emerge from nonintentional self-organizing behavior? We have argued that it does so as a development from primitive purposeful movements of an organism that is able to coordinate all of its components to achieve a goal. The organism masters this ability through representational processes that unify the goal and the means to achieve it, and that are used to trigger purposive behavior. Some purposive behavior can occur prior to consciousness, but when these are represented in action imagery, and when the action imagery then grounds an understanding of the action affordances of objects and situations in the environment, we are finally on our way to intentionality and consciousness. These representational processes, inhibited from triggering overt movements, become thoughts. We are now ready to examine the nature of some of these thoughts—in particular, the mysterious ones that constitute phenomenal consciousness and are so philosophically problematic.

6

The Paradoxes within Phenomenal Consciousness

In order to attack the "hard problem" of consciousness in all its difficulty, it is important to develop a full appreciation for some of the more mysterious and "ineffable" features of consciousness, and show how a self-organizational approach can have a better hope of explaining them than the traditional information processing models. We begin with the problem that any physical explanation of consciousness seems to leave unresolved certain "mysteries" of consciousness. As we have seen, these include:

a. The dual location of phenomenal properties "out there" yet "in here" in consciousness.

b. The mysterious "thickness" of the specious present.

c. The feeling of "free agency," that we can voluntarily direct our actions, including the act of conscious attention, while at the same time attention and the emotions that direct it seem responsive to physiological substrates with physical causes.

These paradoxes, which formed the central core of Kant's *Critique of Pure Reason,* can be resolved by relating each of them to three elements of consciousness:

i. Organismically interested anticipation.

ii. Sensory and proprioceptive *imagery* generated by the interested anticipation rather than by sensory input.

iii. *Resonating* of these activities with activity stimulated by sensory data, where the interested anticipation *precedes* the processing of the input.

Each of these elements is bridged to physiological processes such that, if they occur in a certain relation to each other, we can understand why they would inevitably be accompanied by the corresponding elements of *conscious* experience.

1. The Ineffability of Conscious Experience

In an earlier chapter, we began to identify the specific elements of phenomenal experience whose absence in ordinary "physical" phenomena makes consciousness seem to be such a mysterious phenomenon from the physical standpoint, and thus produces Levine's "explanatory gap" (1983) in understanding consciousness. In this chapter, we attempt to face up to the full seriousness of the difficulties that make consciousness seem so "ineffable." We then develop a theory capable of addressing these paradoxical features of consciousness, and thus build a bridge from conscious experience to the physiological events that subserve it. This task will require directly confronting those paradoxical aspects of consciousness that make it difficult to describe in terms commensurable with those of empirical science. This examination will suggest what kind of physiological events are inseparable from the phenomenon of consciousness itself, and why they are inseparable. As we have already seen, Chalmers(1995), similarly to Levine, raises the problem that, confronted with any physical mechanism purported to explain conscious experience, one could always ask, "Yes, but is it not conceivable that a physical system could behave in those same ways, or process information according to those rules, without being accompanied by consciousness?"

Such a response seems possible in the case of consciousness because the sort of phenomenon philosophers want to explain is essentially an experience. Being conscious is feeling a certain way, to oneself, and the feeling is effortlessly at hand the instant we decide to think about it. We need not construct it intellectually, or take pains to form a mental image of it in specific experiential modalities, as we do when thinking of objectively existing mechanisms. Indeed, we have no "objective concept" of phenomenal consciousness other than our own experience of it. Being conscious does not give the impression of having a mere partial acquaintance with an objective state of affairs, one that can be captured more fully by further information.

Consciousness thus inevitably *seems* to be a distinct kind of thing from any physical mechanism, no matter how detailed and well supported are the empirically discovered correlations between the operations of that mechanism and instances of conscious experience. No matter how strongly you may think you reject dualism, can you honestly say that your own conscious experience seems to you fully accounted for by (a) a physical description of your brain, and (b) a physical description of the world it senses? Would such a combined account prompt you to exclaim "Right! That combination captures the qualitative nature of what I feel!" Most say not (for example Chalmers 1995; Davidson 1970; Goldman 1969).

There is a good reason why this explanatory gap appears unbridgeable in principle. Any *objective* mechanism can be *analyzed into components*, and the mechanism can be completely understood in terms of those components and their interrelations, whether or not the properties of the mechanism can be "reduced" to the properties of its components. Even if properties of a mechanism are "emergent" out of properties of its components and their interrelations, such as in the case of convection rolls in heated liquids (Clark 1997, 112), as soon as we have explained processes of self-organization on the part of the components, and their causal history, then the properties of the whole have been explained with no nonphysical residue. By contrast, in the case of conscious experience, such an explanation appears impossible, because the experience does not lend itself to analysis such that its history and its components can be matched to those of a physical mechanism. Indeed, conscious experience seems altogether unanalyzable. Even though it seems possible to identify distinct *aspects* of conscious experience, such as its temporal and emotional aspects, these do not combine additively, or constitute components of the experience that are in any way analogous to the components of any physical mechanism.

We believe, however, that the experience of phenomenal consciousness can be analyzed. The appropriate analysis will do two things: it will prompt the intuition that the experience of consciousness has been captured in all of its "ineffability" (in contrast to most functional or physical accounts); and it will make the experience available to be mapped onto known brain mechanisms. What sort of analysis could accomplish both of these tasks? Is there a combination of physical mechanisms that could "add up" to consciousness itself, in any modality?

If there is to be any hope of bridging the explanatory gap, it is not enough to say that consciousness is indefinable except through direct experience; that would leave the gap unbridgeable. We must identify elements that, on the one hand, are necessary aspects of the *subjective experience* of consciousness, and on the other hand can be bridged to the empirically observable world of neuroscience in such a way as to understand *why* those brain processes are inevitably accompanied by the corresponding elements of consciousness.

In the first part of this chapter we sketch a way of describing conscious experience that directly addresses the features of the experience that make it appear ineffable. We believe that there exist three equally important aspects of conscious experience: the spatial, the temporal, and the causal/motivational. Each of these aspects, as experienced, involves what is conceptually a contradiction, and hence presents itself (misleadingly) as mysterious and unanalyzable. With a bow to Kant, we refer to these three phenomenal aspects (which Kant believed were simply inapplicable to the subject of experience) as "paradoxes." Our prediction is that once these phenomena are analyzed and their mechanisms described, the apparent contradictions will disappear, and with them the belief that phenomenal consciousness is empirically unexplainable and fundamentally unanalyzable.

In section 2 of the chapter, we propose a formal characterization of consciousness that can serve as a bridge between the phenomenal experience and its brain correlates. The characterization will include the results of the phenomenal analysis of section 1, and discuss recent work in the neurosciences offering supporting evidence of an inseparable correlation between those functions and conscious experience.

But the first step toward solving a problem is to admit that we have a problem, and admit the full extent of it. So let's begin simply by laying out a full description of each of the three main paradoxes that we take to be crucial.

a. The Paradox of Spatiality: The "Objective" and the "Subjective"

Conscious perceptual experience presents objective states of affairs: we experience objects, including our own bodies, as being in the world and experiencable by others. Even the qualitative properties of those objects are experienced as public properties: we invite others to feel the softness of a fabric, or taste the flavor of a dish. Properties of things seem objective and not created by our own subjectivity. Colors seem pasted to the surfaces of objects, rather than constructed by the subject's visual apparatus.

But at the same time, the experience is presented as *mine*. "Secondary" properties, such as colors or sound qualities, which I perceive as belonging to the object, are actually produced by my own sensory mechanisms in a way tacitly acknowledged in my own behavior. I look at the room from *this* angle, where "indexicality"—the fact that it appears this way only from a particular, unique point of view, and would appear different from another point of view—is essential to any description of my experience (Perlis 1995). That is, my own experience, *even as naively experienced,* already acknowledges that the room would look different from someone else's point of view. I adjust my focus, shift my attention, squint, turn my head; each of these actions alters my experience in ways that I am at home with. My body understands that perception is both an activity that it performs and a state that it achieves; it is not just something that *happens to me* as a result of the object's existence. In describing the visual features of an object that I see as an independently existing entity in the world, I am actually describing my subjective experience.

Part of the ineffability of conscious experience thus results from the fact that, in phenomenal consciousness, the responses of our bodies to external stimuli are projected outwards, onto the external sources of the stimuli. Internal responses are, as it were, *reified* as objective properties of external objects. In effect, when we observe what we think of as external objects, we are really "observing" part of the activity of our sensory mechanisms (Edelman 1989). This activity is the "constructing" of a world of objects as solid, enduring, and separate from our selves. We interact with this world through direct experience of what its objects "are like." But what they are actually "like" is not objective; it is the product of our subjective response to them. In this way, conscious awareness of the world is a type of illusion in which the objective is not clearly separable from the subjective, although it appears to be.

When I observe an object in the world, the object *as I observe it* is entirely a product of my sensory (and conceptual) mechanisms. It *appears,* however, to exist entirely independent of me; even its color appears as an intrinsic property of the object rather than as a mode of my perception. As a philosopher, I must continually remind myself that color is *not* pasted onto the surfaces of objects, since no amount of theoretical commitment allows me to *experience* it otherwise. It is true that certain properties of objects actually present themselves as requiring the perceiver for their realization: texture, taste and smell call attention to our bodies as color does not. Our bodies, however, also appear to us as public objects. The fingertips that detect the rough bark of the tree are physical entities, spatially contiguous to the tree. The sensation of roughness, like that of color, is an event that takes place in the brain, but the brain does not appear as the locus of the property in either case.

Even philosophers and scientists can be victims of the illusion of objective perception, as Akins (1996) argues in a discussion of recent "naturalistic" theories of how brain states represent external objects: "What I wish to show is that the naturalists' project, as commonly conceived, rests upon an intuitive and seemingly banal view of what the senses do—that the senses function to inform the brain of what is going on 'out there,' in the external world—and that this 'banal' view about sensory function is false" (337–38). Akins describes the naturalistic view as holding that a representation is "about" an object in the sense that it "bears a specific kind of relation—call it the *aboutness relation,* to an object or property in the world" (339). But in fact, she holds, most sensory systems are "narcissistic": they evolved to direct motor behavior, not to answer ontological questions about the external world. To look for answers to such questions through our sensory systems is to look in the wrong place.

It might be objected here that sensory experience could easily be *both* "narcissistic" *and* ontologically accurate—after all, would such a happy arrangement not be favored by natural selection? But for our purposes, the moral of Akins's argument is not that contemporary philosophers are wrong about the functions of the senses, but that being right requires overcoming a powerful illusion produced by those very senses: that they are showing us the world (including our bodies) as it exists independent of ourselves.

At this point a different objection could be made: if the senses present us with a consistent illusion that the internal products of our sensory mechanisms are really external, then there is no experienced incompatibility, no paradox *intrinsic* to the illusion. There is nothing self-contradictory about the fact that a straight stick in water appears to be bent. What is paradoxical about conscious experience *per se,* however, is that it not only presents subjective qualities as objective, but also does so in such a way that on the one hand assumes that the subjective qualities are clearly distinguishable from the objective ones, while on the other hand cheerfully acknowledging that such a clear distinction between subjective and objective elements of sensory experience would be a hopeless endeavor. We know full well that the redness of an object can be located neither "in here" nor "out there," because we experience it both as a subjective response ("in here") and also as if it were an objective primary property of the object ("out there").

Even though common sense indeed presupposes in its everyday functioning that reality must be constructed piecemeal from misleading appearances—that the bent stick is really straight, that the foreshortened boxcars are really rectangular—it also continues to present the shapes of the stick and the boxcar as realities "out there," independent of subjective processing. If the objects as seen really were completely independent of us, then we should not expect to experience them as they really are. All we should expect to experience is the way they affect our own bodies, and that would tell us nothing about their intrinsic properties except through very complicated intellectual inferences. We would expect to experience the boxcar as an asymmetrical trapezoid of solid material, which we would then tell ourselves is "really" not asymmetrical and not solid, but rather a movement of light with a certain symmetrical, rectangular overall pattern. But we feel that we do *experience things as they really are;* that is precisely the illusion. Our senses produce this illusion because data that have already been processed by primary and secondary cortical mechanisms appear to us as though they were not already processed—as though they were coming to us in just the way that they exist before being processed. This means that there is in principle no way for us to distinguish within experience between (a) aspects of the object that are independent of their effect on us, and (b) our subjective responses to the object. "The object," therefore, *as we experience it,* consists of both.

Thus, paradoxically, the redness of an object appears to be like a physical pigment mixed into the matter of the object, yet we also experience it as a subjective quality within ourselves that is "caused by" the object and experienced in our head. The red seems both "in here" and "out there" at once.

This constitutes a *paradox within* experience, rather than just an illusion produced by the senses, because even common sense views subjectivity and objectivity as opposites. The same object can have both subjective and objective properties, but a single property cannot be both subjective and objective. Color, as a secondary property, and size, as an objective property, can co-exist in an object, but the color of an object (the redness *as it appears to us*) cannot be both a subjective and an objective property, and common sense holds that experience conforms to that fact. Literally, however, it does not. If we try to combine the components of our experience in a consistent description—if we say, for example, that we *experience a red cube* sitting several feet away and *separate from our bodies*—what we describe cannot be objectively or literally true. An object completely separate from our bodies could cause experience only by acting upon our bodies. And experience would then present itself only as a response of our bodies to that action. The cube would then not appear as red in itself, but only as accompanied by a subjective *feeling* of redness—as red only for me. Yet in experience it invariably appears as red in itself.

An adequate theory of consciousness must address the paradox that, if consciousness behaved according to the causal principles that seem to describe physical reality, one would expect redness (or any property) to be experienced as a *subjective feeling*, *"in here,"* an effect produced *by* and thus distinguishable *from* the external event that acts as its cause; an effect is not the same thing as its cause. Thus the consciousness of red would have to be a separate phenomenon in a separate location from the "red" object, yet we do not experience the "redness" in our consciousness as a separate phenomenon, or in a separate location from the red object. Instead, redness seems to be *out there,* in the world.

In our experience of other persons, the paradoxical quality is even easier to see. Cognitive psychologists have been exploring the development of the concept of a person, or of what is sometimes called a "theory of mind". Meltzoff and Gopnik (1993) propose that there exists in normal infants a representational framework incorporating *both* input from the infant's own body (proprioceptive and kinesthetic sensations) *and* input from the perception of others as external objects. They stress that the representation is not just associative; it blends, or superposes, input from the two sources into a unity, experienced as such by the infant. The other person appears both as a physical object (an objective entity that we experience) and a subject *of* experience (which cannot directly show itself as an object, but is experienceable from its own subjective standpoint, as the subject of the experience of other objects). The infant understands the person as a physical object because of its impact on the infant's perceptual system; and the infant understands the person as a subject by referring to the infant's own bodily proprioceptive and interoceptive feelings. This unified representation of another person as both subject and object of experience, which Meltzoff and Gopnik call a "supramodal body scheme," forms the experiential basis for the concept of a person as a unique kind of entity: a physical object with subjective experience. This concept can be applied both to the self and to others, because it is based upon data from both sources.

Barresi and Moore (1996) discuss the nature of our understanding of *intentionality,* or the ability of something to be "about" or to represent another thing, from this angle. Intentionality, considered a defining characteristic of human mentality, can be conceived in terms of an "Intentional Schema," defined as "An intermodal perceptual and conceptual structure with the capacity to coordinate and integrate first and third person sources of information about object-directed activities into representations that link agents to objects through intentional relations. Because first person information . . . consists primarily of kinesthetic and proprioceptive information, whereas third person information consists primarily of visual information, the intentional schema is a special case of intermodal schema [which] preserve[s] the quality of both forms of informational contribution" (Barresi and Moore 1996, 109).

The existence of such a schema, representing both the self and the other person, would be an extremely exciting empirical discovery. It would underlie the most puzzling feature of both consciousness and intentionality: the unification in a single entity of objective (physical) and subjective ("nonphysical") properties. And it would imply, not that a single entity can actually be a combination of two opposing properties, but rather that we can construct within our own experience the idea of having both a subjective and an objective perspective on the same thing—the other's embodied personhood—at the same time. Recent work on "mirror neurons" suggests that the ability to imagine another person as both physical and mental at the same time, involving the illusion that one could take both the subjective and objective perspectives on the other person at the same time, is a very rudimentary ability in infants (Gallese and Goldman 1998). We have argued elsewhere that the "mirror neuron" phenomenon is due to the fact that we understand what it is like to execute another person's actions by imagining ourselves executing those same actions, and we do this by enacting the motor imagery in ourselves—which requires frontal inhibition of the motor command (in the same area where the "mirror neuron" activity is observed)—corresponding to the motor commands we would enact if we were to actually perform the corresponding actions (see Newton 1996).

But why call the subjective/objective entity—the other person who is perceived, for example—an *illusion?* Haven't we just shown that each of us really *is* such a thing? Of course every sentient being has an objective and a subjective aspect, bearing non-sentient external relations to other beings, and also bearing sentient relations to its own states. So far, there is no paradox. A paradox arises only when a sentient being forms a unified representation of itself, and of other sentient beings, in which the external and the internal relations *merge*. The paradox, or apparent contradiction, lies in the illusion that both the external and the internal relations could be perceived as a unity in a single experience. I appear to sense my feelings from the inside, while in the same conscious act sensing myself as a body in the world, from the outside. But in fact, the two modes of sensing are *not* a unity; they occur separately and "in parallel" in the brain, and are "unified" only in the "Intentional Schema" or "Supramodal Body Scheme." Our bodies present themselves as both subjective and objective entities even while our very *concepts* of "objective" and "subjective" seem to locate them in completely separate spheres—the one in a Cartesian, homogenous physical space, the other in a completely "internal" realm *to* which all such spaces are supposedly presented as "external."

Merleau-Ponty (1964) highlights this paradox by referring us to the experience of what it is like for our own right hand to touch the left hand. If we experience what is happening from the point of view of the right hand, feeling what it is like subjectively to touch the left hand, then we lose the sense of how it feels to the left hand to be touched by the right. But if we focus our attention on what it feels like to the left hand to be touched by the right, then we lost the sense of how it feels to the right hand to be touching the left. Either the right hand is the one from whose point of view we subjectively feel—in which case the left hand seems like an unsensing physical object whose shapes and textures the right hand can feel—or vice versa. We cannot experience either the right or the left hand as *both subject and object simultaneously*. Yet we know that we ourselves, as well as other people, are both subjective and objective (physical) entities, at the same time.

Whether we experience physical objects or other people, there seems to be a contradictory impression that the qualities of the object on the one hand are "out there," but on the other hand are experienced as occurring "in here." The main point of emphasizing this paradox is this: The very act of representing something implies, in a sense, externalizing it—making it into an object *for* and *over against* the consciousness of it. To represent something is to form some kind of image, concrete or abstract, of that thing (Damasio 1994). Images are formed from memory traces of sensory (including proprioceptive and kinesthetic) experience. But imagery always seems to present itself as being the experience of an "external" object, one that was perceived through the sensory channels that tell us about the world, which includes our own bodies.

This constraint upon what we can represent applies to the self as well as to other entities. One can sense and respond to stimuli without forming a conscious representation of one's self (when on "automatic pilot," so to speak), but one cannot be consciously self-aware without such a representation. The raw material for that or any other representation is sensory experience of public, physical objects. Our bodies are such objects. Thus conscious self-awareness, even of a subjective, apparently non-bodily "self," is mediated by a representation of a public object—

the body (Wider 1997). For this reason, conscious self-awareness requires combining conceptually incompatible elements—the "subjective" and the "objective" properties of experience. Realizing this, as we intend to show later in this chapter, can be a first step toward dispelling belief in the essential "ineffability" of consciousness, even though conscious experience itself will necessarily retain its unique qualitative character for its subject.

b. The Paradox of Temporality: "Present" and "Not-Present"

The second set of incompatible aspects involves temporality. Intuitively, "now" is an almost infinitesimal point. In the time it takes to think "Now!", the beginning of the thought has already become past, not-now. More significantly, common sense tells us that experience presents only what is going on now; we cannot experience the past directly, but only through the activity (now) of memory. But if experience did exist only in an instantaneous now, we could not be aware of it. Our presently occurring conscious experience is a blend of three moments—the just-past, the present, and the anticipated immediate-future—such that all are experienced, not as memory and not as anticipated future, but as occurring "now." We experience sensory input from the immediate past, together with sensory input entering now, not as an additive juxtaposition but as a single "specious present." We feel as if we are directly experiencing the enduring object, but while we are experiencing the object, and while it has in fact an enduring presence, our *experience* of that presence is the product of the blending of several distinct components. Our experience is composed not only of newly entering input but also just-past input, retained in working memory and "reentered" along with newly-arriving input, so that we experience an unbroken flow that corresponds to nothing in the input itself (Edelman 1989).

Even from a purely subjective point of view, to experience the object as "enduring" does not feel like a series of instantaneous thoughts in which we would say to ourselves "I experience the object now, and I remember that I experienced it a moment ago, therefore I can infer that it is enduring." The enduringness of the object is not a logical inference based on memory, but an immediate present experience. There is no infinitesimal present moment to which a remembered moment would be added to produce duration; the experienced present moment is already a segment of time that seems to *include* a retained "just-past" and an anticipated "will-continue." We do not experience a series of dimensionless *"now-points,"* which are then remembered and combined in order to make up a view of the world as enduring, as one might expect if the present did not already include a tiny bit of the just-past and the anticipated future.

Besides a retention of the just-past, the specious present also includes an expectation: that the object will be there to be experienced in the future. This expectation is not merely conceptual—it is a felt component of our experience of the present, of what the object is actually like now. The object seems to extend ahead, as well as backward, in time, such that the felt extension is experienced as part of the present moment. The present moment thus has "thickness" for a conscious subject. Husserl distinguishes two sorts of temporal experience: that of the present *as containing* references to past and future, and that of past and future as such:

> Immanent contents are what they are only as far as, during their "actual" duration, they point ahead to the future and point back to the past. . . . In each primal phase which originally constitutes the immanent content we have retentions of the preceding phases and protentions of the coming phases of precisely this content, and these protentions are fulfilled just as long as this content endures. . . . We then have to distinguish the retentions and protentions from the recollections and expectations which are not numbered among the phases constituting the immanent content but instead represent past or future immanent contents. The contents endure, they have their time; they are . . . unities of change or constancy." (Husserl 1917, 110–11)

The paradox of temporal experience is that, while our experience of the past in memory and of the future in expectations is held both experientially and conceptually to be complementary to our experience of the present, in fact the present is constituted by the past and the future, and is so constituted, moreover, as part of the phenomenal, experienceable structure of that experience. Our experience of the present, in other words, can be subjectively recognized to include the past and the future, while at the same time contrasting with them.

For example, consider the experience of looking at your bookcase. You see not just a time-slice of a bookcase, but one that has been there for an indefinite period of time. Part of your present experience of that bookcase is its immediately past existence. At the same time, you expect it to remain there, and this is not a conceptual expectation or reasoned belief that your experience will continue, but a felt sense that the existence of the bookcase extends into the future. It is a sense that the presence of the bookcase has a thickness; that the "time-slice" that is the present is not infinitely thin but substantial. One feels that within a single present moment, *there is and will be time* to experience the temporal extension of the bookcase; that is the temporal paradox of conscious experience. It is the experience of the past, the present, and the future, all blended together to form what is happening "now."

The paradox is well illustrated in perceptual experiments (for example, Changizi et al. 2008) where the subject is presented with a moving object, and a burst of light occurs in the exact location of the object at a certain point in its trajectory. The subject erroneously sees the object as having already moved past the burst of light. This highlights the fact that, even in perception, we are always anticipating the next moment in the flow of experience, rather than perceiving only an exact present. The present includes that anticipated future, which is literally experienced as part of the present, as if it were already present.

It would be useful to offer a concrete example of the way distinct temporal moments can be blended in a single experience such that their distinct natures are disguised. Since our claim is that *all* conscious experience exhibits this character, any specific example could be misleading. The example would highlight a blending process so as to make the blending obvious, but appreciating the example would itself take place in a moment in conscious experience and hence would itself be a blending of distinct temporal moments.

With that caveat in mind, consider the technique of digital delay in sound engineering. Digital delay records both the original sound and one or more simultaneous duplications of the original sound, except that each duplication is delayed by a few milliseconds. If the delay is very slow one hears two or more different instruments playing the same note at the same time. If the delay is quicker, one hears a single instrument whose tone quality is "fatter" and more centered in the space of the listening room, as opposed to sounding thin and "off in a corner." Thus a quantitative variation in the timing of what is heard produces a qualitative difference in the experience. We do not hear separate, overlapping sounds occurring in non-synchronization, but rather a unitary sound that fills both space and a segment of time. The experiential result is not analyzable, simply in terms of the felt properties of the experience, into the separate components that correspond to the quantitative temporal properties of what is heard. The "temporal thickness" of the present moment is something like that. Our anticipation of the future and our retention of the just-past are "heard" as if they were part of the one unitary phenomenon, "the present." In the case of the digital delay in sound recording, when one knows about these temporal properties, then the experience can be understood for what it is, even though the ear will still hear the overlapping sounds as if they were one. Part 2 of this chapter will suggest a similar account of the paradoxical "specious present" in all conscious experience.

c. The Paradox of Agency

We have described two paradoxical sets of features of objects and events as they appear in phenomenal consciousness—the mysteries involving both the spatiality and the temporality of the way experience presents itself. A third mystery is the traditional paradox of agency *versus* passivity. We feel as if we are "free agents"; at the same time, however, we can be fully convinced that some or all of the actions in question are physically determined. For example, if we want to eat, we feel that eating is a voluntary action, yet at the same time we feel that our wanting to eat drives us through a physiological process subject in principle to physical causation. This paradox exists not only in the case of gross motor activity; even our covert, conscious attention toward objects feels like voluntary behavior. Yet at the same time we feel that our attention is "pulled" by the objects, and that our consciousness of them is a passive causal reaction to forces external to us. Hence the traditional paradox emphasized by Kant, Searle (1981), Kim (1992), Wegner (2003), Dennett (2003), and many others, that the system of sufficient causes at the physical level, which our experience presents to us, seems inconsistent with the notion that consciousness itself has causal power—a notion that our experience also presents to us. In other words, physical causation seems to exclude the possibility of agency, yet we experience ourselves as agents, and in some respects (for example the direction of attention) our agency seems to entail causal power on the part of our own conscious being. Moreover, we sometimes *feel* as if our attention were passively a reaction to the stimulus, yet also feel that it is within the control of our agency. And so, I experience two incompatible causal chains: I control the direction of my attention to the world, and at the same time I am subject to a prior, given relevance of the world to me, including the dictates of the causal chains within my own body and nervous system. As in the other cases, we call this aspect of experience a paradox because both incompatible causal chains—world-to-perceiver and perceiver-to-world—are represented in consciousness, accessible within subjective experience.

That this third paradox is a paradox within experience is less obvious than it was in the first two cases. It could be argued that the feeling of free agency is dominant in phenomenal consciousness, and a belief in necessary and sufficient physical causes of behavior is derived from conceptual sophistication, not from anything within experience. There is some force to this objection. Certainly, on the level of conscious decisions about future activities, what is prominent in experience seems to be the existence of multiple possibilities, and the feeling that many of them remain open to us until our choices have permanently excluded them. But the point is that, even if I feel my body driving me to eat a big steak dinner, and thus feel the causal determination of my own need to eat, I still do not feel determined; I feel that I could decide at any time to stop, even if external circumstances remain unchanged. I may also know intellectually that even the *decision* whether to stop eating or not is determined by brain processes, but I still do not feel as if the decision has been predetermined.

In the case of finer-grained actions, such as the direction of attention, the intrinsic paradox is easier to see. Consider our immediate visual field. We feel that, like all other voluntary actions, the direction of our attention is within our control, and we can pay attention to different parts of the visual field at will. Not only that, but we can control aspect shifts: I can see the famous duck-rabbit drawing as a duck or as a rabbit according to my conscious choice, once I know how to recognize the two aspects. But in spite of feeling that I can control what I attend to, in fact I do not feel that I can control the salience of the different features in my visual field. I cannot, in other words, voluntarily vary the importance or the relevance of the various objects to my interests. Something about me that is not within my conscious control determines for me what stands out as significant and what does not; it seems that this salience, in many instances if not all, determines my attention and not the other way around, and I experience this determination.

The world-to-perceiver causal chain is experienced in part through my efforts to adjust my sensory mechanisms to signals from the object. I hear a sound behind me and to my right, and automatically turn my head. In my experience, the sound was there first, the postural and attentional adjustments second. In vision, attention to the bookcase feels like a response to the enduring presence of the bookcase, which I sense as having been there all along, awaiting my response. Conscious awareness of the body's sensory tracking activity seems to reveal a semiautomatic response to a signal. There is a relevance of the object to the perceiver that feels already given; the object presents itself as already belonging to the perceiver's world and as occupying a place on a perceiver-relative scale of values. Either it represents a change in my environment, requiring attention, or else it represents an aspect of the environment with which I must interact in order to achieve some prior goal, or which I *hope* or *fear* to find similar or different from a moment ago. Everything is noticed as already playing a role in my activities and plans.

Because of this pre-established relevance to my interests of what I observe in my environment, some degree of emotional arousal is inevitably part of every conscious experience. In addition to the bare alertness and interest that must accompany consciousness of anything, there are also specific emotional responses whose qualitative feels are the products of associations with remembered stimuli, traces of which are activated in response to current input during categorization. Thus each perceptual experience involves a unique feeling-tone, no matter how often the same perceptual object has been encountered before, and this feeling-tone is intimately connected with the interests and goals of the organism, some of which may be conscious, and some of which may not be. Even though the emotion may not be equivalent with the "felt" quality that we consciously experience, it is still an indispensable contributor to it.

The precise characteristics of each unique "felt" quality are difficult to specify verbally. For example, we can say that the feeling of resolving a philosophical puzzle is similar sometimes to the feeling of finding a long-lost beloved object, or of figuring out how to fix a broken appliance. But specifying exactly how these feelings differ is murky. Part of the reason is that bodily feelings present themselves both as aspects of a public, physical object responding to physical forces *and* as intentions that we direct.

An adequate theory of consciousness must make sense of a paradox here similar to the spatial paradox presented earlier in relation to the secondary properties of intended objects. If the direction of my attention is a matter of free agency, then the salience of the objects I attend to should seem to follow, rather than precede, my attention to them; but it does not. If, on the other hand, pre-existing motives and organismic needs do determine the salience of these objects, then I should not have the feeling that I could direct my attention differently at any moment, independently of any determinant other than my own choosing itself. But I do feel that way. Therefore, the paradox of agency does appear to be, like the others, a paradox within experience.

d. Ineffability and the Function of Conscious Experience

One of our central claims is that the ways in which logically incompatible elements in experience are combined underlie the "ineffability" of consciousness. And the ineffability resulting from these paradoxes makes a coherent description of the phenomenon of consciousness seem impossible. But our next task is to consider the brain mechanisms that produce this experience, with a view to developing an account that will make it obvious that those mechanisms must produce that experience. That is, the account must be such that a description of such mechanisms in action appears *ipso facto* to be a description of a *conscious* organism, and could not conceivably apply to a non-conscious entity. The task will be easier if we have first considered the *function* of this curious combination of elements.

Conscious experience includes data from the perceptible properties of external objects, and information about the states of our bodies during this perception—both brain states that cannot be sensed directly as brain states (as located in the head) and somatic states that can be sensed through proprioception and kinesthesia. Some of this information concerns emotional responses. We have described the result as a combination of subjective and objective aspects within the perception of what we superficially take to be a completely objective state of affairs. In addition, all conscious experience includes information about both the present and the immediately past, as well as expectations about the immediate future. It can also, of course, include memory images from the more distant past, and anticipatory images about the more distant future. Thus the "present" is rich and multidimensional.

We have suggested that the value of such experience to the organism lies in its contribution to action planning. For both the constant short-term decisions that one makes, and the frequent longer-term ones, we must have a criterion for *evaluating* alternative outcomes. This evaluation in turn depends on the effects on the organism itself: how will it be for me if I choose Option A or B? What will each outcome feel like? To make a decision, we must form images of these outcomes, reflect upon them, then on the basis of the emotional values of these images, we choose the one that includes preferred feelings that we also try to imagine in advance (Newton 1996). The overriding purpose of such reflecting is the planning of actions.

The term "image" as we use it requires some further discussion, since our usage is nonstandard. Images, as noted earlier, are commonly understood as visual, and sometimes as a kind of picture in the head, observed by a homunculus. On this understanding, imagistic theories of cognition are rightly dismissed. By contrast, we are treating images not as mental pictures but as multi-modal experiences, produced with the help of the activity of memory traces of past experiences. To image something is to have an internally generated experience similar to actual perceptual experience of that thing. As we have already mentioned, Wittgensteinians and others have good reasons to doubt that *sensory* imagery is present in all mental contents of which we can be conscious. But for us, mental images more generally can include any experience that we can imagine (Newton 1982); that is, there are proprioceptive and motor images (Jeannerod 1994, 1997) as well as visual and auditory ones. Imagery may also sometimes be preconscious until we attend to it; for example, in executing skills, we may not consciously form the sensory and proprioceptive images we had while practicing prior to their execution, but we know that many such images are available to consciousness if we should choose to attend to them, and they often play a role in guiding our present performance. In this expanded sense, images are a primary medium for cognition (as suggested by Damasio 1994), and play a central role in the anticipations of future experience.

In the planning of actions, we must compare future possible experiences not only with each other, but also with our current experience, to evaluate the direction of change. Thus, when we are imagining ourselves performing some action, what is important in the relevant sensorimotor imagery is not physical states of affairs, but our own experiences of those states of affairs. However, when we proprioceptively image states of our bodies in order to plan the action, certain aspects of our own bodies, strictly speaking, are intentional objects of the experience, although not precisely the *same* aspects of the body (and brain) that serve as the substrata for that experience. When we imagine X, we are not imaging the physiological correlates of the act of imagining, but when X is a bodily state, say the tightness in a cramped leg, that aspect of the body *is* the intentional object. Similarly, when we imagine ourselves performing an action, we also imagine the aspects of our bodies that would gear us up for the action—that is, we imagine ourselves-acting, but as if experienced from our own point of view. In these cases, the imaged experiences are always *of* physical states of affairs, both external physical objects and the states of our own bodies.

In reflection, of course, much of this structure is not subjectively noticed: we reflect, not on our experience *per se,* but on our experience of physical states of affairs. Thus in describing what we reflect upon, we describe primarily those physical states of affairs. We also refer to feelings about the states of affairs, but language for those feelings tends to be inadequate. The feelings involve not only named common emotions like fear, but also a penumbra of much more subtle feeling-tones much more difficult to describe, including the "contradictions" discussed earlier: the blend of the subjective and the objective, and the temporal "thickness." It is that vast and murky penumbra that constitutes the ineffability of conscious experience.

Our strategy, then, is to take this seemingly hopeless complex of paradoxes that we call "consciousness," and develop a phenomenological characterization of it that will seem to "match up" with a physiological one, in such a way that we can say "yes, that physiological situation does fit what I phenomenally experience." The next section will show how this matching is possible.

2. Resolving the Paradoxes: Bridging Phenomenal Consciousness with Its Physiological Substrata

Philosophers since the time of Locke, Hume, and Kant have noted the difficulty of relating consciousness to the three main modalities of empirical experience—time, space, and causality. Spatially, the "objective" properties of objects "out there" are not distinct from "subjective," "secondary" properties that result from processing "in here." Temporally, experience does not present an infinitesimal "now" clearly distinguishable from an immediate past and future, the way the temporality of empirical occurrences presents itself. And in terms of causation, our emotional and feeling-tone "responses" to the "stimuli" that supposedly cause them are not separable from our experience of what the stimuli themselves "are like"; yet we experience our emotional-motivational intentions as both caused by and causing our experience of a world separable from them.

Husserl made some headway in clarifying each of these three paradoxes, but without connecting them to the empirical world of neuroscience. Spatially, Husserl (1913) shows that we must distinguish a *physical* object independent of us from an *intentional* object "in consciousness." Temporally, he shows that there is no experience of a "present moment," but only a "specious present" that includes the "retention" and "protention" of the just-passing and just-emerging moments (Husserl 1917). And causally, he sharply distinguishes between the psychophysical cause of a subjective response (for example, a motivation of the organism) and an *intentional object* of the response—what the state of consciousness is *"about"* (Husserl 1913).

These three dimensions of perceived physical reality remain intractably paradoxical whenever philosophers and scientists try to relate consciousness to physical correlates; the corresponding paradoxes have thus been at the heart of the "mind-body problem" throughout modernity. Each of the three paradoxes revolves around the difficulty in conceiving of consciousness as a physical mechanism, and thus as conforming to spatial, temporal, and causal principles that we attribute to physical events generally. Many are thus tempted to reject the underlying assumption that consciousness can be understood in terms commensurable with the physical and empirical-scientific realm at all. But, before making such a hasty sacrifice, we should also examine another underlying assumption that we have already seen contributes just as much to the paradoxes surrounding consciousness—the assumption that external objects function as "stimuli" which *cause* a "response" in the organism, on which an understanding of the consciousness of the object is to be based. If consciousness were like a physical mechanism, one would expect that the causal reactions of the conscious being would be distinguishable from the causal inputs that bring them about, and that a systematic correspondence would exist between causal inputs and their effects. But, whereas consciousness seems to be a "receiver" of "information" from the world, the perceived "information" cannot be clearly attributed to the perceptual objects from which the experience originates; color seems to be embedded in the surfaces of objects but in fact is not. By contrast, in the case of clearly physical mechanisms, we can distinguish cause A from effect B and identify a direct, systematic correspondence between aspects of A and their causal effects on aspects of B, with causation clearly flowing in one direction, not in both directions simultaneously.

To be sure, red light waves from the object play an important part in causing responses in the occipital lobe (Hubel and Wiesel 1959). But, in the first place, we have already seen that this occipital activity by itself does not result in *consciousness* of red (Posner 1990; Posner and Rothbart 1992, 2000; Damasio 1994; Farah 1989; Aurell 1989). And in the second place, the red in our consciousness seems to be *out there in the object,* and thus does not seem distinguishable from the object's redness in the way that a cause should be distinguishable from its effect. In sum, consciousness does not seem to behave like a physical mechanism, both because it is unanalyzable into constituent spatiotemporal components, and because aspects of consciousness cannot be correlated in a systematic causal correspondence with aspects of the analyzable physical mechanisms that supposedly elicit them.

Heidegger came a step closer than Husserl to connecting phenomenal and physical realms by emphasizing that human subjects are born not *into* the world, but *out of* it. We therefore are part and parcel with the world, interacting with it as if with something of our own fabric, rather than standing over against it and observing from without, like a pure "subject" (Heidegger 1927). This *a priori* familiarity with the ways of the world out of which we were born is what Heidegger calls "being in the world." From this standpoint, the key to resolving the dilemma of consciousness might be a recognition that emotional feelings and subjective "responses" are not responses to a physical realm of stimuli "out there in the world." Emotional motivations arise from purposes that already exist in our biological organisms prior to presentation of any environmental stimulus or situation—from what Ludwig Binswanger calls the "existential *a priori*" or "emotional categories" that condition experience (Needleman 1968). We don't experience the world merely by passively reacting to it, but also by *acting upon* it as agents.

This step suggests that the seeming incommensurability between the phenomenal and physical realms might be bridged if we begin by considering what it means to say that consciousness is associated with an "organism." The concept of organism is crucial in this context because organisms are physical phenomena, yet are driven to act *upon* their environment rather than merely reacting *to* it. As we hinted earlier, it may be that the physical correlates of consciousness are to be found not by looking at the information inputs from the environment and the brain's "responses" to those, but rather by looking at the emotional motivations arising within the organism itself, which has its own physical substratum. This physical substratum differs from stimulus-response mechanisms in that organic processes function in an active, self-organizing way rather than merely allowing their patterns to be dictated by the passive, *partes extra partes* mechanisms that seem so incommensurable with the structures of conscious experience.

It is the organism's emotions that motivate it to act on its environment rather than merely react; the *phenomenal* aspect of conscious experience requires the organism's emotionally motivated action in relation to the perceived world, particularly in its interest in selecting for attentional focus. If the organism's knowledge of its environment is to involve a *"felt"* dimension, in the sense that there is "something it feels like" to have a state of consciousness, the conscious processing must first flow from an emotional process within the organism, which *preexists* any particular input, and puts its qualitative stamp on each selected input.

We are suggesting that the "felt" aspect of experiencing is tied in with the fact that organisms are emotionally motivated to "look for" elements of the environment that are significant with respect to the organism's motivational purposes; that the organism "anticipates" experience in terms of motivational categories that pre-select for attention; and that the emotions that guide this anticipation and selection process are a major contributor to the conscious feeling of "what the consciousness of such-and-such an object is like."

When we formulate questions about whether such-and-such type of object is in our vicinity, we are already forming a rudimentary image of the object, or at least an "image schema" in the sense of vague parameters of the anticipated object. The emotionally motivated anticipation of the object is what *gives shape* to this image and forms it. For example, when subjects in perceptual experiments are instructed to hold in consciousness the image of certain objects to be flashed on a screen, and to continue to look for those types of objects as they are flashed intermittently with other objects, the attempt to "look for" the designated type of object is indistinguishable from holding in mind a more or less vague "image"; and this anticipatory image formation enables the subject to *see* the object more readily when it is actually presented (Corbetta 1990; Legrenzi et al 1993; Lavy and van den Hout 1994; Mack and Rock 1998; Posner and rothbart 1992, 1998, 2000).

To feel the full impact of this point for what consciousness "is like," try the following thought experiment: suppose we imagine a pink wall at which we are actually looking as blue. By doing so, we put ourselves into a state of readiness or vigilance to see blue if it should occur. We can observe within ourselves that what we do when we imagine the pink wall as blue is very similar to what we do if we look at the pink wall and anticipate actually seeing blue in the wall. We scrutinize the wall, as if searching for any blue that might show up there, or as if prepared to see the blue if it should suddenly appear. If this were not true, then subjects asked to imagine an object would not see it more readily than those who are not already actively imagining it at the point when it is presented. Even subliminal priming studies bear out this point, because the "looking for" process need not be conscious in order for it to shape the attention pattern and therefore the content of consciousness. When we look for something, either consciously or unconsciously, we *prepare ourselves* to see what we are looking for. For example, if I want to find my glasses among other objects on the dresser, I will fail to find them if I do not first form some sort of mental image or a general image schema of how they might appear—at least in rough outline.

This is why we say that the process of anticipating a certain type of object, which is grounded in emotional motivation and in the adaptive purposes of the organism in general, actually *gives rise to* the anticipatory image of that type of object, and in effect *forms* the image. As noted earlier, "imagery" can be preconscious as well as conscious, a point whose implications will be considered more extensively below. The important thing for now is that the realm of emotional and biological purposes that motivates conscious attention also permeates the act of consciousness through and through.

The suggestion that the process of forming an image is not only motivated by, but in fact *permeated* by emotion might sound absurd until we remember that even attentive perceptual consciousness presupposes that we have first "looked for" the object in the sense just mentioned. Even the act of selective attention must be emotionally motivated in *some* way, even if only by the emotion of curiosity or the need to find out what is going on in the environment in general. When the eye naturally directs its gaze toward a moving light in the visual periphery, there are strong motivational reasons for this attentional tendency, relating to the organism's survival needs.

If we can combine the roles of emotional motivation, anticipation, and imagery in a coherent characterization of the *structure* of phenomenal experiencing, so that this structure can be mapped to the corresponding physiological substrata for its constituent elements, then we can entertain some hope of seriously addressing the explanatory gap. To do so requires that our concept of consciousness must not only be framed in phenomenally experienceable terms, but also can be broken down into specific enough elements that these elements can be correlated with physiological substrata which, in the final analysis, will turn out to be inevitably inseparable from the corresponding elements of consciousness.

Based on the above considerations, the following characterization of phenomenal consciousness should be able to meet these requirements, because on the one hand it characterizes consciousness not by arbitrary fiat but as *phenomenally experienceable,* while on the other hand the elements of the description lend themselves to being correlated with empirically observable physiological substrata, so that at the end of our analysis it should be clear why this particular combination of physiological substrata cannot be unaccompanied by its conscious correlates. We propose that anything recognizable as consciousness, and not merely information processing, can be described as exhibiting the following structural character:

> Conscious experience (by contrast to unconscious information processing) entails an emotionally interested anticipation of possible sensory and

proprioceptive input such that the pattern of the subject's interest determines the modality, patterns, and emotional significance of the anticipated input. Incoming data, when combined with anticipatory imagery in conformity with structures specific to the capacities of that organism, becomes conscious perceptual experience. The intentional referents of consciousness are experienced with vividness to the extent that the activity constitutive of the interest in the future resonates (in terms of holistic patterns of activity) with the activity of incoming (afferent) imagistic data and with activation of memories of past imagistic or conceptual data.

In case anyone thinks these aspects of consciousness are not directly experienced, let's consider them in reflection. The sense in which consciousness is an "anticipation" of a possible input is experienced clearly by subjects in perceptual experiments instructed to imagine an object before it appears on a screen, or to continue looking for the object while other objects are flashed intermittently. The object being imagined or looked for *is in fact perceived more readily* (Corbetta 1990; Pardo *et al* 1990; Logan 1980; Hanze and Hesse 1993; Legrenzi *et al* 1993; Rhodes and Tremewan 1993; Lavy and van den Hout 1994). This attentional process "increases the probability of being able to detect the relevant signal" (Posner and Rothbart 1992, 97). Subjects in such experiments anticipate the object being looked for by imagining what it would be like to see the object. To imagine the object is to be on the lookout for it, and vice versa. This is the sense in which to form a mental image of a wall as blue means to "look for" or "anticipate" blue in the wall. This observation is highly consistent with Nigel Thomas's "perceptual activity theory" of imagery, in which images consist of organism-instigated neural actions in anticipation of possibly resonating input (Thomas 1989). When presented with a collection of objects, we are conscious of those on which attention is not focused only to the extent that they serve as ground for the figure to which we are attending. Normally we do not pay attention to the motivations and expectations that guide attention, but if they were not there, there would be no general regularities as to what kinds of objects tend to hold our attention in what kinds of contexts.

We need not be presently feeling an emotional need, consciously and attentively, in order for that need to direct attention and lead us to have expectations about the perceptual environment. A suddenly moving object in the periphery sets up cortico-thalamic loops that quickly direct consciousness to the object because it is vital for the organism's emotionally-defined purposes to be aware of such objects, even though the specific object usually turns out not to be important for the organism's goals. Any object that suddenly appears is emotionally important for the same reason. Thus it is difficult to direct attention away from the moving lights on a TV screen, because it is normally important for us to pay attention to sudden movements in our peripheral environment. As Merleau-Ponty says, "It is necessary to 'look' in order to see" (1941/1962, 232). "When I read the word 'warm'. . . my body prepares itself for heat and, so to speak, roughs out its outline" (1941/1962, 236). Helmholtz (1962) makes a similar point: "We let our eyes traverse all the noteworthy points of the object one after another." In other words, the organism must actively search for information; vision is active, not passive.

Someone may think that no anticipation is needed for very disinterested perceptual experiences, such as vegging in front of TV commercials. But if the TV should suddenly begin expanding, or turn into a pigeon and fly away, the subject would become acutely aware of the system of expectations that had already been at work guiding the direction of conscious attention.

Abstract thought, at least when executed by conscious beings, always involves subjunctives referring to things that are not immediately present particulars, and thus requires an understanding of subjunctive relations. That is, we imagine what it might be like *if* such-and-such were to happen. These subjunctive relations in turn involve anticipation as much as does consciousness of sensory or perceptual imagery. For example, as we argued earlier, anticipating that if I throw a ball at something in certain circumstances, it *will* knock it over is very similar (linguistically, neurophysiologically, and phenomenally) to believing that "If I *were* to throw a ball, it *would* knock something over." Anticipation of the future grounds our understanding of *subjunctives* and thus of abstract concepts at the most basic level of phenomenal experiencing (Ellis 1995b, Chapters 3–4; Newton 1996, Chapter 2).

Abstract logical or mathematical entities can be the intentional objects of cognition when represented by bodily or action schemas. When we think about arithmetic, we think of relational structures that are isomorphic with the familiar structures of our actions: we say, for example, that 3 "goes into" nine three times. We could say that concepts of mathematics are related metaphorically to action types, and that working out math problems involves interested anticipation of correct results of the calculations (supporting this view, see Kitcher 1985).

By *"interested* anticipation," we mean one that is emotionally motivated. The main feature that distinguishes conscious information processing from the kind of processing that non-self-organizing computers accomplish is this emotionally *interested* anticipation, which computers (and indeed all non-self-organizing systems) lack (Cytowic 1993). We are conscious of incoming afferent data only to the extent that we actively "pay attention" to something, and this process of directing attention is *motivated* by the needs of the organism. (From an empirical standpoint, afferent processing, for example in the occipital lobe, never results in conscious awareness of the object unless accompanied by corticothalamic loops instigated by midbrain motivational activity, and including frontal-limbic activity—see Bachmann 2000; Lethin 2002, 2004; Posner and Rothbart 1992, 1998; Damasio 1994; Farah 1989; Aurell 1989; Luria 1980.) In the figure-ground relationship, we may be conscious of the ground without "focusing" our attention on it, but neither figure *nor* ground would be in our consciousness if there were not some motivation (for example, curiosity, survival motives, etc.) to get us to direct attention in one way or another.

According to our hypothesis, the primary organismic need that motivates consciousness of objects is the need to *anticipate future* data that are considered important for the organism's purposes. As Dennett (1996) says, "Animals are not just herbivores or carnivores. They are . . . *informavores*. . . . Without the epistemic hunger, there is no perception, no uptake. Philosophers have often attempted to analyze perception into the Given and what is then done with the Given by the mind. The Given is, of course, Taken" (Dennett 1996, 82). And again, "The task of a mind is to produce future. . . . A mind is fundamentally an anticipator, an expectation-generator" (57–58).

It might be suspected that by explaining the "felt" quality of consciousness in terms of its being permeated by "emotion" we are sneaking in the phenomenal dimension through the back door, since an emotion may be thought of as already *being* a state of consciousness. So the question as to how an emotion can have both a felt quality and a physical substratum seems as unclear and ineffable as ever.

But emotions are not necessarily already conscious, all by themselves. They can be unconscious, in at least two senses. First, we may unconsciously "want" to electrically neutralize the ionized molecules in the nervous system; in this case, the emotion doesn't yet have any representation of what it is about until it begins to become conscious, and forming this representation (for example, the image of something to drink in the case of thirst, and also the proprioceptive image of *what it feels like* to get something to drink) is what makes the difference between consciously desiring something and non-consciously desiring it.

Secondly, emotions may also be "derivatively unconscious" (see Ellis 1995b), that is, *derived from* earlier processes in which consciousness *did* play a role—for example, when we unconsciously but purposely use a diversion technique in argument because we unconsciously *want* to cover up a mistake in our own reasoning. These "derivatively" unconscious processes have been learned through earlier conscious experience, and then habituated (see Posner and Rothbart 1992), just as we gradually cease attending to the process of "figuring out" each note as we learn to read music.

Remember that both emotion and motivation, as we use the terms, involve purposeful action in the micro sense—the action of a self-organizing system to achieve and maintain dynamical basins of attraction. Emotions are different from motivations because not only can they motivate further action, but they can also monitor how well the body is doing overall in achieving the goals of motivations, and this monitoring can be done either consciously or preconsciously, as when a boxer finishes a fight and then realizes he was afraid. The fear was an emotion that was helping the fighter to monitor his bodily well being and also projecting courses of action to maintain well being, but the boxer did not have to be consciously thinking of the fear while fighting. So, as we are using the terms, neither emotions nor motivations are necessarily conscious by definition or by their very nature. The important point for our purposes is that emotions are used in planning or monitoring. This not only means that they can be preconscious or conscious, but also it implies that emotions can be aroused by very specific states of affairs, to act in the interest of long-term motivational purposes, and also in the short term to test the suitability of a possible action.

Emotions and motivations are characterized by purposive strivings, and there do seem to be *non-conscious* yet *purposive* phenomena in nature, especially in biological organisms. The human organism purposely does what is needed to regulate heartbeat and blood pressure, yet normally is not *conscious* of doing so. Merleau-Ponty defines a "purposeful organism" as one that changes, replaces, or readjusts the functioning of its own parts as needed to maintain or enhance the functioning of the whole organism. Monod (1971) and Kauffman (1993) have used this definition as a leading concept in the attempt to show how biological processes tend to maintain their pattern of activity across very multiply realizable replacements of their components.

When we speak of the relationships between conscious and unconscious emotions, we should be careful to avoid a simplistic "appendage" view of consciousness. An emotion experienced at the conscious level is *not* simply the corresponding unconscious one, plus an extra layer of consciousness superadded to it, as though the conscious emotion, X, were nothing but the unconscious emotion X plus our awareness *of* X. The process through which X becomes explicated as a conscious phenomenon is complex, and it changes its structure and its assessment of its goals and intentions as determined by organismic needs in the perceived context. A man who is jealous but unaware of the jealousy may merely direct an unconscious anger at innocent bystanders; after reflecting, he is no longer angry, either at the world generally or at the object of jealousy, but only "hurt" or "sad" at the perceived loss of intimacy (Gendlin 1992a, b). Both the intentional object and the felt quality of the conscious emotion differ from the unconscious one that gave rise to it. Thus if X is a conscious emotion, X is not simply the *same* bodily response that could occur unconsciously (Ellis 1986, 1995b, 1996, 2005; Jackendoff 1996).

Since there can be unconscious emotions, saying that the phenomenal dimension of consciousness depends on an emotional process is not circular. In fact, emotions are conscious only to the extent that we form some sort of representation of what they are about and of how they are manifest in our bodies. Usually, this entails imagery of some sort, especially when we consider symbols as a kind of imagery, as Damasio (1994) does—not only sensory or sensorimotor imagery of the referents of symbols, but also sensorimotor imagery of ourselves saying the words (as in Joseph 1982; see also Ellis 1995). This view is consistent with the fact that the part of the left prefrontal cortex that is specialized for symbolic utterances is exactly symmetrical to the part of the right prefrontal cortex that controls simple images (Faw 2003).

Both emotion and representation are needed for phenomenal consciousness. Without emotion, we might have unconscious information processing, as in a digital computer or thermostat or thermos bottle; and without the representation, we might have unconscious emotions, as in "wanting" to fill or empty the outer electron shells of atoms in the various biological systems, so as to restore chemical homeostasis; but, in this case we would not feel a *conscious* wanting of this outcome. Both emotion and representation must be present for phenomenal experiencing to occur.

For example, if a person is hungry, but does not know that the feeling is a feeling of *hunger,* then there is no consciousness of the hunger. A hypoglycemic who is hungry, for instance, may not realize that she is hungry, and instead may become vaguely restless or irritable. The person is not conscious of her hunger because she is not *representing* the feeling in terms of a desire for some kind of sustenance or edible objects, and in terms of a bodily sensing (proprioceptively) of the *phys-*

ical sensations that go with being hungry. She *is,* of course, conscious of *other* feelings, but the feeling of hunger is also there, *un*-consciously, which is the key point. In order for the feeling of *hunger* to move from an unconscious to a conscious status, she would have to represent something (for example, edible objects, or the empty feeling in her body) to facilitate this movement. (As far as the *other* feelings that she is *conscious* of having are concerned, those *are* being accompanied by representations of various sorts, and this is part of the reason why *they are* conscious.) This representation could be a little "off target" as far as bodily localization goes, and still accomplish the purpose of representation. The further off-target it is, of course, the less well it will serve as a representation capable of bringing *that particular* emotion to conscious awareness; it may instead result in bringing to awareness *other* emotions.

Because emotions are not conscious until they result in some sort of sensory or proprioceptive "imagery," the above characterization of conscious experience also emphasizes the way the emotionally motivated anticipation of input leads to such "imagery." By "image," again, we do not mean a physical replica of some object, or some sort of holographic image floating around the subject's head, but rather the felt sense that one is looking for (or listening for, tasting for, proprioceptively feeling for, and so forth) some object or state of affairs that would take the form of an intentional object. The role of imagery in action planning involves forming (not necessarily a visual or auditory image, but) a sensory *and/or* proprioceptive *and/or* sensorimotor image of oneself performing the action in the way planned (Newton 1996).

This implies that the consciousness of an image involves much more than the traditionally understood stimulation of the "primary and secondary sensory areas" (for example, the occipital area and area V4 for visual images). We have already mentioned that all these areas can be stimulated without *conscious awareness* of the perceptual object, resulting in a correspondingly less complete *processing of the information.* Before any perceptual consciousness can result, corticothalamic loops must be activated which involve much more extensive brain areas than the primary and secondary sensory areas (Posner and Rothbart 1992, 2000; Aurell 1989). *Understanding* the perceptual object means that we imagine what it would be like to use or deal with the object in the context of purposeful action, which involves the emotions and a process of *actively directing attention,* as well as activation of brain areas corresponding to motor activity. Thus understanding can be viewed, physiologically and phenomenally, as a sort of imaginary and truncated process of purposeful action planning, involving an emotional component as the organism's motivation for the imagined action. But this process still constitutes an "image" in that through it we are *representing* something—not just sensory data, but also the execution of bodily actions.

Some might object that this definition of "imagery" makes it a conscious phenomenon by its very nature: explaining consciousness in terms of "imagery" already *presupposes* what is to be explained. It is true that imagery in the sense intended here is a necessary component of all conscious experience. Our purpose is not to explain consciousness as causally resulting from imagery, but to show how consciousness can be broken down into interacting elements recognizable as involved in the phenomenal experience of consciousness. The point is that all three elements—emotional motivation, anticipation, and imagery—are necessary aspects of every conscious experience. Once we have understood how these three functions interact, we will then be in a better position to see why certain combinations of brain processes are inevitably accompanied by conscious experience, whereas no one of them in isolation would have been conscious.

Postulating a central role for imagery also requires that we show how language and logic use can be grounded in "imagery" (in this broadened sense). The expansion of "imagery" to include proprioceptive and sensorimotor images in the context of action planning, combined with the understanding of language as a type of *tool* (Newton 1982, 1996) is a key step in this direction. As we pointed out earlier, when we understand the meaning of an abstract term, a key part of what we are doing is to feel confident (at a marginally conscious level) that, if we wanted to, we *could* imagine what it would be like to execute the operations involved in making the observations necessary for the fulfillment of the ostensive conditions that define what it means to be that type of object. We do not actually imagine all these ostensive conditions each time we use the word, but we do feel confident that we *could* imagine them. As Damasio puts it, we form a "partial activation of a dispositional concept" (Damasio 1994, 104). Words are then used as tools in the context of action planning schemas, where the words can also be understood as *objects* in terms of the kinds of action planning schemas relevant to object understanding.

Notice that any of the *elements* of our dynamical characterization of consciousness, if they were to occur in isolation, could occur on a *nonconscious* basis (and therefore would be susceptible in principle to being bridged to empirically observable physical processes). For example, we can and do often have *interested anticipations of the future* without consciousness. Throughout nature we find purposeful activity without conscious awareness of anything. We can also have *processing of afferent data* without consciousness (non-conscious "experience," as in blindsight). We can have *holistic processing* without consciousness (as in holograms which are not conscious). We can have non-conscious *interests* alongside of non-conscious *data processing*, with no consciousness resulting from the mere *additive juxtaposition* of these elements. We can have non-conscious *anticipations of the future* (as in operant conditioning, or as when a computer predicts the future), juxtaposed with non-conscious activations of stored *information* or of *present afferent activity*, with no consciousness of the process.

Consciousness occurs only when the conscious or unconscious interest in the future acts in such a way that the pattern of its own activity *gives rise to* an image (or concept) of a possible or alternative future; and *perceptual* consciousness occurs when this activity *resonates* with afferent activity and with activation of imagistic (or in some cases conceptual) memories. In other words, the interested anticipation (which may include evolutionarily adaptive organismic interests), the forming of the image, and the processing of the sensory (or sensorimotor) data do not merely occur *alongside* each other in additive juxtaposition, but instead the interest *gives rise to* the image; at the same time, the image, the interest, and the sensory (or sensorimotor) data all resonate with each other. The degree of *resonance* among these activities corresponds to the *vividness* of the consciousness. Also, the three elements of consciousness—interested anticipation, image-formation (of a possible future), and (perhaps "re-entrant") activation of past afferent data (either as sense experience just having occurred, or as memory of sense experience long ago) constitute the three temporal moments, past, present, and future, so that every conscious experience seems to be stretched out over a very short but extended interval, rather than encapsulated in an infinitesimal "present moment."

Most of the experienced properties of objects are attributed to the object because of subjective processing (for example, bats apparently "see" certain sounds), yet these subjective attributes are ineffably blended and blurred with the apparent objectivity of the object. This blending results more basically from the way the organism blends the three temporal moments through anticipation and re-entrant signaling. The motivated anticipation of blue gives rise to the neural patterns that constitute the imaging of blue, which, in resonance with those motivated anticipations, constitutes the consciousness of blue. Motivations for such an activity can vary widely, but what they all have in common is a desire for some sort of action planning. The organism is thus conscious of its environment by acting in relation to it, not by reacting to it. When we "see" the roughness of a concrete driveway, we imagine ourselves acting upon it—running our hand over it or crawling on it—in anticipation of how such interactions would affect our purposes as an organism. Thwarting of certain purposes (for example, circulation in the skin of the knees when crawling, or electrolytic balances in the nervous system, which are affected by the way our nerves interact with the concrete) results in painful consciousness.

We are now in a position to resolve the three paradoxes of phenomenal experience described earlier. First, the paradox of the spatial location of qualities: What we anticipate is an imagined resultant *activity of our own organism,* yet this anticipation is partly constitutive *of* the consciousness of an image—for example, as a subject prepares herself to see a blue triangle flashed on a screen, resulting in her entertaining a vague or sharp image of the blue triangle before it is actually flashed. When it is flashed, her *afferent* occipital activity ("afferent" in the sense of "reacting to external stimulation") reflects the activity of the object as it reflects light oscillating with certain frequencies and in certain patterns. But, in order for perceptual consciousness to occur, this afferent activity also must resonate with *efferent* activity that the organism itself has already initiated in much more extensive brain areas (Lethin 2002, 2004; Luria 1980, 82ff; Ellis 1995b, Chapter 2)—"efferent" in the sense of "generated by the activity of the organism itself to direct its actions" (Luria 1980, 82ff). The efferent cortical activity alone would correspond to the mere mental image of a blue triangle; but the resonating of these efferent patterns of activity with the afferent patterns of the occipital region signals that the image is now a perception rather than merely a mental image. Yet the imagistic activity of the efferent system (which, in the sense of "efferent" used by Luria and others, includes midbrain, limbic, and frontal activity) had to occur *before* conscious attention could be directed to the percept. Active imagination in a subject-initiated process is *presupposed* by perceptual consciousness, yet also is a constituent component of the perceptual consciousness. Hence the paradox that the perceived property (for example, blue) seems to be "out there" in the world, yet at the same time "in here," in my subjectively generated imagination. The anticipation of interacting with blue is inseparable from the conscious experience of blue as a mental image.

The paradox of the specious present can be understood in terms of this same mode of analysis. Because the conscious act occurs as we *anticipate* a possible percept in the context of action planning, any momentary slice of conscious activity seems already to subsume past, present, and future. Since anticipation of the percept partly *constitutes* the consciousness of it, the *future* state of the percept seems to be included *in* the present moment, rather than merely expected to occur later, and the image that is anticipated is not distinguished from the image of what is present "now." Hence the perceived paradox of the intermingling of present with non-present. This explanation applies clearly to the Changizi et al. (2008) perceptual studies in which subjects see a moving object as being ahead of where it actually is at each point in time. When a light flashes at the current location of the object, the subject sees the object as already having moved past that point, suggesting that the object is seen to be where it is just about to be, rather than where it literally is. If the phase of experience that creates our consciousness is actually the *anticipatory* phase, whereas the reception of that which we anticipate lags behind the anticipated location, then of course what we are looking *for* would appear to be where the object currently *is*, even though it is not there yet. The looking-for phase is the conscious phase, not the receptivity phase. And yet, of course, if the receptivity phase *doesn't conform* to what we were looking for, then we do not experience what we are looking for as literally *being there*, but instead we experience it only as something we imagined *might* be there. Also, the surprise shocks us, so we become confused for an instant about exactly what we did see—as in the case of the soccer player who is deceived by the opponent's deceptive move. After recovering, the player then is able to find the ball again by looking *for* it in its new trajectory rather than the previously expected one.

Finally, we can also see why phenomenal consciousness would involve a paradox surrounding the confusion between an emotional response and the "what it's like" sense of the object's perceptual properties. In anticipating perceptual objects, we are anticipating the way they may or may not interact with our motivating organismic purposes. There is no attention without motivation to attend, and no motivation without organismic purposes. Furthermore, part of the anticipated outcome in action planning is the hoped-for or feared subsequent emotional state of the organism. In anticipating that the concrete would be rough to crawl on, we anticipate being thwarted in the desire to maintain optimal circulation in the skin of the knees and optimal electrolytic balance in the nervous system. The anticipation of the resultant emotional state of the organism is thus partly *constitutive* of the consciousness of the object. Hence the paradox that "what it's like" to experience a given object presents itself on the one hand as attributable to the object itself, and on the other hand as completely generated by subjective emotional processes.

What we have proposed is a characterization of consciousness, taken in part from our phenomenal experience of it (and, as we will argue in the next chapter, compatible with phenomenology in every respect), which can be broken down into elements that in turn are explainable in rational and empirical terms, but which, when they interact in a certain way, are inevitably accompanied by consciousness. These elements, essentially, are 1. an emotional motivation that grounds an interest in anticipating the future; 2. sensory, sensorimotor or proprioceptive imagery (which, by itself, can occur preconsciously) activated by this emotional motivation; and 3. a resonating between the activity of emotionally-motivated imagery and the activity stimulated by incoming sensory data and data reactivated through memory. If consciousness is characterizable as a certain kind of interaction of these elements, then the corresponding interaction of the necessary and sufficient patterns of activity in the physiological correlates of these three elemental processes will be inseparable from the corresponding conscious processes.

To appreciate how impossible it would be for this combination *not* to be accompanied by consciousness, consider a thought experiment. Imagine an organism whose actions are being guided by a need to quench its thirst. Imagine that this organism is neurophysiologically sophisticated enough that its desire to quench its thirst leads it to select from incoming perceptual data only those items whose form seems to it relevant to the thirst. At this point, we still have not *necessarily* imagined a conscious being; it could still be a cleverly designed but unconscious machine. But now imagine that the pattern of activity in the parts of the organism's nervous system that *represent* the thirst-quenching item *resonates* so completely with the pattern of activity in the part that *desires* the thirst-quenching item, that a unified pattern of activity occurs which *simultaneously*, and *by virtue of one and the same pattern of activity,* both desires *and* represents the thirst-quenching item (because the desiring pattern has *given rise to* the representation of that which is desired or of related imagery). At this point, we are no longer imagining a machine that contains a representation in one of its parts, and a biological need in another of its parts, but rather a unified activity that blends representing and desiring in *one unified* activity that permeates *one unified* system within the organism.

In the next chapter, we shall go further and argue that to imagine one unified activity that both desires and represents *in the same act,* because its desire gives shape to its representation, *is already to imagine a conscious being.* To be sure, such a being *might* still be a cleverly designed machine, but it is now a *conscious* machine. Is it possible that one activity which simultaneously both desires and represents, and whose desire has given shape to its representation, could be a *non-conscious* activity? What we shall suggest is that such a thing is logically possible only in the sense that Clark Kent might not turn out to be Superman, after one has already seen Kent repeatedly deflect bullets with his fists, hurl missiles into space, put on his Superman suit, fly away, and leave fingerprints which conclusively match Superman's fingerprints. Even if we can still "imagine" Kent as not being Superman in this case, we can do so only by purposely forgetting the empirical facts that have already established the probable identity of Kent with Superman. Certainly, the idea that Kent could be Superman is no longer "ineffable" in the way that consciousness seemed in our earlier discussions. Similarly, the argument of our next chapter will attempt to show that the idea of a biological system that, in one unified act, both desires and represents a thirst-quenching item, and for this reason is *conscious* of the thirst-quenching item, is not ineffable. Yet the desire and the representation and their resonating can also be conceived of as activities that take *physical* events as their substrata. Such a characterization of conscious experience can present the hope of connecting with both the phenomenal and the physical realms in a way that is not ineffable.

Obviously, if the elements just enumerated must all be present in order for any conscious experience to occur, then the subject of experience will not be able to experience any one of the elements as separable from the others. A subject does not *experience* her own consciousness as broken up or analyzable into these elements. Our characterization therefore is not simply a phenomenological description of conscious experience as it immediately presents itself to a subject. In what sense, then, is this characterization somehow "true to" phenomenal experience, or a characterization of consciousness *as* it is phenomenally experienced?

Our characterization can be thought of as a "dynamical" or "functional" characterization, in the following sense. While one of the most familiar features of conscious experience is its apparently essential unity—the resistance of the experience itself (as opposed to its sensory content) to analysis in terms of components—this experiential unity is necessarily connected with brain events separated both physically and temporally. It can be fragmented by brain damage, and tests show that brain events underlying conscious experience are more widely separated in time than is apparent to subjects, who consistently underestimate time lapses between moments of consciousness (Libet 1999; Libet et al. 1983). Thus the internal structure of consciousness is opaque to the subject.

But while the structure of conscious experience is not a part of the experience, it shapes the experience. Consciousness can feel the way it does only if certain brain events occur in certain ways. This means, in principle at least, that scientific knowledge about those brain events should shed light, for a subject, on different aspects of that subject's experience, and help the subject distinguish those aspects as products of distinct brain events. The hope that increased neuroscientific sophistication would supplant the phenomenal dimension of consciousness has guided eliminativists for two decades (for example, Paul Churchland 1985, 1989). In practice, however, the "illusion" has proven highly resistant to being dispelled, and the eliminativist program has not made much headway. Note that Patricia Churchland (1986), unlike Paul, tends toward a more modest psychophysical identity rather than such a flamboyant eliminativism.

In our view, there is too wide a gap between consciousness and brain events, described in neuroscientific terms, to be phenomenally bridged by the subject of the experience being examined. But this very width provides room for an intermediate description of conscious experience, one that is only partially—and yet crucially—accessible by the experiencing subject. This intermediate description uses phenomenological terminology to describe *dynamic relations* among anatomically and temporally distinct components of experience. The description is formulated in such a way that the subject can identify these relations with aspects of her own experience. Then, when a phenomenological description is provided of the experiential results of the blending of the elements we have described, the subject is able to say "Aha! That's it!" While the description analyzes the experience into components separately associated with distinct brain events, both the components and, more important, their dynamic relations, are described in familiar, phenomenological terminology. Our view is that consciousness is not a static entity or state, but a goal-directed activity on the part of the subject. A conscious subject is actively involved with the sensed world, and is emotionally motivated toward this activity. Only if a description represents this motivated activity *vis a vis* the sensed world will that description be phenomenally recognizable. If it is recognizable, as we believe it is (or will be, by the end of the next chapter), then this recognition will bridge the epistemological gap between the physical and the experiential aspects of consciousness, since the elements in the description can be objectively shown to be mediated by brain events.

7

The Self-Organizing Imagination: A Fuller Resolution of the Mind-Body Problem

We now need to show how an action-based approach can actually explain why and how non-conscious ingredients can be combined to create consciousness in the familiar phenomenal sense. The previous chapter showed how a self-organizational approach can address the *paradoxes* of consciousness. But we have not yet shown conclusively how the action-based theory can explain why there is a difference between conscious and non-conscious processes. If we are to hold that consciousness is a type of activity of a self-organizing creature (in agreement, for example, with Gallagher 200; Humphrey, 2000; O'Regan and Noë, 2001), then we must also face up to some serious challenges to this way of thinking. Is it not possible, after all, that an active system with self-organizational "purposes" and representations could occur on a physical basis, yet still without being conscious?

We have seen that viewing consciousness as an activity—rather than as a passive state in which the subject is affected by afferent stimuli while being somehow aware that it is so affected—seems to offer hope of avoiding certain difficulties of the latter view. This latter view is still the traditional one in recent information processing theory, and ultimately traces to the Cartesian passively-observing subject. We can refer to this traditional information-receiving model of consciousness as the "perceptual model." It thinks of consciousness as being like a recipient of perceptual inputs, observing intentional contents as a perceiver observes that which is perceived. In this model, as we pointed out in our introduction, consciousness tends to take on the role of the end point of a causal chain, and often seems to be a ghostly *observer of* information that has already been processed within the physical brain-body system.

By contrast, if consciousness is an activity, in the sense of being "enacted" by the organism in the ways we discussed earlier, then its inaccessibility to objective observers is no longer a problem. Only the *agent* of an activity can *perform* it. On the traditional model, consciousness is a way of experiencing things, a special way of receiving information; in that way of thinking, the question immediately arises of why only one particular conscious subject is able to "receive" this information. As Jackson (1986) points out, an experimenter's empirical knowledge of someone's brain, even if complete, would not by itself reveal what the person's subjective experience "is like," or what it feels like for that subject—or indeed that it feels like anything at all. By contrast, in the action-centered approach, asking why only the subject can enjoy her conscious experiences is like asking why only a dancer can perform a particular token action of dancing. It is conceptually meaningless to suggest that a second person can simultaneously perform a given agent's bodily action.

We have not yet addressed the objection, however, that the move from a passive to an enactive view, by itself, is of no help in crossing the explanatory gap between physiology and phenomenology: "'ways of acting' are by no means closer to experiential features than 'internal representations' are" (Kurthen 2001). The zombie argument concerning phenomenal consciousness can easily be applied to a crude claim that consciousness is an activity, just as well as it can to the perceptual model. That is, it seems possible that a creature could perform this, or any, sort of activity with no associated phenomenal experience.

In this chapter, we sketch an action-centered way to address, in addition to the functional aspects of consciousness, the question of *phenomenal experience*. We must clarify in more detail how consciousness can "emerge" from an interplay of processes that, *taken in isolation*, would *not* be conscious. The account is emotivist and action-centered in holding that anticipation is an essential component of the more global activity of self-maintenance and growth or development in the face of challenging environmental conditions. Complex creatures like human beings are able to test possible actions in advance of performing them by means of sensorimotor imagery—activated memory images of the experiences of such actions and their past consequences, understood not in passive perceptual terms, but in terms of sensorimotor and proprioceptive imagery *of the consequences of actions for the organism* (Newton 1982, 1993, 1996; Ellis 2005). The consequences in question are in turn understood, not primarily in external terms, but in terms of potential future organismic actions that they would or would not afford.

Images of objective events in the world are secondary in this context, and they are not presupposed by the sensorimotor imagery needed for this anticipatory process; on the contrary, perceptual imagery of the world, in our view, is a *consequence* of the sensorimotor understanding of the environment's action affordances with respect to types of objects. The activation of the sensorimotor action imagery is subserved by various brain areas, such as the motor cortex, the cerebellum, and subcortical regions that control the neurotransmitters needed to energize the organism for action. This action-initiating brain activation is normally the precursor of actual performance of actions. But as we have seen, even when we *imaginatively contemplate* the actions, their initial stages are activated and then inhibited from overt realization by effector systems (Jeannerod, 1994, 1997; Stippich 2002). We are arguing, then, that conscious experience *is* fundamentally and essentially this imagined performance of sensorimotor activity, explicitly or implicitly. Explicitly, in that much of conscious experience is the explicit contemplation, through proprioceptive and action imagery, of things that we might do (Newton, 1993, 1996, 2000, 2001). Implicitly, in that conscious experience can also involve implicit contemplation of action, in cases where action imagery underlies reasoning about abstract matters, such as logical or mathematical questions (Johnson, 1987; Newton, 1995; Ito, 1993; Ellis 1995a, b). For example, a musician imagining a melody may implicitly imagine what it would be like to play the melody on an instrument. In the same way, understanding the "either-or" connective in logic might involve implicitly imagining touching each of two objects in alternation, or making two movements in alternation.

The above claims do not address the question of why such activity "is like" something for the organism—why it results in phenomenal experience—but they do provide a basis for such an explanation. In this chapter, we propose a fuller account of phenomenal experience. In anticipating actions and their possible outcomes, subjects must make use of working memory of previous action images, in which multiple sensorimotor states are represented. It is necessary for these alternative states to be held "on line" simultaneously, or nearly so, so that the subject can compare them for selection purposes (Damasio, 1994, 1999). Not only are possible future states of the active organism represented, but past and present ones as well. When we think about what to do next, we must be aware of what we are doing now, and what we were doing in the immediate past, since future states are constrained by the past and present ones. This simultaneous representing of different temporal moments is a crucial part of the explanation of the ineffable experience of phenomenal consciousness. But again, remember that the relevant action imageries themselves can be implicit as well as explicit.

We begin with a general discussion of the ontology of consciousness viewed as an enactive process, and we outline a way the process emerges from its component processes. Then we look in more detail at the specific sense in which consciousness is an "emergent" property. At that point, we can show how it is that this kind of emergence can provide the familiar but ineffable phenomenal experiences.

1. Connecting First-Person and Third-Person Definitions

As explained earlier, consciousness is "emergent" out of physical realities and, because of its self-organizing nature, is capable of exhibiting "downward causation" once it has emerged. That is, consciousness is a *relational pattern* of activity capable of controlling and rearranging many of the background conditions that must be in place in order for a causal sequence at the micro-level to be necessary or sufficient for a given outcome.

This emergent consciousness, as we have emphasized, is not a novel substance in the universe, exerting a force on a passive subject; on the contrary, it is a novel *activity* of the subject considered holistically. Structural patterns in the activity of a dynamical system can make a causal difference to the efficacy of various micro-constituents in the holistic context, and sufficiently complex systems can select, appropriate and replace micro-components as needed to maintain structural continuity across replacements and recombinations of the micro-constituents of the structure (Kauffman, 1993; Ellis, 1986, 1999, 2000, 2001a, b, 2005). Consciousness corresponds to such higher-order processes, and thus has certain causal powers over the parts that make up the whole.

For reasons that we shall now show, it turns out that this self-organizational structural stability across various micro-level causal constituents is precisely what provides a unique phenomenal state that alters the subject's experience, and hence her behavior, and in that sense is the source of causal power. Phenomenal consciousness is a unifying process in sufficiently complex creatures—a process continuous with the way any living organism can sense or have access to proprioceptive and environmental stimuli, and have its actions influenced by them.

The "ineffability" of phenomenal consciousness results from the necessary failure of a conscious subject to identify, in her conscious experience, the components of physical reality that have formed the components of this organizational unity. Since these components can be both predicted and identified from an objective standpoint, it is less useful to think of consciousness as a novel form of existence than as a novel *configuration* of more elementary states and processes.

This notion of *dynamical* emergence—the result of a novel combination of quite lawlike physical phenomena in a self-organizational structure—should be distinguished from *metaphysical* emergence—the notion that consciousness cannot be a combination of physical processes that, in isolation from each other, could have existed without consciousness. In our view, consciousness is a combination of several other processes that in some natural contexts do occur in isolation from each other, and in the absence of consciousness. Yet when these processes interact within a certain structure, this interaction necessarily results in consciousness; metaphysical dualism is thus avoided.

In essence, it is obvious from natural observations that a kind of "proto-desire" can exist in some self-organizing systems that lack consciousness; similarly, in some living and non-living systems, there can be non-conscious "proto-representation," not only of actually existing things, but also of non-present logical possibilities. Our argument is essentially just this: when the same living and self-organizing system both proto-desires *and* proto-represents an unactualized logical possibility, within the same framework of purposeful action, consciousness is *necessarily* the result. In this case, desire and representation occur in their full *conscious* sense, not just in their "proto" and non-conscious senses. Before elaborating our argument for this claim, let's be careful not to over-commit to an unrealistic type of "explanation." We already noted above that Chalmers and Levine are right to insist that causal explanations alone are not adequate for our purposes.

a. What Kind of "Explanation" Is Needed?

When we ask for an "explanation" of consciousness, what are we asking for? Do we need only a description of the physical conditions such that, whenever those conditions are met, and only when they are met, there is consciousness? This listing of necessary and sufficient physical conditions alone would not be a satisfactory explanation, because as Levine (1983) points out, we still would not have explained *why* those physical conditions necessarily exhibit the property of consciousness. For a description of the physical conditions to explain consciousness in a way that would provide real philosophical understanding, it should ideally be possible for someone receiving the explanation to relate it to her own experience; to recognize that *that* description fits what she knows her conscious states to be like.

There is one useful alternative to an explanation that merely lists necessary and sufficient physical conditions: one that would enable someone hearing the explanation to understand not only the physical conditions themselves, but also why those conditions should create an experience whose subjective character is not captured by the description of the *physical components that subserve* consciousness; and yet, while the explanations of the separate components do not entail consciousness, their *combination* must be *unimaginable as unaccompanied by* consciousness. In other words, we should recognize at the outset that the ineffability of conscious experience might be an unavoidable feature. It might be impossible for a conscious subject to analyze her own experience, while she is having it, into a combination of states that are the inevitable result of certain underlying brain mechanisms. But if this is impossible, then that impossibility itself should be explicable in a way that is intuitively acceptable, subjectively as well as objectively. Our view is that the latter state of affairs is the case with our own (human) type of consciousness.

Our goal, then, is to explain why certain physical features, *when combined in a particular way*, will inevitably entail the familiar experience of consciousness. The entailment here will be an inductive entailment between physical events and phenomenological experiences, not a deductive inference from the physical events to the experiences. To put it another way, the equivalence between consciousness and its separable physical components is "extensional" rather than "intentional." That is, the *meaning of the terms* "Clark Kent" and "Superman" is not equivalent, yet the two are "extensionally" equivalent in that, *as a matter of fact,* they are the same. To use a different example, the Morning Star and the Evening Star are *extensionally* equivalent, because they happen to be the same object; but they are not *intentionally* equivalent, because "Morning Star" does not *mean* the same as "Evening Star." So the equivalence of the Morning Star and the Evening Star is not something to be logically deduced, but rather something to be *discovered empirically*, just as someone might discover empirically that Kent is Superman. A sweeping explanation that would allow consciousness to be *deduced* from physical observations would require them to be *intentionally* equivalent, but that kind of equivalence is not called for in philosophy of mind. What is called for at most is only an *extensional* equivalence (or even more modestly, a sense in which mind and its physical substrates are ontologically inseparable in some strong sense—see Ellis 1986).

So if we can support the modest claim that consciousness as we phenomenologically experience it would inevitably have to result whenever certain third-person physical ingredients are combined, then we would provide an explanation that bridges the explanatory gap, but without entailing that the existence of such a thing as consciousness is *deductively entailed* by some particular physical description (here we are in agreement with Kelso, 1995, 260). Given this aim, it will be necessary to begin with a definition of "consciousness" that is framed in first person terms—that is, a phenomenological description of what consciousness is like. Only then can we hope to bridge a scientific story to what is really meant by "consciousness."

Obviously, a phenomenological description of what consciousness "is like" must distinguish it from the non-conscious processing of information that is accomplished by digital computers, robots and the like. With this contrast in mind, a phenomenological characterization will include essentially the same elements that were contained in the third-person "functional" characterization of consciousness in our previous chapter. These can be quickly summarized:

1. Consciousness is colored by an ongoing *affective* dimension, and this affectivity seems to motivate us to "anticipate" experience in the sense that a perceptual event cannot be conscious unless we "look to see" what is there, as Merleau-Ponty (1941, 232) says. This point is consistent with the Mack and Rock perceptual experiments in which subjects are not conscious of perceptual data in their visual fields when their attention is distracted by an irrelevant mental task. Receiving input is not enough to create consciousness; "attention, when otherwise engaged, must be captured *before* perception can occur" (Mack and Rock 1998, 18, italics added). We experience things consciously only if we are engaged in a "looking for" and not just a "looking at" (Ellis 1995b).

Christina Schües (1994) describes this affective-anticipatory element in consciousness this way:

> The continual course of experiences takes place as a process of actual anticipations followed by subsequent assurances in which the same object of perception, remembering, etc., is held in awareness and is determined more closely. If an anticipation is not assured, but disappointed, then I might be

surprised and a modalization of my experience takes place.... We find here the possibility of a meaning which may even retroactively *inhibit* the already constituted meaning and overlie it with a new one, and hence, transform the experience accordingly.... When an object of experiences affects me, it seems to have an affective power which motivates me to perceive it. ... a movement of interest aiming at the object.... If the anticipation is disappointed and its motivational power diminishes, then the original mode of the experience is transformed into negation. (Schües 1994, 12–14)

2. This first point by itself may not be enough to distinguish consciousness from the information processing of a cleverly designed biological yet non-conscious computer or robot, but the distinction becomes more sharp when we see how this point combines with our second and third points. The second point is that consciousness includes an "imaginative" dimension in the sense that it requires that we contemplate some sort of vague notion of what might be presented *before* it is presented; and this means that consciousness, at least in part, is always *imagining possibilities* independently of whether they are actually presented to us. It is true that our expectations might be surprised, and they frequently are; but the important point is that, in either case, we are contemplating (anticipating, imagining, wanting, fearing, interested in . . .) a *non-present* event, as an as-yet-unactualized possibility, and only as a consequence of this *awareness of unactualized possibilities* can any actual state of affairs enter our consciousness when we are aware of it. Computers can register events without representing unactualized possibilities, but consciousness of events always requires that we also motivatedly anticipate data by imagining, desiring, or otherwise envisioning, *that which is not yet present.* We are always comparing the actual with the possible when we are conscious of it. This is seen clearly in the Changizi studies discussed earlier, in which subjects always see a moving object as being slightly ahead of where it actually is, at the point when it passes a flashing light (Changizi et al. 2008).

While it is true that computers can compute logical possibilities independent of the actual, they do not require a motivated anticipation of the imaginary in order for the computations to occur. If someone could construct a computer with motivation, such a development would take us closer to conscious "robots." But we also have already emphasized that such robots would have to be *biological* ones in the sense we have defined—a type of self-organizing system. It is not enough to draw box diagrams and then program those into a traditional nuts-and-bolts computer.

A similar emphasis on anticipatory imagination of objects of perception is found in Husserl's thinking. In Husserl's terms, every experience must include a "meaning intention" if the corresponding "meaning-fulfilling intention" is to register in consciousness (Husserl 1913, see especially Investigation V; see also Husserl, 1931, 1962). The meaning intention is simply the *imaginative entertaining of a possibility,* which then becomes actualized when we perceive, remember, or further articulate the intentional meaning *in terms of which* the meaning-fulfilling event (for example, perceptual input) achieves its experienced meaning for consciousness. The meaning intention thus "anticipates" an imagined possible fulfillment. If consciousness includes an anticipatory imaginative element of this sort, then we can also say that it always contemplates the possible, not just the actual.

3. In addition to its affective, anticipatory, and imaginative capacities, phenomenal consciousness is also able to unify the elements into "thickness" that combines emotion toward and imagery of the *logically possible,* not just the actual. Consciousness is thus experienced as having a paradoxical relationship to the experienced objective world in at least the three main ways that were introduced in our previous chapter:

> A. As Locke discussed at length (and probably failed to explain adequately), many perceptual properties seem to be physical properties of their objects or of the spatial array of objects, but in reality are created by consciousness itself. For example, color does not exist until our nervous systems operate on the perceptual signals that the light frequencies produce only after they reach us. Thus properties like "red" involve the eerie and ephemeral feature of seeming to be "in here" in our consciousness, yet at the same time "out there," at the surfaces of the objects.
>
> B. Consciousness is similarly paradoxical in the way that it seems to be *temporally* extended. In Husserl's (1905/1966) terms, we seem to be experiencing a minimal amount of anticipation of the continuation of a momentary experience, however brief, in the form of a "protention," along with a minimal "retention" of a just-past dimension of the experience, all rolled into the one "present" experience. Memory and anticipation seem on the one hand to be included *in* the present experience (no matter how brief), and yet also seem to stretch out *from* it in both directions. Just as in the paradox of spatial experience, the paradox of temporal experience seems to locate aspects of the retained and protended content both "within" and "external to" the present experience.

C. We also discussed in the previous chapter the paradox of causality and motivation. We seem able to direct our movements, yet we also experience our bodies as physical objects, which we observe are subject to regular patterns of causal determination. So we experience ourselves as both free and caused at the same time. Objects seem to "pull" our attention, as if we could not help seeing them, yet we also feel that we are in control of our own attention, and even that we would not have seen the object if we had *not* directed our attention. We also experience our attention as directed by *motivational* concerns, yet the motivation itself is an aspect of our bodies, which again appear to us as both free and determined.

In the previous chapter, we encapsulated these mysterious phenomenological qualities that characterize conscious experience in a summary description. The description was justified on the grounds that each of the features in it is needed to take account of the mysterious aspects of experience—the specious present, the apparent causal power of consciousness, and the necessarily motivated aspect of this agency, which gives rise to anticipatory efference as a crucial component of conscious states. We therefore characterized consciousness as importantly including three features that give rise to difficult philosophical problems: 1. It entails an emotional interest that determines the anticipation of experience; 2. it involves representing the world in some way; and 3. it involves imagining *subjunctive* states of affairs, that is, states of affairs that are *not yet the case,* and that in some cases are *merely possible,* not actual.

Given these features of phenomenal experience, we can now ask ourselves: Is there some combination of physical events that are describable in third person terms, and which could occur *without* consciousness when they occur in isolation from each other, yet whose *combination* cannot be imagined by a phenomenally conscious being as occurring in the absence of all of the features of conscious experience that we have just described? If there is some such combination, then it will bridge the explanatory gap, at least to the extent that our phenomenological description of consciousness has been adequate. I.e., we will have specified a combination of *third person* events that cannot be imagined as not accompanied by the phenomenal experience of consciousness as we have described it in *first person* terms.

b. Conscious States and Their "Proto" Counterparts

The explanation we offer is one in which both the juxtaposition of certain physical components of consciousness and the components themselves can be explained by known physical principles. For the purposes of this explanation, we shall make certain ontological assumptions about the physical realm. These assumptions will be aspects of process philosophy (for example, Whitehead 1925) and of the theory of self-organization (for instance Kelso 1995; Kauffman 1993) that we think are minimal enough to be relatively *non-controversial*. The essence of this argument has three parts.

i. Proto-Desire

Many processes in nature show a robust and resilient tendency to maintain themselves across replacements of their components; these tendencies in nature we shall call *"proto-desires"* (and proto-aversions), because they are functionally similar to our conscious desires (and aversions) in all physical respects except for those that entail consciousness. Proto-desires, that is, impel an organism to alter its states and environment until a goal state is reached, and then to relax those particular efforts. All self-organizing living systems seek out replacement components on the basis of "proto-desire." Like desires in the psychological sense, which can be conscious, they tend to seek out conditions favorable to a certain homeostatic outcome for the systems that proto-desire them, and to react in such ways as to incorporate the proto-desired conditions when those are available. Especially important for our purposes are the following properties:

> Proto-desires have an active tendency to maintain not only inertias of motion, but also inertias of organization.
>
> Proto-desires reflect the tendency of a system to seek out substratum elements needed in order to maintain the system's definitive patterns.
>
> Proto-desires tend to convert available substrata to their ongoing patterns of organization.

We do not claim that a proto-desire is a *desire*. But when both the second and third elements of our explanation *co-occur with* proto-desire in the same unified act, then the result is desire in the conscious sense.

ii. Proto-Representation

Consciousness entails that a currently non-actualized possibility is "represented" by a system that has desires and aversions in relation to those possibilities, where the process that desires and averts is the *medium in which* the possibility is represented. Even in some non-conscious systems, there are *"proto-representations"*—situations where a copy, replica, or isomorphic encoding of an event occurs. But these proto-representations lack "intentional" reference, in the traditional philosophical sense of being "about" the states of affairs that they proto-represent. There is nothing about the system in which they occur to make them any more than a very similar or analogous version of the original, as when a xerox coy is made from an original.

Even proto-representation, however, can occur either in a trivial or in a non-trivial sense. For example, a digital computer can non-trivially proto-represent something without consciousness. The proto-representation occurs in a non-trivial sense because the proto-representational state does more than just be "isomorphic to" an input to which the state is causally related. The computer also *uses* the isomorphic state to achieve a "goal" that has been defined for the computer (but not *by* the computer, since digital computers are not living, self-organizing systems capable of defining their own goals). A digital computer, then, can have proto-representations in a non-trivial sense, but it does not have representations in the full sense. Representation in the full sense requires that the system doing the representing should at least be able to form proto-desires, so as to establish purposeful goals in a non-trivial sense of "purposeful."

Proto-representations are often usefully referred to *as if* they were representations in the full sense, but most such references fail to make the crucial distinction between the two senses. Philosophers and brain physiologists frequently use the term "representation" to refer to a state that in some physical way reflects, or maintains a trace of, its cause. As an account of intentional representation proper, this notion is grossly inadequate, as we saw earlier. Not only will any effect of any cause be a representation on this account (Thelen et al. 2001), but it offers no explanation of how a physical state can represent just one among many of its causes, one that is picked out from among all the rest. It fails to provide, moreover, any role for the *activity of meaning*, which is at the root of the traditional sense of intentionality. Symbols refer to something when they are meant to do so by their users. Physical causation and isomorphism alone cannot explain this relation.

It is necessary to develop a non-trivial concept not only of intentional representation, but also of *proto*-representation. If a cancerous cell replicates itself in my brain, the one cancerous cell does not "represent" the other one, or even "proto-represent" it in a non-trivial sense. The reason is that my system is not purposefully *using* this activity to represent the original cancerous cell with which the new ones are isomorphic. There must be a purposeful activity whose aims are served by some similarity between the original and the copy in order for the copy to bear an intentional relation to the original—to represent it in the full sense. Thus proto-desire is presupposed both by genuine representation in the full sense and by proto-representation in any non-trivial sense. If there were no proto-desire to establish the purposefulness of the activity for which the isomorphic activity is being used, isomorphism alone, even in the presence of a causal relation, would not constitute an intentional relation of representation. Nonetheless, we shall argue in this chapter that when proto-desire and proto-representation (in a non-trivial sense) *of an unactualized possibility* are executed by *the same elements* of a physical system, intentionality and consciousness can result.

Proto-representation in a non-trivial sense differs from representation (in the full sense) in that proto-representation uses the isomorphic state to achieve goals defined *for* the system, but not *by* the system. A similar point can be made with regard to knowledge and proto-knowledge in general. Proto-representation is a specific type of proto-knowledge. Many systems in nature include the property of proto-knowledge. Proto-knowledge occurs when a system gathers information about its environment, but does not entail the "what it's like" component exhibited by the knowledge that conscious beings have. Proto-knowledge occurs any time information is transmitted, as in a digital computer. But such proto-knowledge can occur in either a trivial or a more significant sense. Proto-knowledge occurs in a trivial sense when any causal force is transmitted: the causally affected system "knows" that it has been affected in a certain way, because the information that it has been so affected is "encoded" in the output of its behavior (Jackendoff 1996). This is *trivial* proto-knowledge, however, because any outcome can have a number of possible causal antecedents, so the system does not know which possible antecedent has caused the behavioral outcome. More important, to extend the notion of "knowledge" to include all causal processes would render the term "knowledge" virtually meaningless. We would lose the distinction between the mental and the non-mental.

A more significant form of proto-knowledge occurs when the system forms a proto-representation of the causal antecedents that have affected it in the relevant ways. Remember that a system *non-trivially* proto-represents a causal antecedent when it not only forms a pattern isomorphic to that which it proto-represents, but also at the same time associates that pattern with the outcomes that it produces for the system. Digital computers, for example, have proto-knowledge in this more significant sense, because not only are they *causally affected* by that which they "proto-know" about, but they also *proto-represent* that which causes these effects by contextualizing the information in terms of purposes that the system is trying to achieve.

In general, proto-knowledge occurs anytime there is non-conscious information processing. But non-conscious knowing, while it is not trivial, is still only *"proto"*-knowledge, because, as in the case of proto-desire which we just discussed, it does not intentionally refer to its object in a non-trivial sense. If an input causes a computer screen to display a picture, P, of the environmental object, EO, from which the input is derived, the fact that P is a representation of EO, rather than EO being a representation of P, or both P and EO being representations of some third thing, is known *by us,* the *users* of the computer, because we know enough about the structure of causation that we can establish that EO is the cause while P is the effect. Thus the difference between knowledge and proto-knowledge (in the non-trivial sense) is that in proto-knowledge a system (a) is causally affected by its object and (b) proto-represents the object that affects it in this way in a non-trivial sense, and also (c) is guided in its action by the information that the object in the picture it forms is functionally similar to the one exerting the causal effect. Knowledge in the full sense is similar to this account of proto-knowledge except for item (b); rather than merely *proto*-representing its object, knowledge in the full sense represents its objects in the full sense. (And this difference remains the same as defined above.) But even to *proto*-represent the object in a non-trivial sense requires more than just isomorphism plus causal relatedness.

As we have already suggested, to say that something is represented in the full sense requires more than that it proto-know that an input has caused a reaction. It requires that the subject of the representation also form conscious or preconscious sensorimotor imagery of *possible actions* that could be performed in relation to the environmental object or situation, and this also entails enacting the motivations for those actions. Moreover, it requires that the subject imagine actions toward a symbolizing element that are connected to those that could be performed toward actual environmental elements. For example, in thinking the word "blue," I not only imagine myself saying the word "blue" (Joseph 1983), but also imagine performing the attentive act that could prepare me to form the visual image of blue (Ellis 1995b). In other words, I motivatedly "look for" or "anticipate" blue.

It might seem superficially that non-biological computers could have true knowledge rather than mere proto-knowledge. A computer can be programmed not only to represent a causal input, but also to "know that" the representation resulted from the actual causal input and not merely from the logical possibility of the environmental conditions in question. By "knows that" (in quotation marks), we mean "acts in a way that is determined by the causal relation between the proto-representation and the object." But to call this full-fledged knowledge would be to assume that computers do actually represent rather than proto-representing their objects. As we saw earlier, digital computers only proto-represent, because the goals they use the isomorphic states to achieve are defined *for* the computer, but not *by* the computer. So it would seem more appropriate to characterize a digital computer as proto-knowing (in a non-trivial sense).

Of course, as always, terms can be defined however one likes, and there is no "correct" meaning of any word in the dictionary. Someone could define their terms differently to allow referring to the computer's proto-knowledge as knowledge in the full sense, but this difference in terminology would have no effect on the present argument. The situation we have defined as "proto-knowledge," regardless of what someone wants to call it, cannot result in consciousness unless combined with proto-desire and directed toward unactualized possibilities.

iii. Unactualized Possibilities

We hinted earlier that consciousness must not only desire and represent, but must also desire and represent *unactualized possibilities*. This additional essential ingredient of "unactualized possibility" must be stressed. It is not enough merely to add proto-desire to proto-representation in order for consciousness to result; what the desire and representation are about must include not only physical environmental objects, but also the unactualized logical possibilities that can be anticipated, sought out, or imagined, against which *existing* states can contrast and in terms of which they can be used and understood (Ellis 1995b).

In a sense, consciousness is nature's way of allowing unactualized logical possibilities to have causal power in the real world. However, this causal power must be understood in a physical way if we are to avoid an untenable Cartesian dualism. Our thesis, then, is that consciousness can occur only when the elements of proto-representation and proto-desire (or proto-aversion) *of unactualized possibilities* are co-present in the same pattern of activity. At that point, they become both a representation and a desire (or aversion) in the full senses of those terms.

Since the elements of proto-desire and proto-representation are present throughout nature, with or without consciousness, and since the essence of consciousness is that it executes a unified activity that both represents and desires a currently unactualized possibility, we can say that the existence of consciousness necessarily follows from the unified execution within the same system of proto-desire and proto-representation of an unactualized possibility.

Those who have a bent for phenomenological reflection can feel this effect by means of a thought experiment. Suppose you find yourself blankly staring at a familiar object, such as your kitchen stove. Try imagining for a second that the stove is not there: suddenly your consciousness of the stove becomes more vivid and intense. Such examples illustrate that consciousness is facilitated when we imagine the mere possibility or impossibility of something, and perceptual consciousness in particular requires comparing what is with what we (interestedly) *imagine* as a possibility. When we fail to do this, light may impinge on the retina, and signals may be sent to the occipital lobes, but we do not consciously "pay attention" to what is there. Again, we can see this effect in the Mack and Rock inattentional blindness studies: the subjects are interested in looking for one type of object, and thus do not consciously *see* what they are not looking for. To look for something is to anticipate it, and this means imaging it (as merely possible) before we see it.

The notion of a desire that represents an unactualized possibility can be described in purely objective terms, and the three elements whose combination in the way just mentioned realizes consciousness—proto-desire, proto-representation and unactualized possibility—are *third-person* phenomena. If the explanation captures *both* the functional purpose of consciousness as described above, *and* the phenomenological, "what-it's-like" character of the third-person phenomena involved, *for the subject* of the phenomena, then the explanatory gap will have been bridged. In other words, we will have physically explained components that, when combined, inevitably must equal consciousness. This claim is asserted, however, not as an analytic one, but as an inductive one that allows all relevant evidence and argument to cohere in a consistent theory.

Given these definitions, we can now clarify what is needed for an explanation of consciousness that bridges the explanatory gap. Essentially, we can begin with certain elements—proto-desire and proto-knowledge, which exist in many places throughout nature and can be given purely objective descriptions—and then show that when these elements come together in a certain way, all the elements in the definition of consciousness are satisfied.

2. Fitting Consciousness into the Ontological Picture

Consciousness must involve more than mere computation, in the sense of information processing, knowledge, or proto-knowledge. We can approach the explanation of consciousness by asking what is needed for consciousness above mere computation, while at the same time computation seems to be an element in consciousness, since it involves a kind of proto-knowledge.

a. Kinds of Computation

First let's be clear as to what is meant by *"computation."* Computation can occur in an important or a trivial sense. In the *trivial* sense, computation is based on the correspondingly trivial type of proto-knowledge. In this sense, any transfer of causal effect from one physical event to another involves "computation" or a processing of information. For example, when we run hot water onto a jar lid, the jar-lid "computes" the temperature of warm water we run onto it and "responds" to this "input" by expanding to the appropriate extent. In the same trivial sense, a thermostat "computes" the desired temperature and "responds" by throwing a switch for the necessary amount of time. To equate "computation" in this trivial sense with thinking *per se* would constitute what we might call "jar-lid computationalism"—a view that would ultimately equate any cause-and-effect mechanism in nature (such as the expansion of a jar-lid in response to a temperature increase or the thermostat's throwing of the switch) with a "computation," and thus would fail to distinguish genuinely "mental" events like thinking from completely non-mental ones like the response of the jar-lid to the temperature increase (Ellis 1995b).

But we must also work toward a more significantly *mental* sense in which the brain "computes" (which is more reasonably equated with "thinking"); in some cases this mental computation is indeed unconscious, but these unconscious computations are often habituated or sedimented from past conscious processes (as the Donoghue monkeys clearly illustrate at the point when they have quit consciously imagining moving the joy stick, yet are still implicitly doing so). Other cases of mental computation are straightforwardly conscious, as when we purposely use a logical principle to help us make an inference—although this purposeful use of logical principles may often be *minimally* conscious (like the deciphering of written music) because it too can be more or less habituated and sedimented. Of course, very simple computer systems "compute" only in the same sense in which jar-lids and thermostats "compute"; but more elaborately programmed ones, like the human brain, compute in a more important sense, and it is this more important sense that is of concern for our purposes here.

The more *important* kind of computation occurs when not only does the computing system exhibit behavioral outputs resulting from transformation of the input (as occurs in the trivial example of the jar-lid), but the system accomplishes the transformations by using not only its knowledge or proto-knowledge of the inputs, but also by applying a knowledge or proto-knowledge of unrealized logical possibilities to a transformed representation of the inputs. For example, a digital computer, after transforming the input that we key in into an isomorphic proto-representation vis-à-vis one of the computer's "languages," then operates on that information by making use of its proto-knowledge of a system of *logical possibilities* which are "understood" by the system independently of the specific input received on that occasion—for example, by means of a proto-knowledge of certain logical principles such as *modus tollens* or *modus ponens*, or mathematical principles such as the theorems of algebra or calculus.

Halfway between the important and the trivial sense, there is an *intermediate* case. A computing system may make use of logical or mathematical principles on a "rote memorization" basis rather than with a knowledge of the epistemic derivation of them (as unfortunately many math students are encouraged to do). Although the theorems are not known to be true in this case, the system does still use them *as if* they were known to be true. To the extent that the epistemic bases of logic and math are still in doubt, this is what we humans do as well; but we can *feel confident* in using the theorems as if they were known to be true, because we also know that they and the assumptions on which they are based have proven somewhat reliable. So there can be various degrees to which "computation" occurs in the significant rather than the trivial sense, but in all of them, there are fundamental elements and relations between them that are not found in computation in the most trivial cases.

To the extent that computation occurs in a non-trivial sense, the system is doing more than simply reacting to inputs, and what it knows about the input is known *in relation to more than just the input*. The input is known in relation to knowledge or proto-knowledge of logical possibilities. To know (or proto-know) something about a logical possibility is to know more than is exhausted by any *current input*. It involves knowing about *uninstantiated* possibilities as well as those that are instantiated. And it involves comparing any current input with a previously known system of possibilities which the specific input may instantiate, fail to instantiate, or approximately instantiate.

In some computational systems, the uninstantiated possibilities themselves are not represented, or are not represented very vividly. In others, the uninstantiated possibilities are entertained as phenomena in their own right, independently of the instantiated possibilities to which they are being compared. As a hint to where these distinctions are leading, we shall soon see that the element of *proto-desire* is the crucial determinant of whether the entertaining of an uninstantiated possibility is fully representational, or only proto-representational.

b. Proto-Desire and the Computation of Unactualized Possibilities

There are some instances in nature where an unactualized possibility is computed (in a non-trivial sense of "compute") as an essential part of the sequence of events that leads to the actualization of that possibility or prevention of its actualization (or to the actualization of some possibility related to the one in question—for example, an approximate actualization of it, or the closest feasible approximation). Consciousness is one such instance. We shall now argue that a computation is a *conscious* one if the relevant unactualized possibility is represented through the medium of the *self-organizational need* (a type of *proto-desire*) which *anticipates* the unrealized possibility as desirable or undesirable, or in some way emotionally meaningful or having an emotional relevance. In other words, the representation and the self-organizational need are not two *separate processes,* but rather the self-organizational need *itself* enacts a pattern that is intentionally isomorphic to the represented state of affairs.

In order to accomplish such a unified activity, the organism also must be able to include quasi-perceptual imaginative events (representations or proto-representations of unactualized possibilities) and anticipatory emotional ones (desires or proto-desires) into *one process*, and this requires re-entry of perceptual processing into a feedback loop with the emotion-laden anticipation of events, in such a way that the "just-past" phase of the flow of proto-representational activity is superimposed over the present anticipatory phase of this same activity, resulting in the two phases' being fully represented as if they were one. Thus a temporal thickness is necessary to consciousness (Ellis and Newton 1998; Newton 2000, 2001).

Non-actualized logical possibilities acquire the ability to *affect the actual world* when the computation that X is possible leads to a different outcome from any that otherwise would have occurred. For example, the realization on the part of Magellan that it might be possible to circumnavigate the globe led him to make the attempt, with subsequent effects on the course of history. This causal impact of unactualized possibilities is reminiscent of the Popper and Eccles (1977) 'World III objects' such as the logical processes in the minds of scientists that causally affect experimental and technological events. But in light of our causal analysis of the role of consciousness, we must reject the Popper-Eccles dualistic conclusions. The important point for our purposes is that only through *computation* of this sort (in the non-trivial sense of "computation") does the fact that something is *possible* have a direct effect on the *actual* course of affairs (except in the trivial sense that things cannot be actual unless they are also possible).

Although computations involving unactualized possibilities (which thus affect actual ones) originally occurred only in self-organizing systems (living creatures), they can also occur in non-self-organizing ones, such as digital computers. A computer's "realization" that a certain chess strategy is possible may lead it to actually try the move, thus causing an effect in the realm of the actual. (For example, the computer may defeat a grand master, thus changing the future flow of Artificial Intelligence grant monies.)

We may therefore think of computation in the important sense as nature's way of allowing a computational consideration of what is possible to have a causal effect on what is actual. Why would nature "proto-want" to do this? Because, as we have seen, proto-desires exist in many places throughout nature, and seek ways to satisfy themselves. This is why the first computational systems (in the important sense of "computation") were also biological ones driven by proto-desire. These proto-desires in turn were merely tendencies for self-organizational processes to seek out the material components needed to sustain their inertias of motion and, at a higher level, to sustain their patterns of activity.

c. Proto-Desire Does Not Necessarily Proto-Represent a Non-Actualized Possibility

Although very primitive biological systems may "compute" in a trivial sense, they do not compute in the important sense. That is, they do not even non-trivially proto-represent the unactualized states of affairs that they proto-desire (let alone represent them in the full sense involving intentional referral).

Then as biological systems become less primitive, they do proto-represent *actual* states of affairs in their environments, but they do not proto-represent the *unactualized possibilities* that they desire to any significant extent. Instead, they simply proto-desire an outcome, and wait (perhaps moving around in the environment while they wait and automatically executing certain foraging patterns hardwired or learned through a blind natural selection process) until the right *actualized* possibility occurs. The actualized possibility may at this point be non-trivially proto-represented in a perceptual system, but computation in the important sense is still not occurring because the organism did not consider the actualized possibility in relation to a system of knowledge or proto-knowledge of *unactualized possibilities*. Nor did it proto-represent the anticipated but as-yet unactualized possibility in terms of perceptual or sensorimotor imagery of the not-yet-actualized possibility.

In these cases, we cannot say that the conditions needed for the existence of consciousness have been met. In principle, nothing has happened to distinguish such a system's mode of information processing from the information processing of completely inorganic self-organizing systems such as ecosystems or forming crystal structures. There is a proto-desire (that is, a mere tendency to maintain a certain pattern across replacements of substratum elements) and a naturally-selected method of registering the presence of the proto-desired outcome, *when it does present itself,* through a proto-representational (but not fully representational) system. At this low level of organizational structure (amoebas and various kinds of worms and insects, for example), the organism is not aware of the relation of intentionality between the image created in its perceptual system and the corresponding image in the environment, because it has no understanding of what the object is, nor any feeling toward the object qua intentional object. To be sure, as Damasio (2003) suggests, it has affective responses—further proto-desires (or aversions) or satiation of proto-desires (or aversions)—as *effects* produced *by* the object. But to respond in this way with satiety or further proto-desires or aversions is not to feel intentionally toward the object. If I feel depressed because of chemical imbalances in my brain, but have no idea that the feelings occur with reference to the chemical imbalances, then it is obvious that the feelings do not take the chemical imbalances as their *intentional object*. Similarly, if there is no intentional relation between the feeling and its environmental causes, then the feeling is not a consciousness of that intentional object, even if the object is proto-represented in a nervous system devoid of conscious status.

d. Mere Co-existence of Proto-Desire and Proto-Representation Does Not Equal Consciousness

We can easily imagine a mechanical device implanted into a very primitive organism, such that the mechanical device non-consciously proto-represents environmental objects in the device's "nervous system," and helps the organism direct its movements toward the object in question, with no more consciousness occurring in the organism than if the device had not been implanted. Nor is there consciousness in the mechanical device in this case, because it is not the device that proto-desires the object, but rather the organism. So in this case, the proto-representation of the device plus the proto-desire of the organism clearly do not add up to consciousness of the object.

In what case, then, would it be clear that consciousness is present?

3. Consciousness: Representation-through-Desire of Unactualized Possibilities in One Unified Self-Organizing System

We defined phenomenal consciousness above in terms of its functions—as a process in which we have some (proto-) desire (or aversion) toward an as yet unactualized state of affairs, and also non-trivially represent unactualized possibilities relevant to the (proto-) desire. In this case, we argued that the proto-desire becomes simply *a desire* in the familiar sense that conscious beings have. We can drop the "proto" prefix. To non-trivially represent in relation to unactualized desires (or aversions) is what it is like to be conscious.

If this definition of consciousness is applied, we can see that consciousness can result from a computational process when a system purposely intends to introduce certain possibilities into the realm of the actual. In primitive self-organizing systems such as amoebas and worms (which we admit do make primitive computations), the system does not *intend* to introduce a non-actual possibility into the world, but merely *tends* to do so. In other words, the system has no advance knowledge or intentional anticipation of the desired possible state of affairs. The non-actual possibility is not represented by the system as a possibility that it desires (or averts). In a primitive organism, the actual is represented, but the possible is not; and while the possible may be proto-desired (or averted) in such organisms, it is not even proto-represented in any significant sense. Only when the same non-actual possibility is both desired (or averted) and represented-as-desired (or averted) is there consciousness.

In order to desire and represent the non-actual possibility, an organism must compare the actual with the envisioned possibility, and be aware of the difference. Thus it must cognitively represent an actuality simultaneously with the representation of a non-actual possibility, and bring the two into juxtaposition. It is this juxtaposition that produces the ineffable experience of phenomenal consciousness.

a. The Phenomenal Feel of Consciousness

We have presented a functional analysis of consciousness, in terms of brain mechanisms that coordinate and combine component states—proto-desire, proto-representation, and proto-knowledge of unactualized possibilities—into a higher-order unified organismic state that is capable of meeting complex and long-range goals. But we have not yet explained why that state should feel the way it does, or, indeed, feel any way at all. We have argued that phenomenal conscious experience plays a crucial role in the attainment of goals, by presenting the organism with anticipations of the experiential outcomes of the various possibilities. But we have not examined the mechanism by which such an experiential state could come into being with its familiar but ineffable qualities. Only an account that explains such a mechanism can bridge the explanatory gap.

We want to argue that phenomenal experience is characterized by a kind of illusion—the illusion of a "temporally thick specious present"—produced by simultaneous representational activities involving distinct temporal moments. What we experience in phenomenal consciousness is time itself, as it affects our self-organizing activity. The experience is unique, in that it occurs only in consciousness, and consciousness is the only state in which we have phenomenal awareness. But while it is unique, it is not incomparable; within conscious experience, an analogous phenomenon is the visual experience of spatial depth perception.

Binocular vision is necessary for seeing our spatial environment in a single, unified visual experience. Not only the breadth and width of a visual scene is portrayed as existing at a single time, but so is depth, stretching out before the perceiver. Our physical existence in three-dimensional space is functionally relevant to us only with respect to bodily movement: we can extend our limbs, and propel our bodies, indefinitely in three dimensions. The ability to do this, however, is represented not only in bodily action imagery, but also in visual experience. Depth perception presents us with almost infinite possibilities for movement, even when we are relatively inactive: the information necessary for planning actions is given in vision, even though vision itself does not move about in the world. The experience of depth perception is not normally experienced as mysterious, but a little thought will remind us of how remarkable is our ability to project possible movements into our environment by means of a sensory modality that does not itself, literally, project into the environment. What is remarkable is not that we receive information that allows us to calculate possible movements, but rather that the information we receive visually allows us to experience, in a visual modality, what various movements would be like. Vision can do this because the overlapping of two slightly offset visual fields creates an emergent property in our experience. It does not create an ontological novelty, but rather an experiential novelty: we experience or "see" possible movement without actually moving. (The necessary eye movements, of which we are not conscious, are a different matter; here we are referring to gross and deliberate bodily motions.)

The mystery of depth perception is highlighted by the fact that, when we combine two slightly different perspectives on a cylinder to give it depth, this means that we can see slightly *more* than fifty percent of the circumference of the cylinder *all at once*; so what we represent to ourselves is one side of the cylinder—fifty percent of it—which nonetheless shows *more* than fifty percent of it (because we have combined two different perspectives on it). So what we see the cylinder as looking like is actually a geometrical impossibility—a cylinder with more than fifty percent of its circumference showing from one single perspective. Yet all the while, we feel that what we experience ourselves as seeing is a geometrically possible state of affairs.

Another way to notice the paradoxical nature of depth perception is to try the following simple experiment: close one eye while holding up two cylindrical objects such as dry-erase markers, of equal size but different colors, in such a way that one marker completely blocks the other one from view. Now open both eyes, and you notice that the edges of the "hidden" marker *cannot be completely blocked* by the one in front of it, no matter how much you try. Your depth perception is allowing you to see "around" the edges of the front marker, making the marker in back appear *larger than the one in front,* even though they are the same size. If the red marker is in front of the blue one, the blue one appears larger; but if the blue one is in front of the red one, then it is the red one that appears larger. As long as we keep both eyes open, the front marker will always appear *smaller* than the one in back of it, even though it is *closer* to us.

In spite of the paradoxical nature of what depth perception presents to us, the ability to see depth does not normally strike us as an ineffable mystery, but rather as the natural outcome of mechanisms of sight. Why should the same not be true of the experience of temporal extension?

Phenomenal consciousness, in which we experience past, present, and future in a single "specious present," need be no more mysterious than visual depth perception. Arguably the most striking aspect of phenomenal consciousness is the fact that we can linger over it and savor the experience. If phenomenal consciousness lasted only during an instantaneous "now," forever vanishing and being replaced by a completely new "now," consciousness would not be the rich experience it is, and consequently would not be so mysterious. We would not have time to know that we were conscious. It might be that such a fragmented form of experience occurs in some other species. What is striking in us is that we can dwell on our present conscious experience; it is this ability that allows us to say that consciousness is "like" something for us. We cannot articulate what it is like, except in terms of the sensory qualities of the objects that we consciously experience—properties of external objects and of our own bodies. But there is nothing more to articulate than the very fact that those properties have enough endurance and stability for us that we can know about them, anticipate them, and relate them to prior anticipations that are still vivid for us, while we are sensing them: this is the natural result of the combination of past, present and future in a single representation of the "present." And remember, the reason we can do this is because of the overlapping of anticipation with retention of the just-past anticipation.

The experience of seeing spatial distance cannot be articulated except in terms of the *possible motions* that this depth makes possible for us. The fact that it is vision that presents us with those possibilities is a striking and important fact, but it is not an ontologically emergent kind of entity that can be verbally characterized independently of its components. This fact does not bother people, but our inability to nail down consciousness with a precise verbal definition does bother people. Not only should the ineffability of consciousness not bother us any more than the ineffability of depth perception, we argue, but rather this ineffability is exactly what one *should expect,* given the self-organizing processes that go into presenting us with both our desires and the means for bringing them to fruition. If a type of organismic state is unique in its effect on the organism, then it stands to reason that it cannot be characterized in exactly the same terms that also refer to other types of organismic states. But that does not mean that it cannot be fully comprehended, from an objective, scientific standpoint.

Notice that the same solution also applies to the paradox of freedom and determinism. If we *are* self-organizing systems that represent possibilities for our future action, then it makes sense that we would feel ourselves as having a choice. In fact, we do make choices, and in self-organizing systems these choices may be free from currently external determination, although this does not entail that they are free from the *past* causal determinations that may have led the self-organizing system to have the particular kind of structure it now has, which in turn frees it *from* many *current* determining influences, so that it can act somewhat freely of them. Moreover, if consciousness *is* an aspect of a self-organizing system, this would also imply that consciousness can have every bit of the same *causal powers* as the physical system of which it is an ontological feature. To say that consciousness can have no causal powers is actually an incoherent claim, unless one wishes to embrace dualism, because if consciousness had no causal powers, then it would have to be separate from any physical system, since all physical systems *do* have causal powers.

b. Conclusion

Our proposal is that phenomenal experience, the subject of the "hard problem," can occur as a result of the juxtaposition or superposition of distinct temporal moments of a single experienced event. This thesis by itself does not require a self-organizational view of consciousness. If we are right in our theory of the phenomenal result of this mechanism, then in principle such an explanation could be part of a variety of different accounts of brain activity, not just self-organizing ones. But in any sort of theory that is *not* enactive and self-organizational, the explanation would be *ad hoc*; it would not follow naturally from the goal-seeking activity of a self-organizing creature. It is because a conscious being must anticipate future experiences, and compare them to past and present ones for purposes of evaluation, that the superposition must occur. When this happens, then the world around us "lights up" in the familiar way of conscious experience. The explanation of this "lighting up" is not complicated or mysterious. It is the inevitable consequence of the prolonging of motivated anticipation, imaginative activity, and sensory stimulation for a subject, so that the qualitative properties of the objects stimulating the sensory systems can interact with the imagining of unactualized sensory activity and with the sensorimotor imagining of desired (or averted) actions—and thus inform the subject's conceptual activities. In this way, they acquire a substantive presence that is familiar to us as conscious experience.

The inevitable objection to such a proposal raises questions about computers. If a computer were designed so that "sensory" stimuli affected it in the same way that has been described here—complete with motivated anticipation of as-yet-unactualized possibilities—then would we have to grant the computer consciousness? We see no reason why not, if all the complex functions required by self-organizing conscious entities were present. It would be easy enough to say "I can imagine a machine doing all the things described, without being conscious." But what is really being imagined here? If someone were to take the trouble to describe every function performed by a living conscious being, and propose a machine counterpart for it, then a simple claim that the machine still would not be conscious would not carry much weight. Consciousness might "feel different" to the computer from the way it feels to a flesh and blood creature, but that fact alone is not sufficient to deny it consciousness. And to claim that such a machine would feel nothing at all, in spite of all its animal-like functions, would require more argument than has yet been offered in any literature that we have seen. At the degrees of complexity we are now discussing, intuitions about the imaginability of "creatures who are just like us physically but are not conscious"—zombies—provide feeble evidence indeed.

At the same time, a computer meeting all the requirements of a self-organizationally structured being with proto-desire and non-trivial proto-representation of unactualized possibilities would be very different from the nuts-and-bolts computers with which we are now familiar. In effect, they would be man-made *biological* organisms. And this point is merely a corollary of our overall argument, that "computing" is not the essence of consciousness, but rather a component of it. Consciousness occurs when a self-organizing system represents (imagines) itself as acting toward unactualized possibilities that play a role in terms of organismic desires or aversions.

8

Introspection and Private Access

PART I
The Mysteries of Introspection and Reflection

Perhaps the worst misunderstandings engendered by the passive-perceiving model of consciousness, as opposed to the action model, have to do with introspective private access to one's own conscious states. The subject of experience on this model would somehow direct an "inner gaze" toward some internal or behind the scenes aspect of the information that is being processed. This exacerbates the problem of the homunculus that is implied by the passive-perceiving model, in two crucial ways.

First, the classic model of introspection reduces the experience of a subjective state to a mere "knowing that" we are in that state, where the "knowing that" process is either an unexplained appendage to the processing of the information, or else presupposes subjectivity in the homunculus who receives the knowledge. In the latter case, there must of course be a second homunculus who "knows that" the first homunculus feels or senses such and such a subjective quality, and so forth, creating an infinite regress. For example, it is generally assumed that pain can exist in the organism with or without our actually "feeling" it, as when we pull our hand away from a hot stove before feeling the pain. What, then, makes pain conscious? The traditional passive-receiving model of consciousness posits that the *feeling of* the pain is a mere matter of "knowing that" the body is in that state (Damasio 1999)—as if feeling emotional pain, for example, were the same thing as intellectually affirming the proposition "I am in emotional pain." This is, in fact, the way an alexithymic—a person unable to consciously feel his or her own emotions—would respond to the question "Are you in emotional pain?" The alexithymic, while unable to consciously *feel* the emotion, may still be aware *that* the emotion exists, because of empirical evidence and logical reasoning. An alexithymic patient reported by Sundararajan (2000) was well aware that he must have had angry emotions when he killed his father, but he could not directly feel the anger. The notion that feeling an emotion (or any other "introspected" quality) is reducible simply to registering the fact that one feels it would reduce us all to alexithymics.

A second difficulty with the passive-perceiving approach to introspection is that it tends to equate consciousness of feelings with proprioception or interoception of internal states in the viscera of the body, and then posits that this process occurs by means of some physiological homunculus in the brain "registering" the signals being delivered by afferent nerve pathways from the body parts. But these afferent signals, as we have already shown, can arrive to the brain *without* consciousness of them, just as afferent perceptual data can make it as far as the perceptual processing layers of the occipital lobe without any visual *awareness*. In short, the passive-perceiving model, which was ill equipped to explain how visual data become conscious, is even less equipped to understand how introspection moves data from a non-conscious to a conscious status.

For example, Locke believed that we can attend to either "outer" or "inner" experience and that, when doing the latter, we "perceive" mental operations such as comparing, representing, and so forth. But why should we believe that there are specific brain mechanisms for processing "perceptual" experiences *of* other brain mechanisms? There certainly must be more parsimonious ways to explain what was traditionally called "introspection" without taking that risky step toward infinite regress, especially without evidence of any corresponding brain structures.

In the action model, introspection is not simply a looking at or receiving of internal data. When we introspect an emotional feeling, for example, we do not do so by looking at proprioceptive or interoceptive data received through afferent pathways. We do it by executing the emotion while paying attention to the *act* of executing it. That is, we pay attention to what the body does to make the emotion happen, and to the way the body is gearing up to do the corresponding action. Similarly, when we "introspectively" focus on the way the left hand feels to the right when the right hand touches the left, what we do is to ask ourselves what affordances the left hand presents for the right, while performing or imagining performing certain movements with the right hand (the imagined movements consisting of inhibited efferent action commands).

We move the right hand relative to the left or push it against the left (or merely imagine doing so) and simultaneously notice that the left hand *gets in the way of those movements* in certain respects, while allowing other parts of the movements to go forward. Knowledge of the fact that the left hand gets in the way is dependent on afferent nervous impulses received from the right hand, but the *consciousness* of what the left hand feels like to the right hand also involves *efferent* action commands directing subtle movements of the right hand. For this reason, when we rest a hand on our knee for a long period of time, we lose our consciousness of what the knee feels like to the hand; but when we move our own hand only slightly, we regain consciousness of what the knee feels like to the hand.

An analogous point can be made with respect to the differences between "reflective" and "prereflective" experience. When we "reflect" on the right hand's experience of the left, what we are doing is to pay more attention to what we are doing to *execute* the actions on the right hand's part that *produce* the consciousness of what the left hand feels like to the right. By contrast, in the "prereflective" experience of what the left hand feels like, we pay most of our attention to the fact that the left hand presents certain obstacles to the right hand's subtle actual movements (or would present obstacles to its covertly imagined movements), without very explicitly imagining what those movements would be like. Thus our attention is focused on the left hand as object rather than the right hand as subject. In general, in reflective experience, we pay more attention to what *we* are doing to produce the experience, whereas in prereflective experience we pay attention primarily to the *object of* the experience.

In both reflective and prereflective experience of an object, truncated action commands are being delivered from the cerebellar-thalamic circuits to the premotor cortex and supplementary motor area, as regulated by the anterior cingulate, although the command is then mostly inhibited—as we have already seen occurs in any conscious perception of objects. In the case of the right hand perceiving the left, instead of overtly moving the right hand, we may mostly only *imagine* moving it, while also imagining the way those movements would be afforded or blocked by the left hand, given the afferent information we have about the left hand's orientation, shapes and contours. But in the case of the *reflective* experience of this perception, we pay more attention to the efferent signals being sent toward the right hand, even while we are inhibiting most of them. This paying attention involves enhancement of anterior cingulate activity as it regulates the efferent signals being sent from the cerebellar-thalamic circuits to the premotor cortex and supplementary motor area (Hatsopoulos et al. 2001). So an action model of reflection would suggest that, in the reflective experience, the anterior cingulate allows the efferent signals to be more amplified prior to their inhibition than they would be in a prereflective experience.

Consider an analogy: While playing the piano, we can hit a note either very casually, in a habituated way, without paying much attention to what the finger is doing, or we can hit it very "deliberately," being very careful to move the finger in just the right way, brushing it against the key to make just the tone quality we want, and so forth. The former case is analogous to a "prereflective" awareness, in the respects just discussed, because we have the afferent data but without much "reflective" awareness; the more deliberate case is more like "reflective" awareness, in that we pay attention to what we are doing to make the finger move in just the right way. In both cases, we are moving the finger in about the same way, but in the latter case we are delivering the efferent commands in a very pronounced, exaggerated way. It would thus be reasonable to suppose that, neurophysiologically, the anterior cingulate is allowing the efferent commands to be more amplified before they reach the motor cortex from the cerebellar-thalamic loops, even though the efferent signal from the motor cortex down to the finger is about the same as it would be in the casual, habituated, "inattentive" and "unreflective" hitting of the note. And there is some empirical evidence to support this hypothesis (Schmahmann et al. 2001).

As a consequence of this reasoning, the action-centered model would also be consistent with the prediction that, in the case of the "very deliberate" hitting of the note, the efferent signal is amplified all the way from the cerebellar-thalamic circuit to the motor cortex. The same thing happens when we "reflect" on an already ongoing experience, except that in this case it is mostly the efferent signal from the cerebellar-thalamic circuit to the premotor and supplementary motor area that gets amplified. Here too, studies by Haines et al. (1997), Hatsopoulos et al. (2001), and Sudnow (1999) support this viewpoint. Haines et al. establish the existence of the cerebellar-thalamic loops, triggered by any perceptual signal, that would be required by our hypothesis, and Hatsopoulos et al., as in the Donoghue studies mentioned earlier, show the involvement of the motor cortex in a case where monkeys' brains are wired to a joystick so that the joystick can be moved simply by means of the monkey's *thinking* about moving it—supporting the idea that similar brain processes are involved in imaging movement and actually doing the movement. And Sudnow actually discusses the difference between habituated and deliberate hitting of the note on the piano and describes the phenomenology in a way similar to our account.

In the "prereflective" or "unreflective" experience of the right hand touching the left, the right hand delivers *afferent* signals to the brain just as intensely as it does in a "reflective" experience. The reflection on the right hand's experience does not make us somehow more aware of the shapes, contours, and textures *of the left hand that we are touching*. What we are more aware of in the "reflective" experience is the feeling *"in"* the right hand as it feels the left. On the action-centered view, this involves directing attention to what we are *doing* that *makes* the right hand's consciousness of the left hand occur.

Instead of talking about introspection as if it were analogous to external "inspection," the action model suggests that we look for subtle sensorimotor/proprioceptive experiences that accompany activities like representing, attending, and so on, and that may be unnoticed but taken for granted as essential aspects of the experiences of those activities together with their sensory objects. For example, when we see a visible object, we can be aware not only of the visible features of the object, but also of the sensorimotor/proprioceptive sensations of focusing the eyes and orienting the body toward the object. These ordinary perceptual experiences may be all that is necessary to ground the concept of reflecting on seeing.

One aspect of experience that has traditionally seemed to require a special form of access like introspection is the experience of agency that accompanies all voluntary intentional activity, even subtle perceptual activity such as ocular control. But even this experience involves proprioceptive and sensorimotor imagery. It appears to be produced by corollary discharge, or efference copy—information about motor commands to the muscles that is sent to the parietal lobe and to the cerebellum from the motor and premotor cortex, for purposes of comparison with the expected movement. This information about motor commands normally is attended to by the subject only when the expected feedback does not match the commands, or is lacking altogether, as when the relevant limb is paralyzed. In ocular motor control, this experience is virtually continuous, since the eyes must be constantly adjusted in response to shifts in the visual field (Houk et al. 1996).

The subjective feeling of agency is strikingly absent when motor activity is initiated artificially in experimental conditions; a subject will then report that the limb moved but that he "had nothing to do with it!" (Ramachandran and Blakeslee 1998). There is evidence that information from efference copy is held in working memory, and hence would be accessible to consciousness like any other perceptual experience (Houk et al. 1996).

In short, in "reflection," we focus on our own (overt or covert) actions rather than on an object's affordances *for* those actions. The same explanation accounts for the difference between "introspection" and exterospective perspectives on "the same" experiential content.

1. Privileged Access

The action theory of reflective experience can help toward an understanding of the respects in which a subject has "privileged access" to conscious states. If reflective experience focuses on the "what it's like" aspect of consciousness, which is tantamount to reflectivity on the subjective actions that produce consciousness of an object, rather than only on the object itself, then it makes sense that the subject would have a kind of privileged access to the "what it's like" aspect of her own experience, because only the subject can be in a position to *execute* her own actions. Reflection of the kind the action theory makes comprehensible is thus a kind of privileged access to a type of data that cannot be accessed as such from any other perspective.

The Cartesian notion that a conscious subject has "privileged access" to inner mental states—that the subject is an authority on the nature of these states because they are her own—has been out of favor for some time in Western philosophy of mind. In part because phenomenology claims something like privileged access, it too was considered by some computationalist philosophers to be irrelevant to the "real business" of constructing a scientifically respectable theory of consciousness and cognition. While it is true that we, qua conscious subjects, lack full experiential understanding of all the causal mechanisms and the seams and faultlines of our conscious states, we do have a certain privileged access. The basis for this argument was supplied by Merleau-Ponty as early as *The Structure of Behavior* (1942), and is also made very clear in *Phenomenology of Perception* (1941). His work establishes two vital facts: that we necessarily understand the basic structure of our consciousness, and that this structure is entailed and elucidated by the physical structures of the brain and body, not by mysterious powers of a Cartesian cogito. Merleau-Ponty brings together the phenomenological and the scientific in a way only now beginning to be appreciated by cognitive scientists. Most people forget that the *Phenomenology of Perception* lists more works on neuropsychology than on philosophy in its reference list.

a. How Privileged Access Fell from Grace

Descartes believed that the mind is better known than the body since the body is known only by changeable external appearances, whereas the mind is known from within by the subject who *is* the mind. In this belief, Descartes was continuing the Platonic tradition that the mind (with its "contents") is at least potentially transparent to itself. No matter what else I must doubt, I cannot doubt my own thoughts.

But Hume showed our vulnerability to false beliefs about our conscious experience: we believe that we experience a unified self, but it is at least plausible that we experience only a "bundle of impressions." William James (1890/1950) famously argued that when we reflect on our subjective experience, we make it into the *object* of the reflective experience. Thus experience never has immediate access to itself in reflection, and the object on which we reflect (our own experience) is almost as far removed from us as any other object of experience, and vulnerable to the same distortions and uncertainties. Sartre also rejected any direct experience of a real self for similar reasons. The view that our self-knowledge may be in large part illusion was popularized in modern times by Freud's claims about the unconscious. Other support was provided by philosophical behaviorists like Ryle (1949), who exposed myths about the "ghost in the machine" that deceive us because of our adherence to a philosophical dogma.

More recently, psychologists like Nisbett and Ross (1980) have studied the phenomenon of "confabulation," in which a subject will invent thoughts to explain behavior of whose real cause she is ignorant, and will believe her own inventions. And much contemporary empirical work has uncovered isolable mechanisms within mental processes such as visual perception (for example blindsight, Weiskrantz 1988) that are subjectively experienced as unitary and unanalyzable. Meanwhile, Millikan (1984), Dennett (1987), and others have argued for an evolutionary account of the intentionality (meaning) of our mental states, one well outside the awareness of most conscious subjects. In the face of all this, the idea that an individual might be an expert on the structure of her conscious states has begun to seem quaint and naive.

The view that subjects have no special knowledge about their own conscious states is in part a result of a twentieth-century tendency toward the externalization of intentionality, attributable in part to a respect for scientific materialism. If consciousness is a physical phenomenon like any other, then it ought to be publicly observable like other physical phenomena. This means that our conscious purposes, like the purposes of a computer program, are a function of circumstances possibly beyond our knowledge. Thus it is widely believed that, in the current jargon, there is no "intrinsic intentionality."

b. Merleau-Ponty and the Embodiment of Meaning

Merleau-Ponty's work contributes two insights that argue against the above view. First, he showed that the actions of a being in its environment are not mechanical, but intrinsically meaningful. Second, he provided a basis for understanding how intentionality is accessible to consciousness. Let's look first at his position on intrinsic intentionality:

> [P]hysical stimuli act upon the organism only by eliciting a global response which will vary qualitatively when the stimuli vary quantitatively; with respect to the organism they play the role of occasions rather than of cause; the reaction depends on their vital significance rather than on the material properties of the stimuli. Hence, between the variables on which conduct actually depends and this conduct itself there appears a relation of meaning, an intrinsic relation. (Merleau-Ponty 1942, 161)

For Merleau-Ponty, the way to view the actions of a living organism is not as the automatic output of hidden mechanisms, like the turning of the wheels of a car, but as the expression of the purposes of the whole organism. The living being has vital needs, and its actions are organic extensions of these needs; they are not detachable "tools" used by the body. They carry their purposes with them. In performing the actions, the being is enacting the needs; and if the being is conscious, then in intending those actions it is intending that those needs be satisfied.

How can this view be evaluated against the mechanistic view that all intentionality is extrinsic? One very good way is by noting a fatal problem with that approach, which Merleau-Ponty's view avoids: the problem of the grounding of meaning. If the meaning of a symbol is determined by conventional rules, which may be beyond the experience of a given user of the symbol (as with the symbols used by computers), then how can correct usage be assured? Only by external causal links between the user and the symbol. This is the problem faced by Fodor (1987), Dretske (1988), and others who develop causal theories of word reference to explain how meaning is learned by a language-user. But all of these attempts fail to explain how original and creative use of symbols is possible. I can learn that the word "horse" properly refers to a certain type of stimulus pattern that is present when others use the word;

but I can also use the word, not incorrectly, but in metaphorical and other creative ways. No purely objective theory has come close to providing a set of rules for this everyday human practice: appropriating symbols for one's own purposes. Yet it can be argued that it is this creative appropriation, rather than formal identification of stimuli, that is the primary human linguistic activity (Glenberg 1996; Barsalou 1999). External causal theories of reference do not explain how symbols can be meaningful for a user.

Merleau-Ponty locates meaningfulness not in the causality of the external world, nor in the isolated inner self, but in the actions of selves *on* their environment. "Because we are in the world, we are condemned to meaning" (Merleau-Ponty 1941, xix). The idea is that there is an intrinsic intentionality to actions, which encompasses an environmental context, a valuation of elements in that context, a goal, and a plan for reaching the goal. These four components alone can fix a meaning for an action, independent of any wider context or position in a hierarchy of goals. Even if I have evolved for the "purpose" of reproducing my genes, such that my ability to choose actions is "intended" to aid in that purpose, my action of choosing celibacy instead is meaningful on its own grounds.

Others have argued for the intrinsic intentionality of action. Polanyi, for example, claimed that

> We may say in general that by acquiring a skill, whether muscular or intellectual, we achieve an understanding which we cannot put into words and which is continuous with the inarticulate faculties of animals. What I understand in this manner has a meaning for me, and it has this meaning in itself, and not as a sign has a meaning when denoting an object. We called this earlier on an "existential meaning." (Polanyi 1958, 90)

But it is one thing to show that a skilled, goal-directed action is meaningful to the agent. It is quite a different thing to show that this meaning is consciously accessible, that it manifests itself in the conscious experience of performing the action in a way recognizable to, and reportable by, the agent, and that it can serve to ground the semantics of symbols. It could be that, while actions do implicitly express their own meaning in their goal-directed structure, this meaning might not always or ever be salient in the experience of the conscious agent. It might not be necessary, for carrying out the action, that the agent be aware of its actual purpose. Perhaps she is aware only of an illusory purpose, a purpose that she has constructed on the basis of a distorted self-image, or a confabulatory story, that serves psychological needs only indirectly related to the action. I might, for example, offer to help you in order to make you admire my generosity, while telling myself that I am purely altruistic.

To argue this way is to miss Merleau-Ponty's central point, which is so revolutionarily simple as to be easily overlooked. Certainly I may deceive myself about my ulterior motives, or about triggering causes of my actions, or their relation to other aspects of my life (although it might be argued that such things as ulterior motives are at least potentially accessible to consciousness). But there is always a basic existential meaning within every simple goal-directed action, which coincides with the goal of the action itself, and without which the action would not be performed at all. If I am shopping for a present for my sister-in-law, I may want to please her or I may want to impress or embarrass or annoy her. But I *do want to buy her a present,* and my activities in preparing and carrying out the mission are intrinsically meaningful to that extent. I may not know why I am buying her the present, but I know that this is what I am doing. On a simpler level, which is where intentionality begins (understanding "motility as basic intentionality", Merleau-Ponty 1941, 137), an infant stretches her arm in order to grasp the toy, and in doing this movement she expresses that meaning of the action. The way she reaches expresses the purpose of grasping the toy: her eyes focus on the toy, her body is oriented toward it, and her hand shapes itself in advance to fit it. Her whole being knows that she is trying to grasp the toy, because it must support and participate in the action:

> In the action of the hand which is raised towards an object is contained a reference to the object, not as an object represented, but as that highly specific thing towards which we project ourselves, near which we are, in anticipation, and which we haunt. (Merleau-Ponty 1941, 138)

c. Embodied Meaning and Consciousness

The preceding section argues that in principle the meaning of an action is accessible to consciousness, because it is implicit in the performance of the action. But there is a further question: How is such implicit meaning ever made explicit? If we can perform an action, then we know what we are doing, but this knowledge might remain implicit (as, perhaps, it is in nonhuman animals). How do we come to conceptualize this meaning, or "know-how," so that we can report it with some reliability? As Merleau-Ponty notes, "It is not so easy to reveal pure motor intentionality: it is concealed behind the objective world which it helps to build up" (Merleau-Ponty 1941, 138).

It is not a major concern for Merleau-Ponty to answer the question of how it is that introspective reports can be reliable. His anti-Cartesianism leads him to stress the implicit knowledge in action in contrast to the sort of explicit knowledge one obtains from observing an object, and to argue that consciousness is a case of the former rather than the latter: "All inner perception is inadequate because I am not an object that can be perceived, because I make my reality and find myself only in the act" (Merleau-Ponty 1941, 383).

Thus Descartes is partially vindicated: doubt is inevitable except "by actually doubting, involving oneself in the experience of doubting" (Merleau-Ponty 1941, 383). We are arguing, however, that Merleau-Ponty's premises, taken together with recent empirical data about brain mechanisms of consciousness, entail the possibility of some reliable, explicit, conceptual self-knowledge. (By "conceptual" we mean knowledge that can be expressed in symbols, such as words, that we have learned to use to pick out categories of objects in the world; see Griffiths 1997, 176).

The argument that the implicit intentionality of actions must on occasion be explicitly available for conceptual knowledge depends on a crucial assumption that was defended in an earlier chapter: that consciousness always has an intentional object, and to be conscious of anything at all, we must represent something—in the revised sense of "representing" we have defined. Consciousness does not present physical objects themselves to a subject; the subject is aware of them by representing them as intentional objects. This claim is generally acknowledged by contemporary neuropsychologists (for instance Damasio 1994). When I am conscious of any object, I entertain imagery of that object. The imagery is not just visual, but is multimodal. Jeannerod (1994) offers evidence that in being conscious of any planned action one generates a motor image of what it would feel like to perform the action. It is, of course, possible that some form of consciousness may emerge that does not involve activated sensory-motor representations, but at present the nature of consciousness, including basic self-consciousness, is being explored via the study of such representations (Panksepp 1998). In what follows, we assume the thesis defended earlier, that where there is consciousness, there is representation, in the sense that we imagine using the imaged object in an imaged action or action schema.

If this assumption is true, then what representations would have to accompany our intentional states on Merleau-Ponty's account? They would have to be representations of our bodies interacting with objects in the physical environment. If, for example, I have an attitude of fear toward some person, I may entertain imagery of physical attacks by that person, or of getting away from the person. Let us say that in the presence of the person my body responds with the arousal of certain emotional states mediated by adrenaline. How do I know that my emotion is fear and not, say, anger? We would say: by what it is that I want or intend to do. I intend to get away from him, not hit him. I know my conscious states not by their appearance to me as a subjective perceiver, but by what physical actions I find myself desiring or intending to perform. I may not know why I became fearful, or what other psychological states may be shaping my fear, but I know that I am fearful in knowing that I want to get away from this threatening person.

How do I know that I want to get away from him? I know it because the sensorimotor imagery of getting away from him is vivid, insistent, and irrepressible, and is positively valenced. Imagery of treating him kindly, of trying to please him, is experienced as a less desirable option. We say: I feel like getting away from him; and we have learned that when we feel that way, we are fearful.

It might be objected that we are often deceived about our real feelings. Ellis (1999a) gives an example of a man who comes home from a difficult day at work and scolds his son for not taking out the garbage. In fact, however, he is not angry with his son but upset by events at work. How do I know that what I think I want to do, I really want to do? There are two answers that can be given. On one level, I can falsely believe that a given action will relieve my intense desires, only to find that it will not relieve it. Often we try out various actions in our imagination, to discover what it is that we really want to do. It seems plausible to say that we can at least come to identify our desires more accurately in this way. On another level, the question is irrelevant to the present argument, since it concerns the emotional cause of a present desire, which has its own identity. I may be wrong about why I want to scold my son, or whether it is all that I want to do, but I do want to scold him! That is, scolding him is my immediate intention; it is what in the present context I intend to do, and in that immediate sense, I want to do it. I know this not by inspecting a feeling or state of consciousness as though it were an object, but by (imaginatively or actually) experiencing myself performing an action.

d. Privileged Access and Semantical Grounding

The thinking of Merleau-Ponty on the issues just discussed allows for an account of the grounding of meaning that proved impossible with the view of Fodor and others that meaning is *external reference*. If we are to understand the symbols we use in communication, in the sense that they are meaningful to us and hence available for original and creative uses, then their meanings must be grounded in our *experiences* and not just in external causal links to physical objects. If it is true, as we have argued, that we explicitly represent the intentionality of our mental states in representations of the actions that would express them, then these action representations constitute the best candidates for the ultimate semantic content of meaningful symbols. In order to understand a symbol, such as a word in natural language, I must relate it to something meaningful *to me,* and my own represented actions are the only things that bear their meanings intrinsically, and not via relations to something else that is meaningful (this point is elaborated more extensively in Newton 1996).

The theory that action representations (or sensorimotor imagery) ground symbols has become an important and widely influential view, with the seminal work of such writers as Lakoff and Johnson (1987) and more recent work related to "embodiment" (Sheets-Johnstone 1998; Barsalou 1999). Not all of these writers acknowledge the work of Merleau-Ponty, but that is a mistake. His insights are clearly the basis for a major revolution in contemporary philosophy of mind.

2. "Introspecting" Emotional Qualia

Panksepp (1998) includes, among the basic emotional systems, the "seeking" system. Unlikely as it may seem, we believe that understanding this system can help to resolve the mystifying philosophical problem of the intrinsically nonrepresentational qualia of pleasure and pain.

The phenomenology of emotion is central to its effectiveness in cognition. Unconscious emotion is powerful in its influence on behavior, but conscious emotion exists, we may assume, for a purpose. That purpose must be, in part, to help evaluate the effects of possible future actions as a part of long- and short-range action planning. Unlike automatic and immediate actual responses to environmental events, we can evaluate possible actions only if we know what it will feel like for us to do them—whether we are going to like or dislike the results. For this purpose, we need to be able to experience those emotional states consciously. We also need to be able to compare, consciously, those imagined results with our current state: Will the proposed action make things better or worse than they are now? Thus current emotional qualia must also be available to us.

Given that conscious phenomenal experience of emotions is so important, a puzzle arises when we consider the phenomenology of emotional states as detached from their objects. While emotions, we are presuming, normally have intentional objects as well as triggers and causes—they are "about" something—it is possible to separate the experience of an emotional trigger from the true intentional object of the emotion—what it is *"really* about." Moreover, there seem to be generalized emotions with no particular objects, which we call "moods." Even the very vivid states of physical pleasure and pain can, with certain drugs and perhaps by other means, be isolated from their objects as well. In the case of pleasure, certain opioid-induced euphoric states appear to have no objects. In the case of pain, states of objectless "hurting" may seem rare or nonexistent. But Murat Aydede (2001) convincingly argues that, in principle, pain must have its own phenomenology, independent of that of its object, the affected body part. We can describe the way the body part feels independently of the way the pain itself feels.

In general, emotion has objects, and in general, whole organisms do as well. Normally, or at least often, we are involved in specific activities aimed at specific objects—such as reading a book or looking for our glasses. But as Panksepp makes clear, when object-related activities are not engaging us, the "seeking" system puts us into a mode in which we *search* the environment (including our own bodies) for salient stimuli, sometimes having nothing particular in mind at all, and sometimes looking for a particular type of thing to match a mood or ease a particular state of discomfort.

It is plausible to suppose that less generalized "seeking systems" analogous to Panksepp's, or perhaps even identical with it or extensions of it, are at work in the organism, activated not only by generalized moods but also by very specific emotions or organismic needs, when the natural objects of these states are not perceived. In other words, when bodily drives are activated, we look for what will satisfy them. Perhaps more significantly, normal perception involves "looking-for" objects. When activated by endogenous or exogenous stimuli that resonate with motivational states, the organism "looks for" confirmation of the presence of the anticipated object (Ellis 1986, 1995b, 2005).

How do we "look for" something in this sense? Two factors seem clear. First, there is internally generated imaging of the anticipated object or state of affairs; second, there is alert attentional focus on perceptual stimuli that are candidates for satisfying the expectation. Candidates capture the attention and are evaluated, and then dismissed if they do not meet the criteria, or match the image.

An example to illustrate this point is the husband and wife who set their alarm clocks for different times. The alarms have perceptibly different rings, and neither spouse is ever awakened by the other's alarm. Even while asleep, both are able to gear themselves up to "listen for" the sound that fits their motivated interest in awakening at the right time.

There is a phenomenology of "looking for" that is distinct in principle from that of the response to an actual sensory stimulus. The phenomenology is produced by the imagery of the anticipated object together with the conscious experience of focused attention, which is a voluntary action with its own distinctive "feel." Voluntary attention involves an orienting of internal and external bodily mechanisms toward sources of possible or expected stimuli. This orienting is an activity, like voluntary motor activity, that produces "efference copy" that has qualitative properties. It feels like something to be in a state of "looking-for," and what it feels like is a combination of the experience of sensory or sensorimotor imagery and the experience of paying attention.

Both facets of this phenomenology of voluntary attention are representational. What is represented are: 1. imaged objects or states of affairs, and 2. sensorimotor imagery of the embodied subject in its seeking state. Here again, there cannot be conscious experience without representation. If there are no obvious candidates to be objects of representation when the subject is in an alert experiential state, then the activity of "looking for" will be set in motion precisely to give the conscious state an object of representation.

Now to relate this account of "looking-for" to emotion. Like states of sensory perception, emotional states normally have objects, and in particular, pains normally are responses to damaged body parts: the pain is *the way that body part* feels. Thus normally, when in pain we pay attention to that body part, just as when in a state of grief we focus on the object of our grief. But what if, for any reason, there appears to be no object? In that case, what produces the phenomenology of the affective (emotional, painful or pleasurable) state? Or to put the question in another way: the affective phenomenology is *more* than the mere sensory perception of the object, but *what* more?

Our reasoning up to this point suggests that the phenomenology of affective states consists of a combination of imagery with the conscious experience of attending to *candidates* for the appropriate but missing object. These candidates are potentially salient bodily or environmental stimuli that are evaluated and compared with the imagery of the expected or anticipated object. Thus our attention is, although focused, also highly active and flexible: we pay close attention first to one candidate and then another. There might be an almost frantic searching among the various stimuli for one to match the affective state.

Consider an example. I wake up in a bad mood, perhaps because I am getting a cold and did not sleep well. There is nothing in particular to dislike in my environment, but I am ready to dislike something. So, I try disliking whatever I encounter: my cat, the way the kitchen looks, the prospect of the day's activities. At the same time, I am imaging objects and situations that are capable of producing negative emotions, and I try to match the current stimuli with those memory images to determine which of them could be an appropriate object of my mood. Perhaps none of them is; this will be the case, for example, if my mood is really caused by my bad night's sleep. But I will be busily trying them out; attending to them *as if* they are the real causes, to see if that activity produces resonance with my mood. Thus even if nothing "is wrong," my discomfort will be obvious to myself and to others, because of my efforts to pin the mood on some object.

An apparent exception to this explanation is the experience of euphoria induced by agents like heroin or natural opioids. In these states, the overwhelming experience is one of complete satisfaction with *the way things are right now*; therefore, "looking for" would not occur. One might try to explain the apparent peculiarity of this type of state by saying that the aim of the qualitative experience is one of actively prolonging the state of euphoria by protecting oneself from any disruptive stimuli; guarding oneself from distracting invasions. But this suggestion is only partially correct. The full explanation is that states of euphoria are not so radically distinct from other affective states: their qualitative properties are representational in the same way as all others. In cases of extreme euphoria, "zoning-out" as it were, the object is the subject's body (which may be experienced as encompassing the universe), as a positive or good object.

In sum, the phenomenology of a pure emotion is neither that of "experiencing a mental state" in an act-object model, nor of perceiving a single negative or positive object or state of affairs. Rather, it is the experience of a multitude of objects, both imaged and real, as negative, bad objects, or as positive, good objects. It is thus a representational experience. Part of the nature of the experience is looking for and identifying what is represented: that is the "job" of a conscious subject. Since activities of looking-for and paying attention are voluntary intentional activities of the same sort as voluntary motor activities, an essential experience of being a conscious subject is the experience of personal agency. In this way, the search for the nature of emotional qualia leads back to embodiment as the core of subjective personhood.

3. What Are the "Intentional Contents" of Internal Sensations? The Problem of "Pure Feeling"

The introspection of emotional qualia presents an interesting test case for the action-centered account. It is often suggested that the introspection of the "raw feel" of affective states is dissociable, at least in principle, from the objects with which we normally connect them (for example, see Ben Ze'ev 2000, 2002; Griffiths 1997). And if so, then it would seem to follow that the emotional qualities per se cannot be oriented toward any particular object with any specific action in mind, and thus that the action implications of the state would arise only *after* the quality of the state is present and available to feeling. How, then, can the explanation of the "what it's like" dimension of affective states hinge on their *prior* action implications?

In effect, we have emphasized that actions are different from mere reactions in that they are emotionally motivated in terms of the self-organizational demands of the organism as a whole. But now a problem must be resolved by this way of putting the relation between emotion and consciousness. The problem is presented by the apparent fact that some feelings, such as pleasure and pain, sometimes seem to be *dissociable from* any representational or intentional objects. We can feel the pure euphoria of a morphine high, yet the feeling may not be telling us to *do anything* about it. The sheer feeling, as a pure feeling, may not be motivating any action commands at all. So, if there are no action commands being sent, then how are we introspectively conscious of the feeling? Is there any other alternative than a passive receiving of afferent signals?

The relation between emotion and consciousness will not be understood until we have an answer to this central question. What is the experiential content of the consciousness of pleasure and pain? Or, as Watt asks: What gets "valence" into consciousness? This is the question that Plato tried to answer with his theory of the Form of the Good. Unfortunately, Plato set everyone off on a wrong track with his perceptual model: one "sees" the essence of goodness with an "inner eye" as one sees (and absorbs) light from the sun. But Plato could be interpreted in a more useful way. His philosopher already has a sense of the essence of goodness before reaching the Form of the Good itself, because striving for goodness is itself good. Still, if this striving is rewarding, what is the nature of *that* reward? The self-organizational model suggests a direction that might lead to an answer.

Our proposal starts with the premise defended in Chapters 2 and 3, that every conscious state involves a representation of what the conscious state is about, regardless of the "doxic modality" of the representation—whether it presents itself as related to an object of imagination, perception, a merely symbolizing object, or even a hallucination. Consciousness is always consciousness of something or other, although this "something" may not correspond exactly or even approximately to anything in the actual world. This is a widely accepted assumption. The central question for our purposes can thus be phrased in this way: What is represented during conscious awareness of pure pleasure or other emotions that contributes to our understanding of what we feel? If we gaze fondly at a loved one, what is it about the experience that tells us that she is loved and not hated?

If we make a point of dropping the perceptual model of consciousness and substitute an action model, the content of the experience of pleasure is already, in a limited sense, defined. Unlike perception, action is intrinsically value-ridden because actions have goals that are to-be-achieved by the action, that define the action, and that entail success or failure for the action. As we will discuss below, perception also may intrinsically involve value, but on a conscious conceptual level the object of perception can be distinguished from its value. Acting cannot, because every intentional action is an expression of the value of its goal to the agent. For example, you can see something about which your attitude is thoroughly negative, but you cannot strive to attain something about which your attitude is thoroughly negative. A condemned prisoner cannot walk to his execution unless he summons the desire for dignity or some other value to motivate his movement.

The apparent separability of perception and evaluation is not true for the unconscious motivational processes governing nonvoluntary behavior. Seeing something entails having looked for it in response to the organism's needs (Ellis 1995b; Milner and Goodale 1995). The fact that these needs can be unconscious may lead the observer to assume that the object is value-neutral: "It just attracted my attention; it caught my eye." We do not find ourselves performing goal-directed actions, however, without knowing that we *want* the goal, however ambivalently.

An action model will not automatically answer all questions about the experience of value. Within such a model one could still ask: what is it that tells us that the goal is desired and not loathed? The obvious answer, that it is a *goal*, is inadequate if not circular. The goal must have been desired before conscious action began. But before it can have been desired, there must have been a need or desire that it could satisfy. In addition, before conscious action could begin, there must have been a sense of the attainability of the needed goal. That means that the goal of an action is experienced in something like the way we would experience the discovery of a missing puzzle piece. It is good in relation to a need, and it is pleasurable in that it promises that the need will be met. This seems to entail that displeasure is more fundamental than pleasure, and may seem to threaten a regress: how do we experience displeasure? It may be that by the time pleasure and displeasure are experienced at a conscious level analysis of their experienced components is no longer possible; they are experiential primitives. The experience of pleasure and pain in consciousness has the qualitative feel that it has for the same reason that the color red has its qualitative feel: those feels are what pleasure *is*, and red *is*, to the conscious subject. Those answers will not satisfy one who wants a complete verbal characterization of the phenomenal properties of consciousness. But they are good enough for our current purpose, which is to attempt an account, not of what experienced phenomenal properties as such consist of (if such a question is even coherent), but of how the conditions they represent can get into consciousness in the first place.

The suggestion that an action-model yields a framework better able to account for the conscious experience of pleasure leads to an important objection, based on a distinction between two kinds of conscious pleasures. Klein (1981) divides pleasures into "consummatory" and "appetitive." Appetitive pleasures are experienced during the pursuit of a goal; consummatory pleasures follow upon the attainment of the goal. Two different classes of addictive drugs are associated with this distinction. Stimulant drugs (cocaine, amphetamine) enhance dopamine brainstem circuits and norepinephrine circuits mediating alertness to the outside world, and this produces euphoria (Volkow et.al. 1997). Depressant drugs (opiates, alcohol) also trigger dopamine reward circuits but, unlike stimulants, they also enhance GABA inhibitors and the parasympathetic nervous system, and can attenuate the effects of cocaine-induced dopamine release (Dewey et.al. 1997), thus *reducing* alertness and activity. In addition, these drugs reduce pain perception and can, like stimulants, promote euphoria; hence their addictive properties.

The objection raised by this contrast is that the action model could be helpful in explaining the consciousness of pleasure from stimulants, but not for that from depressants—for example, the euphoria of a morphine high. During this experience the subject is passive, dreamy, unmotivated. One could describe this state as one's body feeling utterly peaceful and in perfect harmony with the environment. But what constitutes the intense *pleasure* it provides? If no action commands are being initiated at all, then how can there be consciousness of the pleasure?

A further complication is that the state of rest and peace seems not to be *intrinsically* pleasurable, since people suffering from anhedonia—an inability to be happy or satisfied—can experience a state of rest in the absence of pleasure. Such anhedonics also lack the motivating response to stimulants, because of the lack of appeal of the anticipated goal. Still others, however, are able to experience consummatory pleasures if they are imposed from without, but cannot enjoy actively seeking them (Kramer 1993).

The action model of consciousness can respond to this objection in terms of a more general theory of self-organizing behavior in organisms, or dynamical systems theory. Such a theory holds that organisms are systems that are structured so as to strive continuously for both internal homeostasis and a suitably high-energy basin of attraction, and for external interaction with the environment for purposes of maintaining homeostasis at the desired level of energy (Thelen and Smith 1994; Kauffman 1993; Ellis 2005). The more complex the system, the more the maintenance of internal homeostasis requires ambitious interaction with the environment, culminating in the sort of long-term life plans in which we humans engage.

According to our version of this self-organizational model, consciousness is associated with the action-planning component of a complex, active system. It has been proposed (Panksepp 1998, Watt 1999) that a prototypical form of consciousness emerges along with emotional valence in a "primitive and basic neural representation of the self" (Watt 1991, 1), the role of which is to monitor and preserve the well-being of the organism in its internal and external environment. With simple organisms, well being is maintained by means of nonconscious metabolic adjustments and automatic motor responses. With complex organisms, continued well being requires intentional actions, which in turn require conscious awareness of internal and external conditions, and the formation of action plans. The level of activity common to all self-organizing systems (which include all forms of life) is non-conscious, and does not involve representations or schemas of action sequences. The intentional actions of complex creatures take place on a higher level, and are controlled by representations of the organisms' needs and goals.

The action model of consciousness that we propose involves both levels of dynamical processes. Simply put, this means that a conscious organism is involved in some higher-level activity, not just the lower automatic activities that preserve homeostasis. On that model, the answer to the objection takes the following form: The "passive" euphoria of a depressant "high" is experienced as the active effort *to maintain maximal internal homeostasis with minimal perturbation from external stimuli.*

What this means is that, in contrast to stimulant highs that drive the organism to dynamic interaction with the external world to increase and enhance well being, depressant highs drive the organism to draw inward, to *protect the inner environment* from external impacts. The conscious goal is the *absence of change* in the inner state, as opposed to greater change for the sake of increasing positive opportunities for new levels of well being. Depressant highs tell the subject that all is perfect as it is, and that any change must be for the worse (which is, of course, what the philosopher knows when contemplating Plato's Form of the Good). To maintain this state of perfection, the subject must concentrate on the goal, which is the current bodily condition. Hence the inward focus, the intense pleasure in the somatic sensations of sheer bodily existence, rather than those provided by external stimuli. (We might say, then, that Plato would have liked heroin highs, whereas Aristotle probably would have preferred amphetamines.)

The important point for our purposes is that in both types of euphoria, what is valued is a goal, and what is enjoyed is the activity of attaining that goal. This means that the action model is, after all, applicable to both "active" and "passive" pleasures, and the objection disappears. Recall that the objection was simply to the application of an action model to passive pleasures; it was not an objection to a claim that the action model can provide a complete account of how pleasure gets into consciousness. That claim has not been made. What was argued is that the action model offers more promise of such an account, since valuation is inherent in the conscious experience of action in a way that it is not in the conscious experience of perception. The way in which action grounds emotional consciousness is discussed in more detail in Ellis 2005.

PART II
Hunting for Quale: How Do Qualia "Emerge"?

1. "Emergent" Qualities: Higher-Order Processes that Resolve Lower-Order Contradictions

We can now see how the action model, as suggested in Chapter 1, provides resources with which to bridge the explanatory gap. We have seen that the "knowledge argument" can be resolved only when we get away from the stimulus-response perceptual metaphor for the relation between consciousness and its objects. The "explanatory gap" is a more challenging problem because it results not only from the notion that consciousness could be a passive receiver of information, but also from a problem about the phenomenon of *emergence*. Emergent properties are often unpredictable from the properties of the lower-level micro-events from which they emerge. We have argued that consciousness is emergent from properties that, considered by themselves, are mutually conflicting and seemingly contradictory. Consciousness arises from the forced blending of these contradictory components—for example, the blending of motivated anticipation with the recollected just-past anticipation of the same perceptual object, which leads to Changizi's (2008) paradoxical results in which subjects see the moving object where it is just about to be rather than where it actually is.

These "paradoxical" blendings of contradictory elements, which we discussed in earlier chapters, are further complicated by the fact that consciousness, unlike other emergent properties, is not definable in any of the usual ways that things can be defined—analytically, ostensively, or comparatively. So it is all the more difficult to show how consciousness is entailed through the combination of the lower-level events from which it emerges. We shall return to this "indefinability" problem in a moment.

But first, we should remind ourselves that consciousness is not the only example of a case in which unpredictable novelties arise from the forced merging of contradictory elements. For present purposes, emergent phenomena can be divided into two kinds: collective behavior, such as fluidity, that is part of a scientific description of the physical world; and collective properties, such as wetness, that expressly invoke the sensory experiences of observers. In both cases, descriptions of the emergent phenomena require new vocabularies not applicable to the constituents of the phenomena. In the first type of emergence, however, the novel phenomenon is completely definable in *quantitative* terms. For example, fluidity is the capacity to move or change shape without separating when under pressure. In the second type of case, a description of the phenomenon requires novel *qualitative* terminology; a complete description essentially includes reference to unique sensations produced in observers. Since the sensations are qualitatively unique, the description is not analyzable into descriptions of components of the sensations. In this section, we discuss several examples of novelties that emerge from contradictions. We start with a conceptual novelty as a purely formal example to highlight the general point; we then consider cases involving phenomenal experience.

Russell showed, with the Liar Paradox and other logical puzzles, that no logical system could be complete because it would contain a statement that could not be true or false in that system: "This statement is false," or "I am now lying." But our traditional conceptual framework for statements requires that every statement can be true or false. His solution was a novel rule, unprecedented in logic: A statement cannot refer to itself. That rule emerges entirely from the paradox, without which it would be either pointless or false.

A different example involves both conceptual and nonconceptual aspects. The response we call "humor" is produced by an inherently contradictory juxtaposition of responses to two incompatible states of affairs: 1. an unexpected and disruptive event, such as someone tripping and falling down stairs (without serious harm), and 2. the prior expectation of the opposite sort of event, such as a regal and dignified descent. When the latter behavior is the norm, and it is represented in juxtaposition to the actual tumble, we respond in a way different from what our response would be to either event represented in isolation (being startled and/or sympathetic, and being unaroused). A similar event, being tickled, produces laughter as the expression of a blend of pleasure and fear. A third example is also a blend of conceptual and experiential elements: the anti-contrast "assimilation effect" in the perception of colored areas (Hardin 2000, p. 115). In retinal based color perception, when colored areas are very small, their colors are blended: "Thus, although a large region of red is sharply accentuated when placed next to a large area of green, when the areas are tiny, the retinal receptors blend the red and the green to give the appearance of a pure yellow." In this example, we take the appearance of yellow to be an emergent property whose phenomenal nature—that is, what it is like to see yellow—would not be predictable by the subject from previous experiences of unblended red and green. Of course, the usefulness of this example is limited in that the experience of yellow, in normal subjects, results from the positive value of the activation of the post-retinal yellow/blue channel along with the equilibrium of the red/green channel. Thus we cannot claim that this effect of seeing small areas of red and green would yield the appearance of yellow in the absence of the already-existing yellow/blue channel; it may depend on having already experienced yellow. But in principle, the example serves as an illustration by way of analogy: in attempting to blend in a single experience two incompatible brain states, the subject appears to have a positive experience of a third state: one that is qualitatively distinct from the "sum" of the incompatible parts.

The above examples share this feature: two incompatible states (logical constructions or biological processes) are maintained in juxtaposition. If they occurred only serially, the emergent solution would be unnecessary. We can alternate between the perceptions of two incompatible perspectives, as in the Necker cube. The emergent property requires forced simultaneous processing of two incompatible representations, long enough for the subject to reflect on the incompatibility and attempt to resolve it; the emergent property is the result.

Consider examples more purely experiential. Depth perception, which we discussed as a paradoxical phenomenon in our previous chapter, is an obvious experiential instance of emergence (Engel et al. 1999). Binocular vision presents two visual fields, isomorphic but slightly displaced. The result is not a blur or a confusing double image, but visual depth. It is not deducible from binocular processing alone that visual depth would occur; we can imagine instead the experience of Necker cube-like aspect shifts. Moreover, we saw in the previous chapter that depth perception is *logically* paradoxical: our perception of a cylinder seems to present fifty percent of the curved surface, yet if we were not in fact seeing *more* than fifty percent of the surface, then we would not have depth perception. Each eye is actually seeing a little bit of the *back side* of the curved surface that is inaccessible from the other eye's point of view. But our general phenomenal impression of the cylinder does not seem to announce any such contradiction, just as it does not in the case of the Necker cube.

Visual depth emerged, we may assume, for adaptive reasons. The same is true of motion perception: areas of the inferior temporal lobe blend successive visual stimulations into representations of a single moving object. Ex post facto, motion perception makes sense as necessary for our type of organism, but its phenomenal properties are not predictable from single time-slices of binocular vision considered in isolation. To be sure, if one already knows in advance from one's own case what a qualitative property is like, and if one knows the brain states with which it is correlated, then observing those brain states in another person would allow one to predict, with varying accuracy, the qualitative properties. But strictly speaking, the qualitative properties cannot be deduced only from the objective observations of the brain states without the prior knowledge of what the subjective experience is like.

Let's consider one more emergent phenomenon before discussing phenomenal consciousness itself. Our experience (and concept) of persons is such a phenomenon, and like the others, it appears to result from the forced blending of incompatibilities. Cells in the parietal and motor areas respond to two incompatible or mutually exclusive conditions: the experience of deliberate bodily movement of the subject, and the sight of the same kind of movement by a conspecific. The result is the representation in a single structure of both inside (subjective) and outside (objective) aspects of behavior—what it feels like and what it looks like—a single being as both an agent and an object of agency seen as a visible object (Barresi and Moore 1996; Stanemov and Gallese 2002). Our concept of a person is a concept of such a being, even though such a concept is paradoxical: When our left hand touches the right (to borrow Merleau-Ponty's example), we can either inhabit the right hand subjectively and feel what it's like for it to touch the left, or we can think of it as an object, in which case we feel what it's like to be touching it from the perspective of the *left* hand. When we look at an object, we do not think of the subject looking as a spatiotemporal object, but as the receiver of information *about* such objects (Wohlschläger 2002). As soon as we think of our brains as objects, we are seeing our brains from the external viewpoint of someone else. We cannot see something from the first and third person at once, and it does not appear as having the same properties from the two perspectives. Yet, paradoxically, our concept of another person is the concept of something that does have both sets of properties—objective and subjective. Many now think it plausible that the semantic ground of this concept lies in the activity of the "mirror neurons" (Stamenov and Gallese 2002). The mirror neuron system enables us to imagine ourselves doing actions similar to what the other person does, and activates the action imagery system that we discussed earlier, so that we can imagine "what it's like" to do what the other is doing. We are able to have the concept of the other as a subject because we are able to generate this unique experience.

We can now think of the uniqueness of consciousness as actually representing an example of a more general kind of emergence. For example, we argued earlier that phenomenal consciousness essentially involves synchronous activations of representations of "identical" intentional objects but with distinct temporal tags and valences—the anticipation of a to-be-presented object with the just-past anticipation of the object—and the consciousness is therefore a case of the emergence of novelty from contradiction.

We can understand on this basis why it is necessary, as a logical consequence of the way in which consciousness emerges from the combination of its constituents, that it must be indefinable in the usual ways that other phenomena, even emergent ones, are definable. Most experiences can be made sense of by being related to other types of experiences. They are defined in three ways: 1. by *analysis* into their experiential components (for example feelings of anxiety into bodily sensations and imagery); 2. by *ostension* (as when the experience is of a public object that can be pointed to); or 3. by *comparison* (as with color, which is a particular type of visual experience, each color occupying a position along a familiar spectrum). Any experience that cannot be made sense of in these ways will be a mystery to its subject. And there is only one experience that precisely *cannot* be made sense of in any of these ways, and therefore inevitably must seem mysterious: the experience of phenomenal consciousness itself. All physical examples, even of the emergent kind, are examples of types or modes of phenomena, understandable as one among others of that type. But phenomenal consciousness *itself* is *sui generis*. Nothing else is like it *in any way at all*, because anything other than phenomenal consciousness is unconscious, and hence not "like anything" in Nagel's sense.

At the same time, if we can only understand *why* phenomenal consciousness is so unique for subjects, we will no longer need to find a special ontological or epistemological status for it. Instead, we will understand why there is nothing of the kind to be found, and why the apparent uniqueness of the phenomenon is the predictable result of certain emergent and self-organizational brain activities. Thus Dennett and other eliminativists voice a half-truth that could be better understood if they made this approach explicit; since they do not, they appear not to recognize the rich experiential nature of phenomenal consciousness. It will not do to say: there is no such thing as a *"quale"*—a subjective quality. We must first explain *why there can appear* to be such a thing; and for that purpose we must characterize the experience in an intuitively acceptable way.

The only way philosophers have found to categorize consciousness as "one of many," in any category, is genetically, as an "emergent" property. A property is "emergent" if it holds of its constituents collectively, but not individually, and if it comes into existence only through the combined actions of the constituents. But there the ball is dropped. Many aspects of novel emergent properties are unpredictable from the properties of the constituents from which they emerge. Some emergent properties, like temperature, can be explained in a way that makes it clear exactly how they emerge, and hence can be completely demystified. But emergent properties are not always so tractable. So far, this has been the case with phenomenal consciousness.

We are suggesting that the ineffability of consciousness, as compared even with other "emergent" phenomena, results from its unique indefinability. This is a semantic problem, not an ontological or even an epistemological one. As such, the problem provides no reason to view con- sciousness itself as intrinsically of a different nature from other physical emergent properties. (To say that the problem is semantic rather than ontological or epistemological, of course, does not in itself entail physicalism.)

The indefinability of consciousness is in part a result of its subjectivity. This term, in turn, needs to be demystified. We define a phenomenon as subjective if it is a response to an organism's own proprioceptively-sensed self-generated activity, rather than to publicly-recognized "external objects." Subjectivity on this account can be thought of as limited access of a particular kind, rather than a non-physical form of experience. Subjectivity, moreover, is not the same thing as consciousness. Subjective events as defined above may be conscious or not.

In arguing for the indefinability of consciousness, we presuppose the account offered in the previous chapters: that subjective novelty occurs when an organism, by means of self-motivated acts of attention, *blends* distinct *sensational* components of perceptual acts in a certain way. That is, it blends features of the perceptual *activity* (such as location in the visual field), rather than of the perceptual *object,* into a unified "object" of experience. The resulting blend can thus be viewed as a particular type of emergent property. If we consider consciousness in relation to other types of emergent property, we may understand what gives it the seemingly unique *kind* of "uniqueness" described above: it cannot be defined either analytically, ostensively, or comparatively. Understanding why this is the case will, in turn, demystify it.

As we have seen in the previous chapters, both voluntary and involuntary attention require emotional-motivational brain activity to select biologically useful objects for attention. Even general curiosity, which often motivates involuntary attention to the environment in general, is an emotion orchestrated by Panksepp's "seeking system" in the brain;

curiosity directs our attention to explore in general, because such exploration is emotionally motivated for organisms at our level of organization. But there are also more specific interests that direct our attention, and these are the ones that are normally referred to as "voluntary" attention. Many such specific interests are based on previous learning, rather than being genetically hardwired. But in principle, all acts of attention are motivated by the self-organizational purposes of the organism, and directed according to categories of utility and thus object affordances. It is the self-motivated actions of the organism, rather than the objective features of objects, that are blended to form what we experience as the subjective "what it's like" dimension of phenomenal consciousness.

In self-organizing creatures, internal states can embody inherent contradictions, either in absolute logical terms or relative to the structure of the organism. Sometimes these contradictions are untenable, and one of the states must give way. For example, if an organism is motivated to an immediate satisfaction of two incompatible desires, one of the two must be subordinated to the other. In other cases, however, the organism must incorporate both of the contradictory states into a higher level of organization. Our argument is that phenomenal consciousness is the result of the incorporation, into a single representational schema, of representations of organismic states with conflicting temporal labels. In other words, when for purposes of goal selection and planning I attend to my current situation, I do so by blending memories and anticipatory images of temporally distinct states into a single, extended "present." My anticipation of the action affordances of a situation is experienced as inseparably interwoven with the recollection of a just-prior view of the just-prior situation (the soccer ball where it was a few milliseconds earlier, for example), and the new experience is felt as including all these subjective qualities, including the felt sense of the valenced anticipation. The unification in a single representation of such "contradictory" states ("now" and "not-now") produces a novel state with the experiential properties of phenomenal consciousness. Hence the paradox that subjects see the moving object as always *where it is just about to be,* rather than where it is.

Briefly, our conclusion is twofold: first, that consciousness, like many emergent properties, arises from the forced blending of contradictory components; and second, that consciousness is a unique type of emergent property that is analytically, ostensively, and comparatively indefinable. In order to establish these conclusions, we began by looking at the general issue of contradiction and novelty. In line with the goal of categorizing consciousness as one among other types of emergent property, we have examined a variety of cases in which unpredictable novelties arise from the forced merging of contradictory elements. The point is to show that while consciousness may be unique as a psychological state, its uniqueness is comprehensible in terms of a more general kind of emergence.

We then turned to consciousness, arguing that phenomenal consciousness essentially involves synchronous activations of representations of "identical" intentional objects with distinct temporal tags. Understanding this physiological mechanism allows the prediction of certain experiential properties of phenomenal consciousness that identify it as a case of the emergence of novelty from contradiction. We argue that it follows from the general nature of such emergence that the properties of consciousness would be indefinable and hence seem mysterious. While this analysis does not result in the elimination of those properties from subjective experience, it does make clear why phenomenal consciousness would necessarily be impossible to resolve into its constituents by the conscious subject. As a result, the physiological and phenomenological approaches to consciousness can be reconcilable in a coherent and non-contradictory way.

2. The Contradiction of Multi-Temporal Representation: Further Implications for the "Extended Present"

It is widely held that phenomenal consciousness emerges from synchronous firing of neurons in several cortical areas (see Newton 1996). The synchrony unifies the activities in those areas, such that human subjects report corresponding experiential awareness. If the organism is in a particular state of sensory activation, for example, the subject will report that she sees an object; in normal vision the perceived object is correlated with the external stimulus to which her visual system has attuned itself. The newly conscious state, in turn, allows the organism more degrees of freedom to select future actions, since its own responses can now be represented as explicit goals subject to rational planning, rather than remaining behind-the-scenes approach/avoidance motivators.

What is it about synchronized neural activity that makes such a difference to the subject? The brain change is quantitative only, but for the subject the change is a qualitative leap—in fact, the change *introduces* quality for the subject, where none existed previously. Our proposal is that phenomenal consciousness is an emergent resolution of contradictory elements, because of the way it unifies representations of *distinct temporal moments* into a *single* representational framework, which as a result gains what we earlier called "temporal thickness." The unified representation is experienced as "now" by the subject, but as we have seen, experiencing "now" entails a contradiction. The way James famously put this contradiction is that, at each moment of experience, the "now" of which we are aware is in fact the "just past," the previous moment in which we were anticipating and preparing for "now." From the action-based perspective, in that previous anticipatory moment, we activated anticipatory imagery of what was just about to become the actual "present moment," and this anticipatory imagery is experienced again now, as anticipatory, along with the sensations that were anticipated. Novel sensations, in other words, are experienced as having been anticipated. It is not simply that we remember anticipating them; rather, their anticipation is a part of them as *currently* experienced, which accounts for the feeling that what we are now experiencing has been there "already." That phenomenon is a result of the blending of distinct temporal moments by synchronized neuronal firing. Because our present experience includes (at least) two distinct times, it is experienced not as an instantaneous slice of time but as an extended time, containing elements of both "now" and "not-now," in a unified representation. It is still experienced, however, as "the present."

It has been proposed that the binding via synchronized oscillations is essential for phenomenal consciousness (Crick and Koch 1989). It is not obvious, however, that such binding per se can explain the uniqueness of consciousness, without the recognition that the unification of distinct times in one present moment is a contradiction for the subject, who retains a sense (and, usually, a concept as well) of other past times as past. Past and present remain distinct in experience—the contents of both working memory and long-term memory retain their character as *no longer* present. But the *present as experienced* includes some past times of its own. The past that is part of the subject's experienced present is not identified by the subject *as a memory* of a moment that is past and gone. Instead, it feels like a *part* of the present, one that gives the present a duration, significance, and substantiality that it could not have if comprised only of an instantaneous time-slice. As we experience it, the present moment is a logical impossibility, a chimera. Yet it constitutes reality for the subject. As Descartes observed, it is that of which we can be most certain.

We can describe an artificial slow-motion or frame-by-frame version of what we have in mind (the process would in fact be a dynamic one, not neatly divisible into distinct stages). Imagine that you have just awoken, and your senses respond to stimuli from your environment. You are too confused to identify where you are or what is happening, but your brain may be constructing, at time T1, a representation composed of visual data, somatic data, efference copy, emotion, and other elements of your current state. Then, at T2, your brain constructs a second representation, which contains all of the same elements, updated, *plus* the representation from T1, which is retained in working memory. What do we mean by *"plus"*? It is logical to suppose that the T2 representation is an act of attention to only those elements of information that resonate with the T1 representation. Now suppose we say that the two representations together constitute a conscious state. (We must assume that all other necessary supporting brain mechanisms are in place.) The act of attention binds the two representations into a single "object": the present moment. This single "object" is formed from two components that, by their nature, should not co-exist: events at both T1 and T2. But they are posited as coexisting, in that their combined representation is labeled as occurring only at T2. This means that the representation at T2 is the experience of looking at the past, as it were, not just remembering it. Or to put it another way, it is the experience of the present as extending into the past. The present is therefore experienced as temporally thick.

The experience of this temporal thickness is at least one necessary aspect of the emergent qualitative property that is phenomenal consciousness. Because it is qualitatively distinct from other emergent properties, it cannot be defined analytically, in terms of any qualitative components. It is, moreover, subjective, in the sense that it arises from an act of attention to features of the agent's own perceptual activities, rather than to public features of perceptual objects. Because it is subjective and not public, it cannot be defined ostensively. And because it is unique in applying to all and only conscious experience, rather than being one phenomenal property among others, like color or taste, it cannot be defined comparatively. There is nothing else relevantly similar to phenomenal consciousness. It follows that phenomenal consciousness would necessarily feel like a mysterious and ineffable property; and it also would follow that people unversed in brain mechanisms would be at a loss to explain it in terms of any other property. It does not follow, however, that consciousness cannot be explained in terms of brain processes.

In our attempts to integrate brain physiology with phenomenological description and logical analysis of cognitive processes, we have referred frequently to the thesis that efferent neural streams are especially relevant to action imaggery, and thus have priority over afferent ones when it comes to conscious as opposed to non-conscious cognitive states. The next chapter will elaborate more fully on this kind of neurophysiological perspective. Then the following and final chapter will attempt to integrate that with what can be learned through a phenomenological approach.

9

Action Imagery and the Role of Efference

It is easy to conceptualize a problem in such a way as to prevent a solution. If the conceptualization is sufficiently entrenched in one's culture or profession, it may appear unalterable. But there is so much precedent for the discovery of fruitful reconceptualizations that in the case of most philosophical and scientific puzzles it is probably irrational ever to give up trying. Humphrey (2000) suggests that the mind-body problem results from such a misconceptualization, and that something resembling what we are calling an "action-based" analysis of qualitative mental states will be able to render qualitative states commensurate with brain states, allowing them to be described in terms of the same dimensions.

Humphrey (1992, 2000) argues that consciousness results from active and efferent rather than passive and afferent functions. These arguments contribute to the mounting recent evidence that consciousness is inseparable from the motivated action planning of creatures that in some sense are organismic and agent-like rather than passively mechanical and reactive in the way that digital computers are. This type of view was endorsed in passing by the early Dennett (1969), although he never followed up on it in his later work. According to Dennett, "No afferent can be said to have a significance 'A' until it is 'taken' to have the significance 'A' by the efferent side of the brain" (Dennett 1969, 74). Luria also stressed the neurophysiology of efferent processes as correlated with consciousness (Luria 1973, 82–88). A similar view is defended by Ellis (1986, 1992, 1995b, 1999a, b, 2000 a, b, 2001 a, b, 2005), Newton (1982, 1993, 1996, 2000, 2001, 2002), Ellis and Newton (1998a), Watt (1998, 2000), Thelen and Smith (1994), and Jarvilehto (1999). Merleau-Ponty also stressed the efferent contribution to consciousness, pointing out that the phantom limb of an amputee feels as if it still exists because, even though afferent signals are not received *from* it, efferent action commands are still sent *to* it. Similarly, Merleau-Ponty points out, a blind man feels the contour of a road with his stick by moving the stick; the pattern of efferent action commands reveals the contour of the road. Gibson (1986) picked up on this aspect of Merleau-Ponty's work and carried it forward to the current generation of "enactivists." The basic idea is that, while information can be passively absorbed in the form of afferent input, only efferent nervous activity in the interest of a living organism's homeostatic (yet suitably high-energy and anti-entropic) balance can create consciousness of any information, whether perceptual, imagistic, emotional, or intellectual.

1. Efferent Sensory Awareness

Humphrey argues that mental and physical states seem incommensurable because mental states, conceived as sensations, are described as if they are the objects of experience. In fact, however, they are activities: sensings of the action affordances of the true objects, the physical stimuli with which the organism is actively engaged. Conceiving of the sensations as themselves objects of experience (and then talking, as so many do, of what that experience "is like"), Humphrey reminds us, leads to a hopeless regress. There is no such "mental object" that is experienced, and any proposed candidate for it immediately becomes itself the source of more mysterious "objects": the "phenomenal properties of experiences" which are themselves "like something," ad infinitum.

As long as sensations are conceived of as nonphysical objects that can be experienced, they must remain unrelated to brain states, objects of a completely different metaphysical kind. Humphrey therefore distinguishes between perception and sensation, and points out that while perception is indeed "of" external physical objects, sensations are not "internal objects" which are sensed; instead, "sensory awareness is an activity. We do not have pains; we get to be pained" (Humphrey 2000: 13). Sensory awareness is *efferent* activity, and the experience it provides is not the experience of a mental object, a sensation, but the experience of the activity itself. Humphrey then argues that sensory activity has evolved from responses that in the past did carry through into actual behavior, but with further evolutionary development came to be truncated and inhibited. And the result is that even today the experience of sensation retains many of the original characteristics of true bodily action.

Explaining sensory activity in terms of bodily activity allows us to correlate it with brain activity. As Humphrey (2000) points out, sensation, like bodily action, is characterized by: ownership, bodily location, "presentness," qualitative modality, and phenomenal immediacy. Each of these properties can be understood in terms of brain states, because they are "dual currency concepts," neither purely mental nor purely physical. Humphrey provides a plausible evolutionary scenario that would connect the two sides of the mind-body problem.

Humphrey's proposal is that sensation is analogous to bodily activity, and that the reason for this is that the activity of sensing evolved from the bodily activities of responding overtly and behaviorally to stimuli. He holds that the experiences characteristic of sensation are analyzable in terms of properties of bodily activity itself: activities are owned; activities have distinct modalities (hand waves, knee jerks), and so on. He carefully acknowledges a disanalogy: "it is 'like something' to have sensations, but not like anything much to engage in most other activities" (2000, 14). He accounts for the disanalogy by arguing that sensations are self-resonating, and hence possess a temporal "thickness" that sets them apart and makes them more vivid.

Up to this point, Humphrey's argument is consistent with our view except for one point. There is indeed an analogy between sensation and action. For Humphrey, the analogy lies between the objective features of action and the subjective features of sensation. But he plays down the fact that every one of the objective features of action that he cites is also subjective, even in a context of pure action. This problem is evident in his remark that it is like something to have sensations but not to engage in most other activities. It may be true that we focus our attention most strongly on the sensations that are linked to objects in the external world (sight, hearing, taste, and the rest). But that is not the same as saying that it is not like much to engage in other activities. On the contrary, if our bodily activities were not experienced as sensations, as "like something" for us to at least the same degree as other sensations, we would be unable to experience the latter in many of the dimensions Humphrey discusses.

According to Humphrey, sensation always involves "ownership" by its subject. Sensation, he says, always belongs to the subject. His example is pain, but it could have been visual sensations instead. If Humphrey had picked visual sensations, however, his point would not have been so obvious. Visual sensations do not feel like sensations; instead, sensations like color appear to a naive subject to be properties of external objects (Newton 1989a, b; Ellis and Newton 1998a). Sound, to a lesser degree, also appears to the average listener to exist at the source of the sound waves rather than in our bodies. The same can be said of Humphrey's second property of the experience of sensation: bodily location. Pain is again too easy an example. Seeing a red object does not "intrinsically involve this part of me." There is normally no felt sensation in the eyes when we see red.

If sensations such as red, which appear "velvety and thick," are owned and indexical in the way that pain is, that is because the bodily activities involved in seeing an external object are equally velvety and thick. They may not be the primary focus of conscious attention, but they are integral to the visual experience. In seeing a red apple, I cannot help but see it as something in front of me, as reachable and graspable by me, or else as out of my reach. It is seen, as many have noted following Gibson, in terms of its affordances. Its affordances are the various ways that it does and can interact with my body. If I can see an object only in this way, then my body in its current state is part of the visual experience. To see something, but not see it as an object in front of one's eyes, is difficult if not impossible to imagine.

A second argument that our bodily activities are at least as vividly experienced as sensations is more direct: they underlie our ongoing sense of self as agency. Without a sense of self, sensations of external objects would be meaningless; more important, bodily sensations not only provide a context for other sensations, but they often successfully compete with them for attention. Of course I can forget myself in watching an absorbing movie. But normally my attention is not so securely captured, and I take stock of myself, evaluate my current bodily state, consider how my actions may appear to others, or simply remind myself of my existence. Even in the movie, I frequently remember that "it is only a movie" that I am watching. There have been proposals recently that the ongoing sense of self is mediated by continual processing of information about the current state of the body. Panksepp (1998) argues that this processing is orchestrated primarily by parts of the midbrain such as the periaquaductal gray region. It may also involve conscious awareness of efference copy (corollary discharge): copies of motor commands sent to other processing areas of the brain, such as the basal ganglia and the cerebellum, which return processed signals to the cortical motor areas (Hurley 1998). It should be noted that voluntary direction of attention is also a bodily activity of which we can be aware.

Finally, there has been a surge of interest in recent years in the experience of "embodiment" as underlying cognition in general. Examples are numerous (for example, see Boden 1982; Clark 1997; Jackendoff

1987; Lakoff and Johnson 1987; Langacker 1987; Newton 1996). The common theme is that cognition at all levels of abstraction makes essential use of images of basic bodily actions, and that such action schemas constitute the framework for all conceptual domains, including mathematics and logic. Supporting this view is work by Jeannerod (1994, 1997) showing that action images are essential for performing voluntary action, and that they are consciously accessible. If this new thinking is sound, then experiences of bodily action are far from "flat and papery" (Humphrey 2000, 14). Instead, they constitute the experienced building materials of our conscious life.

In treating the experience of bodily activity as peripheral, and arguing that other sensations are experienced as they are because they evolved from bodily responses to stimuli, Humphrey unnecessarily renders his position vulnerable to empirical refutation in a way that would be actually irrelevant to the thrust of his argument. Evidence that sensations are not "privatized bodily responses" (18) would seriously undermine his claim. But if instead he were to grant that sensations of bodily activity are experienced in the same way as sensations of external objects, then the evolutionary scenario, plausible though it is, would be unnecessary to the main argument. The real issue would then become what he calls the "thickness factor." All sensings are subject to recursive interaction; all sensings, externally or internally (imagistically) generated, are subject to internal loops that create a "self-resonance," allowing the sensing activity to be itself an "object" of experience. This self-resonance is possible not because a sensation is a mental rather than a physical entity, but because the activity of sensing is experienced like any other activity. A sense of ownership is provided by the experience of agency and an egocentric perspective on the sensed objects in the world, including one's own physical body. Feedback loops create a present experience of blended self and world, extended by memory and anticipation, providing the present moment with an illusory solidity and substance that we find mysterious, considering the piecemeal way in which our brains combine elements and temporal components of experiences; but this impression of solidity may actually turn out to be quite straightforward, as we tried to show earlier.

The proposals of Humphrey contain some important insights. The most important one is that the "thick moment of consciousness" can be analyzed in terms of physical mechanisms to provide a bridge between mind and body. This idea, which goes back at least to William James, has never been adequately investigated. It has the potential to bridge the explanatory gap, whereas no competing theory comes close.

In what follows, we shall elaborate on a suggestion that Humphrey emphasizes, and which has also been put forward by Luria (1980) and Ellis (1990, 1995b, 2005)—that consciousness always arises as the result of *efferent* activity, never merely from *afferent* activity. Our proposal, however, is different from Humphrey's in three major respects, though not contradictory and perhaps complementary to his approach. First, we emphasize the self-organizational account of the brain-body system. The importance of efference for the phenomena of consciousness and intentionality stems from the way the self-organizing system drives its own activity by using efferent pathways.

Secondly, we emphasize that the emotional system in the brain must drive computations in higher cortical and sensory processes before those processes can occur on a conscious basis. The kind of efferent activity that is relevant to the action theory stems from this emotionally driven aspect of cognition.

And third, we seek to clarify just what sense of "efferent" is required to make sense of the statement that consciousness is grounded by efferent rather than afferent processes. It is primarily the emotional contribution to this process that engenders consciousness, and the distinction between activity and passivity must be fleshed out philosophically in terms of the concept of self-organization as well as the notion that inhibited action commands lead to sensorimotor imagery and the understanding of object affordances.

2. Why Thermostats Don't "Act"

Superficially, the action theory of consciousness appears to avoid the mind-body quagmire quite easily, because by identifying consciousness with an agent-initiated action, we can describe it in ways that make sense both phenomenologically and physically. The action of an organism can be understood in empirical-scientific terms, as the result of a physical system—a self-organizing system, of which biological organisms are examples. And it can also be understood in terms of something that we can experience phenomenologically; everyone knows what it is like to engage in an action. Moreover, the fact that knowing about others' physiology, by itself, cannot tell us how they feel ceases to be such a paradox, since the enactive approach posits that having a feeling is the same as *executing* an action, not just observing it, and it is obvious that we cannot execute someone else's actions (Ellis and Newton 1998a; Ellis 1999b).

But as we have seen, serious questions must be addressed to make this move work. First, what is the difference between "action" and "mere reaction"? Does a thermostat act, or only "react"? What if it is an extremely complex thermostat, with a number of feedback mechanisms in it? And if "action" means the unified, goal-directed action of a motivated and living being, then questions arise about the meaning of these terms. What is the defining difference between living beings and non-living ones? What does it mean to be motivated, rather than cleverly programmed to mechanically pursue an end, as robots do? A thermostat, one might argue, is not motivated in the sense relevant for our purposes, although it does systematically pursue an end.

If the response here has to do with "purposefully" as opposed to "non-purposefully" pursuing an end, then we are involved in a distinction with which twentieth century science did not do well. There do seem to be non-conscious purposeful activities in nature, as when salmon find their way upstream to return to their spawning areas in order to reproduce their species, or when overpopulated lemmings jump into the sea to avoid overshooting the population niche of their species. Presumably, the salmon and lemmings have no conscious awareness that these are the purposes of their activities, but they are purposeful nonetheless. The problem, then, is that purposeful activity cannot be defined simply in terms of conscious end-directed activity; otherwise, to explain consciousness with reference to its end-directed nature would become circular.

But the problem here is that twentieth-century philosophy has been able to understand purposefulness only as a kind of process that lends itself to anthropomorphism because of its resemblances to the processes that conscious beings can subjectively experience or imagine. On this view, the behavior of lemmings or salmon is not really purposeful, but only *resembles* purposeful behavior. Really, it is just as reactive and causally bottom-up as is the tendency of a thermostat to maintain a temperature. But if a thermostat is not purposeful or living, then certainly building more and more complex thermostats is not going to make them purposeful or living—that was the bitter lesson learned by computationalists who thought that building a more and more complex information processing machine would eventually facilitate building a *conscious* robot, the crowning feat that artificial intelligence engineers had promised to deliver by the end of the twentieth century. But the more general problem, with which we must all grapple, is to understand what it means for something to be "purposeful."

The question of the distinction between action and reaction is all the more important if we are to nail the entire difference between conscious and non-conscious information processing squarely onto this concept.

Our thesis is that humans differ from robots and zombies because our information processing not only is more complex than that of lower organisms, but also is emotionally motivated by the holistic homeostatic needs of a self-organizing system, which is able to plan actions through sensorimotor imagery and look for relevant patterns of environmental affordances. This combination of self-organization and sensorimotor imagery, with the latter organically emerging from the former (rather than added as an appendage), is the way we distinguish between "action" and mere "reaction." Some beings do not act because they are not self-organizing. Others are self-organizing, but do not generate action imagery rich enough to represent the world's affordances as a guide to action.

But two main types of objections immediately present themselves. The most obvious objection from those not familiar with this argument can be satisfied easily enough. Some will object that anticipatory expectations and organismic motivations seem unnecessary for certain types of conscious experiences. While driving a car, we may pay conscious attention to an advertisement on a billboard even though the product advertised has no interest for us. The consciousness seems completely passive, and the notion that it somehow was produced by active, emotionally motivated, and goal-oriented organismic activity rather than from passive and aimless causal inputs seems far-fetched to many people. Is the notion that *all* consciousness always results from agency rather than from passive stimulation really plausible?

But we have already seen that this objection overlooks the *broad, general* organismic interest in the environment. Given that is always *possible* that something in the environment might be important, we must pay a certain amount of attention to objects in the environment in order to *discover* whether they are important for our purposes. A general *curiosity* can motivate the active direction of attention to objects that are only possibly important for the organism's purposes (hence the title *Curious Emotions* for the Ellis 2005 book).

This broad vigilance toward objects in general may not determine attention as precisely as when something happens for which we are already specifically on the lookout—for example, when something suddenly runs across the road in front of us. But without motivational interest, at least of a general sort, there is no consciousness. Even when we are disinterestedly scanning the road ahead, no matter how much it may seem that we have no motivational anticipations for what is going to appear next, this complex network of anticipations will become immediately obvious if something completely unexpected should happen—

for example, if the car ahead should suddenly explode, or turn into a pigeon and fly away. Our feeling of surprise shows that we did have certain expectations about what was going to occur next, very much in the way we do when tracking the movement of a soccer ball. Our looking for the ball is a necessary condition for seeing it, and this looking is motivated by our desire to see it. If the ball turns up where we are not looking, we must reorient our pattern of looking before we can pick it up again.

Another variation on this first type of objection is that attention and conscious awareness are not the same thing. There are studies in which subjects *non-consciously* learn to execute tasks requiring attention, in the sense that an item must be distinguished from surrounding items and thus becomes a focus point for sensory and cognitive processing, while the surrounding items are not focused on in this way (Cohen et al. 1990; Bullemer and Nissen 1990). All of this occurs without any conscious awareness of the item on which "attention" has been focused in this way.

The easiest answer to this objection is that, although there can be attention without consciousness, there can be no consciousness without attention. The Mack and Rock (1998) perceptual studies clearly bear this out. Subjects who were occupied with an attentional task did not consciously see an irrelevant object, even though it was presented at or near the point of visual fixation, and even though it was presented in such a way that under normal conditions (as in control trials) it would have been seen. So, even though we may not be aware that the directing of attention is taking place during every conscious state—just as we may not be aware that we are focusing our eyes, performing searching movements, and so on—it is necessary nonetheless. We are accustomed to noticing the object of our consciousness rather than the subjective events that make it possible.

A related objection might be that we have contradicted ourselves by saying, on the one hand, that we can be oblivious to objects that are irrelevant to or incongruous with our expectations, yet on the other hand that we can be surprised when expectations are not met (for example, we are surprised if the TV set turns into a pigeon and flies away). The answer here is that if the unexpected event *interferes* with our expectation, then it *is* relevant to the expectation, and we notice the mismatch between our expectation and the perceptual input that interfered with it. This interference can work in the same way as when the attempt to imagine an object as pink interferes with the attempt to simultaneously imagine it as blue.

A more serious objection to the enactive account has to do with the distinction we have been assuming between afferent and efferent processes within the brain. It is difficult to designate a process as efferent or afferent when in fact any projection that leads *away* from one brain area also leads *toward* another. Moreover, most brain areas are highly interconnected by means of "afferents" and "efferents" that lead in all directions at once in massively complex patterns. The next section will address this issue.

3. The Afferent-Efferent Distinction

Because of the type of consideration just mentioned, a more serious problem is posed by the need to distinguish efferent from afferent processes. Humphrey posits that conscious processes must be efferent rather than afferent, since efferent processes are in some sense more active, whereas afferent ones are reactive. Afferent and efferent impulses are easy enough to distinguish in the parts of the nervous system that are outside of the brain, the former conveying information toward the brain, the latter away from it. But once we get inside the brain, it is difficult to say what is afferent and what is efferent.

There is of course a trivial sense in which an impulse, say from the motor cortex to the parietal lobe, is both efferent with respect to the motor cortex (that is, away from it) and afferent with respect to the parietal lobe (toward it). But in the sense Humphrey is referring to, "efferent" needs to mean something more general, and neurophysiologists do sometimes use the term in this more general sense: "efferent" can mean "directed by the central organism, toward the periphery," as opposed to "received from the periphery"—and in this sense we could say that an impulse that moves from the motor cortex to the parietal lobe is efferent, since the motor cortex is the prime example of a brain area whose purpose is to command bodily action. Can we meaningfully make this kind of distinction with all brain impulses?

Neurophysiological research shows that the posterior portion of the cortex receives incoming input from the senses (Hubel and Wiesel 1959; Posner and Petersen 1990; Warrington 1985). So we might designate these activities as afferent. And it is known that signals from the brain stem and other emotional subcortical areas spread activation upward into the anterior cingulate and prefrontal cortex (Posner and Rothbart 1992, 2000; Gray 1990; Lethin 2002, 2004; Luria 1980; Olds 1977), and from there to less "central" areas of the brain (if we take the emotional midbrain and PAG areas as "central"). So signals from the brain stem and anterior cingulate (as well as those from the brain stem *to* the anterior cingulate) might reasonably be regarded as "efferent" in the needed sense.

But as for the part of the brain "between" the brainstem areas and the posterior areas, more research must be done. There are of course differences between what happens in the primary projection areas of the various sensory modalities and the secondary sensory areas and the "association areas" of the parietal and temporal lobes (Aurell 1984, 1989; Luria 1973; Sperry 1966). EEG studies, PET scans, and other monitoring techniques show that incoming (afferent) sensory signals, after being relayed through the thalamus, first activate the primary sensory area which is at the surface of the occipital cortex, and then activate the secondary sensory area (Luria 1973; Hubel and Wiesel 1959). This secondary layer adjacent to the primary projection area contains "feature detectors" that react only to specific features of environmental images—some cells reacting to right angles, some to vertical lines, some to horizontal, and so on. So all of this activity is clearly *afferent* as opposed to efferent in the relevant sense.

We have already seen that *consciousness* of an object does *not* occur at the point when only these afferent activities of primary and secondary projection areas of the relevant sensory modality are observed (Aurell 1989; Posner and Rothbart 1992, 1998). Consciousness occurs only with the efferent activation of the limbic, anterior cingulate, and parietal areas, and this activation is not a direct causal result of primary or secondary projection area stimulation. This means that, consistently with the efferent-consciousness hypothesis, consciousness does not result passively from causal stimulation. The nerve impulse from the sensory organs (eyes, ears, and so on) to the primary projection area first passes through the thalamus, which, in connection with emotional processes of the upper brain stem, alerts the anterior cingulate and other frontal brain areas that some motivationally *important* input might be in the offing. If there is a feeling that there may be something worth paying attention to (an emotional value judgment in relation to the entire organism's homeostatic balance), then the frontal cortex begins formulating questions about what kind of information might be coming in from the environment (Luria 1973; Ellis 1995b; Lethin 2002, 2004), and whether it is likely to be relevant or important. If so, this prompts efferent input to the parietal and secondary sensory areas, resulting in the production of sensory and sensorimotor images. When these imaging activities of efferent areas find synchronized patterns of activity in the afferent areas, such as the primary projection area, only then does perceptual consciousness occur. Without the afferent input, the efferent activity would normally be consciously experienced as the mental image of a non-present object.

Agent-directed efferent activity as it gives rise to consciousness is well illustrated by the way the prefrontal lobe, when emotionally motivated, leads to imagistic and cognitive consciousness that also activates other brain areas. Luria sees the frontal lobe as "formulating the problem" to be solved by the brain (1973, 188). Thus, in Luria's view, the prefrontal lobe, which is clearly efferent, is active when we pose a problem or question to ourselves that requires that we do some thinking. Posner and Rothbart (1992) attribute an analogous role to the anterior cingulate (which is clearly efferent) in directing attention—a function that Mack and Rock (1998) find is essential for conscious perception. The Mack and Rock perceptual experiments show that we are unconscious of objects to which we are completely inattentive. The general rule is borne out: Efferent activity is essential to consciousness.

Function rather than *structure* defines the difference between efferent and afferent in all the examples just discussed. There is no boundary between a completely efferent area and a completely afferent area. The brain uses *functional* "modules" (Gazzaniga 1986)—widely distributed overlapping systems not confined to a simple structural location. While efferent activity may be more pronounced in anterior areas, and afferent activity more posterior, this is only because the posterior region receives input from the senses, while the anterior is controlled by the emotional-motivational system, which must determine the direction of attention.

Consciousness always involves efferent activity, defined as neural activity generated by the organism itself, for purposes of its own survival and well being, rather than from passive stimulation by incoming sensory signals. This is the important point. Consciousness results from a motivated searching operation; efferent activity must *select* certain incoming data as worthy of attention. Only after executing this purposeful process can the organism focus attention and produce the "looking-for" process needed for attention and imagery-formation. We know that this imaginal consciousness is associated with parietal activation, driven by frontal and anterior cingulate efferent activity, which in turn is driven by emotional-motivational purposes; this then leads to perceptual consciousness corresponding to the object whose input is activating the primary projection area. The parietal area, when it exhibits the "P300" electrical potential correlated with perceptual consciousness in EEG studies (for example Aurell 1989), is functionally the endpoint of a series of efferent activities.

We suggested earlier that perceptual consciousness, by contrast to passive, computer-like processing, always involves imagining what would happen *if* we were to do something actively (such as rotate the object, squeeze it, or drop it). If the subjunctive imagination of a possible sensorimotor activity is presupposed even by the perceptual consciousness of an object, then imagination is the most basic building block of perceptual consciousness, and the efferent always has primacy over the afferent. We are conscious of objects according to their action affordances, which can be imagined. This imagining of action affordances is facilitated by the motorically-initiated efferent brain commands that Damasio (1999) calls the "as if body loop."

This primacy of the efferent in all consciousness is also consistent with Tucker's (1981) thesis that efferent activity is oriented toward activating *motoric* behavior, and that consciousness is largely a truncated, imaginary motoric behavior. For example, we may remember a piece of music by imagining ourselves playing it. PET scans by Petersen et al. (1990) show that the anterior cingulate and the supplementary motor area—predominantly efferent areas in the relevant sense—are even involved in attention to language. And Damasio (1999), in a neurological tradition dating all the way back to Olds (1977), finds that there can be no consciousness unless the basal ganglia interact in certain specific patterns with the cortex. Imagination thus can be viewed as truncated motor behavior. To imagine an object is "as if" to anticipate acting in relation to its affordances. Motor neurons, in fact, mature earliest in ontogenesis (Restak 1984, 46–47). Moreover, Kimura and Archibald (1974), Studdert-Kennedy and Shankweiler (1970), and Liberman et al. (1967) show that speech evolves neurophysiologically as a truncated form of motoric behavior. To *think* a word is to *imagine* ourselves saying the word. Joseph (1982) emphasizes the role of this kind of self-talk during childhood in the development of adult cognitive skills.

All of this is well illustrated by the Held and Hein (1958) studies in which motoric (obviously efferent) action underlies development of perception in kittens. In essence, the kittens who from earliest infancy had been pulled around in carts by older cats behaved as if they were blind, bumping into objects and falling over edges. Objects "are seen . . . by means of the visual guidance of action" (Varela et al. 1991/1993, 174–75).

4. Agency and Self-Organization

Now if the efferent-afferent distinction is drawn functionally rather than structurally—if "efferent" means initiated by aim-oriented organismic activity—then the efferent-afferent distinction, in the sense relevant to this discussion, is derivative from the active-passive distinction. And this returns us to our original distinction between the living, agent-like, active, and purposeful on the one hand, and the nonliving, passive, merely reactive or mechanical on the other.

What is needed to make these distinctions work is a notion of self-organization that is well enough articulated in terms of causal processes to ground such distinctions. A thermostat is non-living and non-purposeful, not because it is not composed of carbon and hydrogen, and not because everything it does has a physical cause which is ultimately traceable to its external environment (for, if the data of science are to be believed, that must be true of all of us!); the thermostat is not living or purposeful because of the way thermostats and living things are *organized*. Self-organizing systems must have a special kind of causal structure, so that we can say "this process is active—is a purposeful agent—whereas that one is not."

But we saw earlier that the causal power of living organisms is a delicate issue. In a sense, living processes must be made up of smaller processes that are just as rigidly and mechanically caused as anything else in the universe. So the notion of the causal power of a living being—the power that makes it "unified" in such a way that it acts for its own purposes, rather than reacting to external forces—is a logically complex one.

Our approach to this problem is to apply self-organization theory, whose rich but recently neglected tradition traces back through Kauffman (1993) and Monod (1971) to Merleau-Ponty (1942) and the developmental biologists of the early twentieth century who were interested in the way embryos manage to appropriate available physical components to settle into the self-directed pattern of unfolding development (Bertalanffy 1933/1962). As we have seen, a self-organizing process is one whose organization creates a strong tendency to maintain itself across various alternative causal mechanisms at the level of the components making up the system. The structural pattern is not just multiply realizable, but actually plays an active role in appropriating the combinations of substrates needed to maintain the overall pattern. For purposes of applying the theory to the problem of mental causation, and thus to the mind-body problem (for example Thelen and Smith 1994; Mac Cormack and Staminov 1996; Freeman 1975, 1987; Edelman 1989), the problem is to understand how the system is *self-maintaining* across multiply realizable substrates, some available subset of which the system actively seeks out, appropriates, replaces, and reproduces.

All biological organisms are self-maintaining in this sense. There is no assumption here that "artificial" systems could not also manifest such functional patterns. The issue is not whether the system is composed of certain specific elements such as silicon or carbon, but rather the functional dynamics of the system.

Open thermodynamic systems continuously exchange constituent components and energy with their environment, yet maintain homeostatic constancies across these exchanges. These constancies preserve the continuity of the structural organization. The organism learns and remembers new perceptual patterns by creating new basins of attraction structurally related to the learned stimulus pattern (Freeman 1987; Alexander and Globus 1996). It remembers a familiar action pattern that the particular stimulus pattern affords; a particularly surprising pattern throws the system into momentary chaos, until holistic reorganization is achieved.

An implication of dynamical systems theory as applied to emotions is that a specific motivation, say the desire to raise my hand, results ultimately from the organism's self-organizing tendency. This self-organizing structure is therefore present, and embodies a tendency for me to want to raise the hand, even before the desire becomes pronounced enough to be a conscious awareness. Thus the "expectancy wave" accompanying the decision to raise the hand is measurable *before* I am aware of a decision or desire to raise it (Libet 1983; Young 1988, 164ff). Expectancy waves (also manifested in Libet's "readiness potential") indicate that motivational feelings arise out of the organism's generally self-organizing nature.

The upper brain stem area, including midbrain, PAG, and Raphe nuclei, monitors this chemical homeostasis throughout the entire self-organizing system of the body, and sends efferent commands (via the neurotransmitters Ach, DA, EN, NE & 5HT) for action aimed at restoring homeostasis. These commands are sent to the thalamus, hypothalamus, cingulate, amygdala, and so on, and ultimately through the anterior cingulate and frontal lobes to the rest of the cortex. Efferent (anticipatory) imagery at this point has to do with anticipated actions, which automatically correlate with anticipated object affordances. Afferent feedback from real objects can convert the efferent imagery into perceptual consciousness, but the efferent imagery already can be conscious with or without afference. The various deficiencies that can occur in this entire process are illustrated by the different forms of automatism, akinetic mutism, and persistent vegetative states (in which there is minimal consciousness and attention, even if "perceptual areas" are intact) discussed by Damasio (1999).

5. The Mind-Body Problem Revisited

Does such a theory "solve" the mind-body problem? Our view may be more modest on this point than Humphrey's. First of all, it is important to be clear about what the mind-body problem consists of, and to acknowledge its true difficulty. We should distinguish between the mind-body problem on the one hand, and on the other hand the "hard problem of consciousness" that Chalmers talks about. All too often in recent consciousness research, these two problems are conflated.

The mind-body problem, as we have suggested throughout this book, is not just a question that is difficult to answer, but a paradox. On the one hand, consciousness does not seem to be equivalent with its physiological substratum, for reasons of the kind the knowledge argument presents; but on the other hand, if consciousness were not equivalent with something physical, then we would be confronted with the well-known problems of dualism, which as we discussed earlier are formidable.

Let's not forget what the main problem of dualism is. It is that it fails to make sense of the causal power of consciousness. When I raise my hand, certain physical nervous events are completely sufficient to account for the hand's going up. Yet it feels to me as if my conscious decision to raise it is necessary to make it go up. If the physical antecedents were sufficient to make it go up, then nothing else should be necessary to make it go up. So we want to say that the physical antecedents are sufficient for the hand's going up, and at the same time that something else, a conscious decision, is necessary for it. This seems like a logical contradiction, unless we assume that the physical and mental events are equivalent. Of course, if two events are equivalent, then they both can be both necessary and sufficient for the same outcome. This was the main argument that prompted cognitive theorists to embrace psychophysical identity theories in the first place—because they eliminate the problem of mental causation. But by avoiding the Charybdis of mental causation in this way, strict identity theories are consumed by the Scilla of the knowledge argument. The mind-body problem, then, is essentially a logical paradox resulting from the causal role of consciousness.

The fact that mind and body seem indescribable in commensurable languages—which leads to Chalmers' "hard problem"—is really a much *easier* problem than the mind-body problem. The hard problem merely shows that we have a phenomenon, consciousness, that in principle is difficult to explain. If we give a physical explanation for a state of consciousness, X, by showing what caused its physical substrata, Y, the question will always remain as to why the physical event Y has the property of consciousness.

However, this "hard problem," despite its name, is not as serious a problem as the mind-body problem. The mind-body problem does not consist merely in the fact that consciousness is difficult to explain, but rather in the apparent fact that every possible explanation for it will still lead to *self-contradictions,* because no proposed explanation can explain how a mental event can cause a physical one without thereby rendering the physical antecedents of the event insufficient to cause it. While the hard problem points out the difficulty in understanding why some physical events have consciousness, the mind-body problem points out that the very notion of there being both physical and conscious events is self-contradictory, because as soon as we posit this apparent fact, there seems to be no way to resolve its contradictory causal implications.

To solve the mind-body problem therefore requires more than just showing how the same event can be described in a way that makes both physical and phenomenological sense. It requires also that we show how the causal properties of the physical and phenomenological events do not contradict each other.

Now suppose that, as Humphrey has argued, consciousness can occur only as a result of an organismic activity, and is equivalent with efferent rather than with afferent nervous activity. The question remains as to what kind of causal power this consciousness-equated-with-efferent-activity has. Does it resolve Jackson's knowledge argument? Suppose a biologist knows all about self-organizing thermodynamic systems, and all about efferent nervous activity. Will that enable the biologist to know what the subject's consciousness is like? This does not seem obviously to follow.

Monod's and Kauffman's concepts of self-organization seem to present the only feasible way to resolve the problem of mental causation *and at the same time* the problem of private access highlighted by the knowledge argument. Self-organization does not entail a dualism or a causal interactionism: the process does not *cause* the behavior of its substratum elements. Instead, the behavior of each substratum element is caused by other substratum level components that are both necessary and sufficient, under the given background conditions, to bring about that behavior—as shown extensively, for example, by Bickle (2002). But the self-organization of the organism in which this behavior occurs is partly responsible for having set up, at each moment, the given background conditions under which those antecedents are necessary and sufficient for those consequences. If the needed antecedents for a behavior are not available, the self-organizing organism is structured so that it can change some of its other functions to allow some *other* mechanism, such as a "shunt mechanism," to be used as the necessary and sufficient antecedent of that same behavior. A typical example is the reorganization of brain function in stroke recovery. Even though the specific behavior of each substratum element is caused by a substratum level component which is necessary and sufficient to produce it under the given background conditions, the structure of the self-organizing process as a whole is such that those given circumstances will tend to be changed when that is what is needed to maintain the overall process as such.

The complex self-organizing process constitutive of the emotionally motivated efferent processes needed for the subject's phenomenal consciousness are experientially accessible only from the standpoint of the organism that executes them, because conscious experiencing per se entails executing rather than merely observing emotional processes. That is why self-organization is the key to solving the mind-body problem—because it promises to address the paradox of mental causation without requiring an out and out rejection of either horn of the dilemma: causal closure on the one hand (at least at the level of molecules), and the fact of mental causation on the other.

We want to be as clear as possible about what we are saying and not saying about the hard problem. Our point is not simply that correlation has no causal implications. In scientific research and theorizing, well-controlled and scientifically well-reasoned inferences from correlations *do* have causal implications. But our point is this: Suppose we assume that the correlation between conscious state C and physical process P does have some causal implications. The correlation would not imply that P causes C, because that would make P and C into *separate entities,* which would imply dualism, and as we have already seen, there are many problems with dualism.

The point is that the correlation between C and P, if we want to avoid dualism, cannot simply imply that P causes C, since removing all causal power from C would make C into a non-physical entity, if we grant that all physical entities have some causal power. So the other alternative interpretation of the correlation between C and P is that the same antecedents that cause C are also the ones that cause P. This is what leads psychophysical identity theorists to conclude that C = P. Now we saw earlier that Jackson's knowledge argument makes "C = P" into a slight bit of an oversimplification (see Ellis 1986), but we do at least agree with the vast majority of neuroscientists that C and P are ontologically inseparable in some strong way.

Regardless of whether we think that C and P are merely ontologically inseparable, or whether we want to make the even stronger claim that C = P, there is still an aspect of Chalmers's "hard problem" argument that must be addressed. The part of the "hard problem" point that is important and worth taking seriously is that showing that C = P (or is ontologically inseparable from it, or has some other relation to it) is not the *same thing* as explaining what causes P (and thus presumably also causes C). So, when someone says "If we can completely explain P (and all other such brain processes), then we've explained consciousness," they are missing an important element of what is actually needed for an explanation. Besides a causal explanation of P, it is also necessary to show what the *ontological relationship* between C and P is—for example, whether that particular C equals that particular P (and not P2 or P3, or some other complex pattern of Ps). The point is not to say that establishing this relationship is impossible, but simply that it is a *different* project from explaining P, and it is a project that requires some philosophy and not merely empirical observation plus inductive scientific reasoning. Simply put, to show that P = C is not the same thing as scientifically explaining P and then showing that it correlates with C. Even though this is a very modest epistemological point, it is pragmatically very important, because many cognitive scientists in our view are prone to pick out the *wrong* P (a P that is too simple and too linear) to connect with C.

So the point is that there are two things that need to be shown in order to explain C: 1. we must show what the relation is between C and P—for example, that C = P (and not P2 or P3 for example), or that C is ontologically inseparable from P in some strong way; and 2. we must physically explain P. In this book, the part of the job we want to do is mostly 1., which includes choosing the right P to do it with. Any P that is not self-organizing, for example, will be the wrong kind of P. But we can also become somewhat specific about what the nature of P must be in order for it to ground such a thing as C. It is to Chalmers's credit that he recognizes (in one of the many ways he states his hard problem), that accomplishing just 2. without 1. is the easy part of consciousness studies, and 1. is the hard part.

Where we do *not* agree with Chalmers, however, is when he not only thinks we have to show what the relationship between C and P is (for example that C = P), but he also demands that we show *why* C and P have the relation that they do (for example, *why* C = P). Like Levine, Chalmers thinks such an explanation would mean showing that P *deductively entails* C. Such a demand seems impossible because knowing all about P doesn't tell us all we need to know about C, since it doesn't tell us what C would feel like. The problem is that, if we had never felt anything at all, then we would not be able to deduce what C felt like from knowing all the empirical facts about P. This would be a problem even if we could deduce what C would feel like from the conjunction of (a) all the empirical facts about P; and (b) the empirical facts showing what the relation is between C and P (for example, that C = P). But, in order to know that C = P (or any other relation between C and P), we would also already have to know what C *means*, and to know this, we would have to have some idea what C would feel like whenever it did occur.

For example, suppose C is a feeling of poignant sadness while watching a sunset. We can plug in this conscious state in place of the "C" in the above point and it becomes obvious that if we know (a) without (b), of course we have not explained that feeling. And in order to know (b), we would have to know what feeling it is that we are trying to explain. If we do know what this feeling feels like, then we can go about our scientific work, asking ourselves at each point "Let's see if this or that empirical observation correlates with that particular feeling." If we lack the concept of the feeling itself, then we don't know whether a given empirical observation correlates with it, because we don't know what we are trying to correlate the empirical observations *with*.

Suppose we can correlate certain brain processes with a cat's saying "meow" in a certain way when he looks at the sunset. We still would not know that saying "meow" in that particular way was an expression of a certain feeling C unless we already had the concept of what C feels like, and we could not have that based only on empirical observations.

So, in order to know that C = P (or any other relation between C and P), we have to understand something about what C is—intentionally and not just extensionally (in other words, you would have to know *what* it means for something to be a C, and not just that C is the phenomenon that occupies position PQR in space-time). That is, we have to understand what it is for consciousness to be a phenomenal state in order to refer to it, and we cannot understand that without referring to our own experience. To understand what we are referring to is to understand its *intentional* meaning. For example, we may attach different *intentional* meanings to the terms "Morning Star" and "Evening Star," and then subsequently discover that they are *extensionally* the same entity. To know what C means intentionally, we would have to know that there is something C feels like; but if we had never felt anything, we could not know that. This is why we defined the sense of the word "consciousness" we are using by referring to Block's "phenomenal consciousness," and then further spelled it out by saying that phenomenal consciousness includes that there is "something it is like" to have the consciousness.

Of course, everyone, including any observing scientist, *has* felt some things, and thus can know what consciousness is like. But our point is simply an epistemological one: knowing what C feels like is a different item of knowledge from knowing what causes P to occur, and knowing that C = P is still another item of knowledge. Once we have the concept of C, then it becomes possible to show by using a combination of philosophical arguments and empirical observations that C has a strongly inseparable ontological relationship with P, and sooner or later, scientists will be able to show what causes P (and thus *ipso facto* what causes C); but we couldn't know what this relation between C and P is unless we first knew what C is, and this in turn requires having felt something subjectively.

This is why we say that this modest version of the hard problem (which is much more modest than some of Chalmers's other versions, involving zombies, imagining possible worlds, and the like) really trades on the same basic issue as Jackson's knowledge argument—because the problem is to show what the relation between C and P is (which in turn entails knowing what C is) independently of knowing what causes P.

So explaining C involves more than just giving a causal explanation of P. It also requires showing what the relation between C and P is (for example, that C = P), which in turn requires knowing what C means intentionally and not just extensionally. Chalmers goes a step further than this, and argues that we *cannot* show what the relation between C and P is (for example, that C = P), and on this further point we disagree with him.

It is true that even a robot unable to know what consciousness is like could form the concept that "humans act as if motivated by some inexplicable, invisible force," and thus conclude that "that brain pattern must have some unique effect on humans," and thus define it functionally and call it "consciousness." But the robot at that point would not be intentionally referring to what we mean by "consciousness." It would be referring to it *extensionally* but not *intentionally*. That is, it would be pointing to whatever process it is that occupies space-time segment PQR, without knowing everything that can be known about *what* the process is that occupies that space-time segment. The computer would not know what X feels like, or even that it feels like anything at all.

None of this entails that consciousness is an epiphenomenon or lacks causal power. Of course, we can show (using philosophical arguments and not empirical facts by themselves) that consciousness is inseparable from a physical process, and thus has all the causal powers of that physical process. And of course, it is conceivable (though very unlikely) that a robot or even a collection of human scientists could identify the unique set of physical causal antecedents (P) that are equivalent with a conscious state (C), and conclude that whatever C is, it must have the causal powers of P. They could even define C functionally as the thing that has the causal powers of P (although in this case it would seem that the concept of C would just be equivalent with the concept P). But our point is that in order to know that this C with which P is equivalent is a state of *consciousness*, they would have to know what the state of consciousness feels like, or at least that it feels like something, because if not, then they would be understanding what C refers to only extensionally, and not intentionally. This would not be referring to phenomenal consciousness as we have defined it, but something more like "access" consciousness—the ability to receive information or to respond behaviorally, such as is possessed by a computer or robot.

So, when observing the cat's meow (and all the limbic and subcortical processes that accompany it), we know with reasonable certainty that it is feeling C, because we already understand what C feels like, and we know that whenever we feel C (or something close to it), we have similar limbic and subcortical processes to the ones we observe in the cat; thus, with some degree of certainty, we can conclude that what the cat is doing actually feels like something, and is not just a non-conscious behavioral process—as Panksepp (1998) has argued so eloquently.

The enactive approach points us in the direction we must go if we are to solve the mind-body problem, but it only provides a necessary, not a sufficient set of conditions needed for this solution. The additional ingredient, as we showed earlier, is to explain how a self-organizing or dynamical system can have a kind of causal power over its own substrata, which is not reducible to the sum of the actions of the substrata, while at the same time causal closure is not violated at the substratum level. Any such causal analysis must use a theory of self-organization as its starting point, since only a dynamical system promises to offer the possibility of a system's having the power to appropriate substratum elements into its own basins of attraction, rather than letting those basins be merely a *higher-level description* of the independent actions of the substrata. That is why we believe that a self-organizational and action-based theory of consciousness is necessary for any solution to the mind-body problem.

10

Connecting Physiology with Phenomonology

In one sense, it seems obvious that phenomenology has followed a line of development that is extremely divergent from the "path more traveled by" of the physical sciences. In phenomenology, one "brackets off" empirical knowledge of the world in order to focus on purely subjective experience, while the physical sciences by contrast function within what Husserl (1900/1913, 1913/1931) called the "natural attitude." The natural attitude proceeds as if what is revealed through the senses were simply as it presents itself; the categories that work so well for our understanding of the physical are then applied to ourselves and our own consciousness, leading to the plethora of mind-body problems we have been discussing here. So, in the twentieth century, phenomenology and natural science (along with the attendant "analytic" approach to philosophy) tended to be at odds with each other; in practical terms, this meant that for the most part they ignored each other.

Although phenomenology and the physical sciences seemed to have moved along different and independent paths, in another sense they have been on a collision course with each other for at least the past century, because the empirical observations that ground the brain sciences are human experiences that must be integrated into a coherent picture of the manifold of experience, yet these sciences are difficult to reconcile with the subjective data revealed by a phenomenological approach to consciousness. For similar reasons, it was inevitable that, sooner or later, the brain sciences would also have to take phenomenology seriously, because it was impossible to explain the phenomenon of consciousness from within a theoretical perspective so constrained by the natural attitude that nothing can be seen but the objective, so that the purely subjective phenomenon of *consciousness itself* cannot enter the epistemological picture.

At the point where consciousness intersects with brain function, the empirical data of experience have remained incoherent with the fact of experience itself, and a reconciliation is necessary.

Merleau-Ponty always sought *not* to reject physiological psychology, but to integrate it with the experience of the living body. On the one hand, it is important not to confuse the lived body (*Leib*) with the abstractions constructed from empirical observation of corpses and other intentional objects (*Körper*), which can be there only *for* some lived body (Merleau-Ponty 1941/62, 75ff). But on the other hand, as Wertz summarizes Merleau-Ponty, perception itself "is possible only because the body, neither a thing closed within itself nor an unextended idea, is sensitive to things as one among them in their very order" (Wertz 1987, 120). The body as subject must be reconciled with the body as part of the experienceable world.

For a century now, the physical cognitive sciences and phenomenology have tried to avoid this necessary confrontation. Cognitive science, for its part, tried to avoid the issue of consciousness altogether. Phenomenology, ironically, also veered away from studying consciousness directly, because it proved impossible to reflect on experience in a completely unprejudiced way—to perform a complete "phenomenological reduction" of experience to its presuppositionless purity so as to describe conscious states with no distortion due to preconceived categories (Merleau-Ponty 1941; Husserl 1954). Because of this perceived inability to reflect without prejudices, phenomenology gave way, in the eyes of many "continental style" philosophers, to an epistemologically relative "postmodernism" which avoids the constraints of acknowledging that there *is* any reality behind appearances and constructions. To use Husserl's phenomenological terminology, they denied that there is any "phenomenological residuum" left after the attempt to "bracket out" cultural, historical and psychological presuppositions from the "raw data" of subjective experience. This led postmodernism also to eschew the study of consciousness itself, because the very concept "consciousness" seemed laden with Cartesian dualistic presuppositions (see for instance Mensch 1996). Postmodernists have been suspicious of the term "consciousness," because it seems to suggest the existence of a separate ego-subject, standing over against an object that it "represents." In their view, this subject-object relation is an artificial creation of modernity (Globus 1995). They argue that the "modernist" notion of consciousness presupposes such a bifurcated subject-object relation, which has artificially created the need to choose between a mind-body dualism and its equally problematic alternative, reductionistic physicalism. Modernism has encouraged naive-objectivist epistemologies such as empiricism and logical positivism; it leads to misunderstandings of the "unconscious" and of the role of unconscious interpretive (or "hermeneutic") contributions to the ways people experience reality; it exacerbates the problems of psychological egoism and a social science that falsely treats the individual as an "atomist" unit of analysis, with the attendant unworkable approaches to social, political, and even economic theory; and these are just a few of the worst problems that postmodernists argue can be blamed on the subject-object paradigm and the related notion of individual consciousness. So the notion of individual "consciousness" carried too much baggage for the postmodernists, and they became skeptical of it as a concept.

Mainstream philosophers of mind and cognitive theorists have also ignored or denied consciousness, but for different reasons. The computer metaphor, combined with an insistence on reducing "the mental" to something scientifically (and "physically") explainable, have led to an epistemology that allows only the objective to appear. So the computational model of mind, which viewed consciousness as merely an epiphenomenon of unconscious computational processes in the brain, became a strange ally of postmodernism. For computationally oriented neurophilosophers and scientists, the attempt to understand the aspects of experiential systems (such as human minds) that are *not* analogous to computer functioning, or to *partes extra partes* mechanical systems, had to be ignored.

But the time for avoiding a reconciliation of phenomenological and empirical scientific approaches to consciousness has now run out. While the popular intellectual trends of postmodernism and information processing theory have moved away from the attempt to understand consciousness, recent findings in contemporary neuroscience call for the reintroduction of considerations about consciousness and the mind-body problem that are convergent with those put forward by phenomenologists.

After a long struggle, cognitive theorists and neuroscientists finally seem to have produced a revolution against the exclusion of consciousness, and are increasingly receptive to a phenomenological approach to the experiential dimension of reality. This radical change has occurred only within the past few years.

As with any revolutionary situation, the outcome is not guaranteed. Many ways of studying consciousness present themselves as options, ranging from Buddhism to a quantum approach to a revival of Berkeleyan idealism. Our view is that phenomenology, notwithstanding its postmodernist critics, has the resources to ensure that the brain sciences can become coherent with a careful and faithful approach to conscious experience, if only phenomenology can reconcile *itself* to the fact that the data of brain science must be accorded their due respect within a coherent epistemological and ontological picture. It is true that this picture must no longer be interpreted simply within the "natural attitude" and dominated by a mechanical worldview, with its unworkable forms of representationalism, atomistic individualism, naive empiricist epistemology, and consequently incommensurable languages describing the subjective and objective dimensions. This chapter discusses the way we see the action-based approach to the philosophy of mind as finally able to be consistent with phenomenology.

1. Self-Organization and Psychophysical Forms

Neurophysiological studies (such as Aurell 1989; Posner and Rothbart 1992; Damasio 1994; and a neglected but important aspect of the work of Luria 1980, on the attention-focusing role of the emotionally-influenced frontal-limbic system) increasingly suggest that information processing takes place by means of different brain activities depending on whether it occurs on a conscious or non-conscious basis. We have argued that consciousness occurs only when *efferent* nervous activity takes the lead in selecting and directing *afferent* activity; conscious beings are self-organizing, emotionally and motivationally directed beings that actively direct their attention, can imagine things with no afferent input (with neural substrates remarkably similar to those in the imaging activities in perceptual consciousness—see Richardson 1991, for example), and do so as a result of formulating their own questions about reality rather than just passively reacting to stimulus-response mechanisms (Ellis 1995b, 2005). These kinds of realizations about differences between purposeful conscious organisms and passive information-processing machines lead to an emphasis on motivation and emotion as playing some as yet poorly understood role in directing attention, conjuring imagery, and facilitating the unique features of conscious beings just listed (see for example Cytowic 1993; Watt 1998, 2000; Faw 2000, 2003).

Notice the convergence with phenomenology that the self-organizational kind of approach makes possible. Merleau-Ponty emphasized that the solution to the mind body problem hinged on a concept of "psychophysical forms" (Merleau-Ponty 1942/67), which he defined in this way: "'Forms' . . . are defined as total processes whose properties are not the sum of those which the isolated parts would possess. . . . We will say that there is form whenever the properties of a system are modified by every change brought about in a single one of its parts and, on the contrary, are conserved when they all change while maintaining the same relationship among themselves" (Merleau-Ponty 1942/67, 47). For Merleau-Ponty, living beings, of which conscious beings are a further elaboration, can appropriate the needed material substrata to maintain their patterns of life, rather than merely having their forms be caused *by* those substrata. In this way, life and indeed consciousness itself can have causal powers that are not reducible to the sum total of the causal powers of their micro-constituents. There can be genuine activity and not mere passivity in nature, if we look for it in the right places. Thus "the relations between the organism and its milieu are not relations of linear causality but of circular causality" (Merleau-Ponty 1942/67, 15).

But this solution to the mind-body problem must also make sense of the data we find *within* empirical experience, especially within science. For example, any free will we can posit must not demand that brain processes contain ruptures in the regularities that are typically observed in physical and chemical processes, when no such ruptures in fact present themselves in experience. To acknowledge this is consistent with what Merleau-Ponty (1942/63) calls "the truth of naturalism." If the subjective data of experience must be phenomenologically reduced in order to get at their meaning, and if, as Merleau-Ponty (1941) says and the later Husserl (1954) agrees, no complete phenomenological reduction can ever be possible (if there is no such thing as a presuppositionless take on our own subjective experience), then "immediate subjective data" cannot be so completely privileged compared with the most coherent possible accounts of empirical experience as to allow us simply to reject or ignore any empirical experience that is in conflict with subjective experience. We must always seek more coherent resolutions of such conflicts.

The new directions in cognitive theory integrate subjective experience with natural science in a way that is congruent with Merleau-Ponty in still another respect. Instead of sidestepping the empirical scientific observations that present regular causal patterns in chemical and physical phenomena—including those occurring in the brain—the new "embodiment" and "enaction" theories open up natural science itself to the task of coherently reconciling linear causal regularities with the causal power of self-organizing systems, of which living organisms are examples. A notable example is the work of Shaun Gallagher (2005). Gallagher's book is a good example of the second developmental stage of a new theory, in which testable hypotheses begin to be explored. This theory, the embodiment of cognition, holds that our minds are shaped by our bodies. Gallagher's concern is to develop a conceptual structure in which two crucial concepts, *body image* and *body schema,* can be used to undersetand consciousness. This distinction is similar to the way Ellis (2005) also defines it: "body image" is primarily based on information that we have *about* ourselves through perception, proprioception, and various thought processes, whereas "body schema" emphasizes the motor commands that we send to our bodies. In other words, we know ourselves by means of what we are telling our bodies to do. Gallagher applies this framework to matters such as the mind-body problem and knowledge of other people. He demonstrates growing empirical evidence of constraints on consciousness imposed by prereflective body awareness, including temporal structures and intentional perceptual experience. He uses various philosophical issues to refine the schema/image, concluding with some justified optimism about the value of this framework for future exploration of the body's role in human nature.

Approaches such as this entail that the idea of a complex dynamical system which actively appropriates and replaces its own parts, and thus is "emergent" in the sense we have been discussing, does not contradict the observation that a material component within the system can serve as a sufficient cause for each material consequent within the system, under the appropriate background conditions; thus the demand for "causal closure" (Kim 1992) is met. Yet the system as a whole is organized so that it can change background conditions as needed to make use of different causal components as they become available. That a system could be organized so as to consistently accomplish this purpose is perhaps the most astonishing feature of living processes, yet we see it happening in biological organisms all the time.

This is why a phenomenological reflection can reveal that the decision to raise our hand is necessary to cause the hand to go up, while at the same time certain chemical reactions in components of the system can also simultaneously present themselves as being completely sufficient to cause the hand to go up. The conscious decision is an aspect of a broad self-organizing motivational tendency of the organism, and occurs at the level where background conditions can be rearranged. But we can always trace each component physical or chemical event to some prior component physical or chemical event, once the new background conditions for these causal relations have been arranged by the self-organizing system as a whole.

Recall that our view requires that time, as well as three-dimensional space, be incorporated into the model of the mind-brain relation. That is, only if *background conditions* have been organized appropriately in the organism's *past* will the current chemical reactions in system components be sufficient causes of voluntary action. In the same way, the system, when in disequilibrium, reorganizes background conditions in order that in the (immediate or distant) future, those altered conditions will be sufficient causes of voluntary action. In any given time-slice, if we ignorer the organism's past manipulation of those background conditions, the only detectable causes of action will appear to be the immediate biochemical reactions underlying them, which at that moment, and considered in isolation, are both necessary and sufficient for the action, under the given background conditions which have already previously been manipulated by the organism itself.

The point we now want to make is that this conceptualization of the relation between a self-organizing system and its material substrata perfectly fits Merleau-Ponty's notion of "psychophysical forms" as a solution to the mind-body problem. If consciousness is an aspect of a self-organizing pattern of activity, then it is not reducible to the ontological status of its material components—in somewhat the same way that a sound wave is not reducible to (equivalent with or caused by) the material components of the wooden door through which the sound passes. The sound wave could have been the same sound wave if it had passed through a different medium; and rather than the door's causing the wave to have the pattern it has, it is the wave that causes the material components of the door to vibrate as they do. But in the case of living organisms (unlike sound waves), the pattern of activity is not only distinguishable from its medium; the pattern also organizes and appropriates the needed media for its own activity.

Like Merleau-Ponty in *The Structure of Behavior,* the new embodiment theorists, along with the recent dynamical systems theorists in chemistry and biology, are suggesting that an organism, insofar as possible, will purposely rearrange some of its parts if that is what is necessary to maintain the desired functioning of the whole, given a disruption of the functioning of one of its parts. The use of one component can "compensate" for the unavailability of another. There are obvious examples of this in the brain. If a right hemispherectomy is performed early in life, the left hemisphere will take over many functions that otherwise would have been handled by the right brain. After a stroke, new nerve pathways can be developed to circumvent the ones that have been destroyed, insofar as the available materials in the affected brain area permit redeployment, and insofar as the attempt is made. It is well known among stroke rehabilitation specialists that one of the main determinants of speech restoration after a stroke is that the patient must continually *make an effort* to say the sounds corresponding to the destroyed neural connections (for example, see Restak 1984, 256; Springer and Deutsch 1981, 173–212). As Aristotle would have it, the guiding purposes of the organism as a whole allow some of the parts to rearrange themselves so as to maintain the desired functioning of the whole.

One of Merleau-Ponty's examples of this kind of self-organization is that, in cases of development of a "pseudo-fovea," the eyes change the functioning of the cones and rods from their original anatomical programming. In cases of hemianopsia, the subject is rendered blind in half of each retina, so that he now has the use of only two half retinas, yet it is found that the eye re-orients itself so that, rather than each half-retina corresponding to half a visual field, "the preserved retinal sector has established itself in a central position in the orbit instead of remaining affected, as before the illness, by the reception of light rays coming from one half of the field" (Merleau-Ponty 1942/67, 40–41). Thus the subject has the impression of seeing poorly in the entire visual field, rather than seeing clearly in only half of it. Also, as Merleau-Ponty notes, Fuchs (1922) has found that all the colors are perceived by the new fovea even though it is now situated in a retinal area which in a normal subject would be blind to red and green. "If we adhere to the classical conceptions which relate the perceptual functions of each point of the retina to its anatomical structure—for example, to the proportion of cones and rods which are located there—the functional reorganization in hemianopsia is not comprehensible" (41). Merleau-Ponty is arguing that in organisms the whole will readjust the functioning of some of its parts when other parts are disrupted in order to maintain the original function of the whole. Other examples of self-directed neurophysiological reorganization following localized brain injury or trauma can be found in Restak (1984, 360ff). Kandel and Schwartz (1981) also emphasize the plasticity of the brain in reorganizing itself to accomplish its objectives by getting around disruptions in one way or another. For example, if brain cells of an embryo are transplanted to a different region of another embryo, they are transformed into cells appropriate to that region. Sometimes this can be done even across species.

2. The Interdependence of Emotional and Perceptual Consciousness

What may be really exciting about the new developments in cognitive theory is that they not only show a new openness to a genuinely phenomenological investigation of subjective consciousness, but they also point toward a coherent integration of phenomenological data *with* those of empirical science. They make possible a way to think of the brain as a physiological substrate of consciousness without reducing consciousness to the action of those substrates, *and at the same time* without contradicting the empirically experienceable data, which seem to leave no room for ruptures in the regular behavior of chemical and physical phenomena as they are observed in scientific experience. Moreover, as we have seen, the paradoxical aspects of the way subjectivity creates apparent properties of objects can be systematically respected.

In large part, the new approach arose from modern science's failure to solve several anomalies that arise for mechanistic approaches to consciousness within the natural attitude, necessitating an entirely new way to think about consciousness, not merely a deletion of the concepts of consciousness and subjectivity from the philosophical and scientific vocabulary: First, as we have already noted, consciousness presents itself as an *enacting of* rather than a *passive reaction to* the physical events that serve as its substratum; but neither is it the nonphysical half of an ontological dualism. A related anomaly was that mechanistic causes at the empirically observable level seem to *underexplain* consciousness, because as Chalmers (1995) points out, even if we can show that some proposed empirically observable mechanism correlates with consciousness, this does not explain why those same mechanisms could not occur *in the absence* of consciousness. Thus the physical mechanism by itself cannot serve as an explanation *for* consciousness, since the question as to why such a physical mechanism should be accompanied by consciousness would ipso facto remain *unexplained*.

But, ironically, still another anomaly for mechanistic cognitive science was that mechanistic causes also seem to *overexplain* consciousness, in the sense that they provide necessary and sufficient physical antecedents for any given event, so that no causal power is left for consciousness; yet we know that conscious intentions do play a role in bringing about many movements of our bodies. Mechanism's best attempt to avoid this anomaly was the thesis of psychophysical identity, which failed in its classic versions because it is impossible to know what a state of consciousness is like merely by knowing everything that can be known empirically about its underlying physical mechanisms.

3. The Phenomenology of Conscious Attention

We have argued that the needs of the organism as a whole first motivate the *asking of questions* about what kinds of environmental stimuli *might* be important for the organism's purposes; at this point, the frontal lobe becomes active, and the categories in terms of which these questions are posed are not in terms of lines and angles, but rather meanings—the sinister smile, or the disorganization resulting from the unnoticed crooked picture frame. As these preconceptual questions are formulated with the help of the frontal lobe, the brain then begins to form vague images and/or concepts of the kinds of potentially important objects that *might* be present. When all of this frontal-limbic-parietal activity, once having been developed, finds itself *resonating* with activity in the occipital lobe (which reflects sensory stimulation)—only then does perceptual consciousness of objects occur. The parietal lobe (which is active when we are *conscious* of visual images) is not activated in *response* to the occipital lobe's activity, as in the causal-chain, stimulus-response paradigm. Instead, the organism must purposely activate the frontal and parietal lobes to "look *for*" potentially important categories which the thalamus has already alerted the organism *might* be relevant, from the standpoint of action affordances, and this "looking for" activity has already begun the forming of visual or conceptual imagery (including proprioceptive and sensorimotor imagery) *prior to* any occipital activity's having any effect on our perceptual consciousness (since at this point the impulse has not yet "traveled" from the occipital to the parietal lobe). The frontal-parietal system is not a *response* to an *occipital stimulus,* but rather must *already* have taken place before perceptual consciousness is possible; the frontal-parietal pattern *determines* whether any given sensory "input" will even *register* in consciousness, in other words whether it will be attended to.

It is true that the imagery to which attention will be directed may be *triggered* by some stimulus input. But the trigger stimulus is not the intentional object of the resulting consciousness. For example, when a soccer player kicks the ball, we know from the direction of his approach, his body posture and his foot movements where to look for the ball. And at each moment of the ball's trajectory, we know where to look because of where the ball was at previous moments. This is why, in experiments involving the visual tracking of moving objects, there is no delay in the registering of the stimulus in consciousness when the subject has already been tracking the object, which is moving in a continuous trajectory (see Aurell 1984, 1989; Srebro 1985; McHugh and Bahill 1985; Changizi 2008). But if something surprising should happen—if for example the soccer player through some deceptive movement manages to kick the ball backwards while appearing to kick forward, we fail to even *see* the ball for an instant, until our motivated interests trigger us to look in other likely places for the ball.

In the case where someone behind me unexpectedly calls my name in a crowded room, I pay conscious attention to the sound because my organism is habitually geared up to be on the lookout for the sound of my name, since being called by name is a potentially important situation for the motivational purposes of the organism. In some cases, he afferent data may linger non-consciously for a few milliseconds before its motivational salience attracts attention. But if it were someone else's name being called, it would not be motivationally important, and thus I would not be on the lookout for it. Physiologically, my thalamic-limbic-frontal brain system would not be geared up in such a way as to activate the imagery of the sound of the name. What happens here, then, is that my interest in the prospect of someone's calling *my* name, combined with the vague stimulus input of a sudden auditory change, triggers my vigilance as to the possibility that my name is being called. But in principle, I must *become* vigilant in order for the name to register in consciousness, and this vigilance results from a motivational interest.

The more recent empirical observations about brain functions are therefore consistent with phenomenological reflection. When I look at a pink wall and *imagine* it as a blue wall, I find myself "looking-for-blue" in very much the same way as I would if I were to focus on a wall fully "expecting" it to be blue. This "looking-for" phenomenon enables us to think about both the similarities and the differences between the physiological correlates of the perceptual and the imaginative consciousness of essentially the *same* cognitive content ("blue wall," for example). Every looking-at must be accompanied by a corresponding looking-for, even though the looking for may also be triggered by a motivationally salient event (such as a sudden change or a sudden movement toward us). Thus, consistently with Merleau-Ponty's (1941/62) "We must look in order to see" (232), Luria says, "The stationary eye is virtually incapable of the stable perception of complex objects and . . . such perception is always based on the use of active, searching movements of the eyes, picking out the essential clues" (Luria 1973, 100). In the Summerfield (2006) studies discussed in our introduction, subjects cannot consciously "look-at" something without having first "looked-for" the object. But we can "look-for" the object with no afferent input, when the relevant *efferent* brain processes are active, and in this case a mere mental image of the non-present object occurs.

In Husserl's (1913) terms, a meaning-*intention* must be in place before a meaning-*fulfillment* can occur. The meaning-intention is a category or concept, and is accompanied by vague mental imagery or image schemas. The meaning-*fulfillment* presupposes this meaning-intention (i.e., this motivated, anticipatory "looking-for"), but adds to it the actual perceptual data that facilitate a feeling that we are actually looking *at* the object, not merely *for* it. This difference between meaning-intention (looking-for) and meaning fulfillment (looking-at) is accompanied by certain phenomenologically observable earmarks, many of which are described by Sartre in his *Psychology of the Imagination* (1966). For example, Sartre notes that a mere mental image of the Pantheon does not have a specific number of columns, whereas an actual perception of it does. A "vivid imager" may insist that her mental image of the Pantheon *does,* necessarily, have some specific number of columns. However, even for such a vivid imager, there are still certain earmarks that allow her to easily distinguish mere mental images from actual percepts: They are not indistinguishable, as in hallucinations.

Wertz (1987) thematizes the difference between a mere image and a percept not so much in terms of the vividness and precision of the image (as would Sartre), but rather in terms of the way the perceived world always includes our own body as part of the ground for its presencing, and thus catches us a little more off guard than a mere image. We feel "in control" of mere imagery, in a sense that is lacking in the case of the percept. We can feel ourselves as *producing* the mere image, whereas in perception we feel that our bodies participate in a realm over which there is some lack of voluntary power. We are in the presence of the world rather than constructing it out of "inputs" or "hypotheses." This characterization too is consistent with the new enactive and embodiment approaches to the neurophysiology of imagery and perception. Although we do often control the act of conscious *attention* to a percept (and thus are not completely powerless as to whether we are conscious of it or not), this attention is also driven by real organismic motivational concerns that are not easily suspended. But at the same time we can phenomenologically observe the difference between *merely* "looking-for" (forming a meaning-intention) and "looking-at" (forming the meaning-intention *and* being in resonance with actual physical *contact* with the world, which makes us feel that we are in the actual *presence* of an object, and not merely imagining it).

The phenomenology of this situation is consistent with the finding of Aurell (1989) and Posner and Rothbart (1998) that, when some sensory stimulus activates the primary projection area in the brain, no *consciousness* of the object is yet present. There is consciousness of the object only when the frontal and parietal areas are activated, and this is the same kind of activation that would be associated with the *imagination* of the object (Richardson 1991; Stippich 2002). Activation of these areas without any corresponding sensory input corresponds to a mere imagination of the object; in this case, efferent activity occurs in the parietal, secondary-sensory, and frontal areas, but no matching afferent signals are found in the primary projection area. Relating this to the phenomenology of the experience, we can say that the efferent system has geared itself up to look *for* a certain image, but this image is not found in the pattern of input from the environment. Logan (1980), Corbetta *et al* (1990), Pardo *et al* (1990), Hanze and Hesse (1993), Legrenzi et al. (1993), Rhodes and Tremewan (1993), Summerfield (2006), and other cognitive psychologists also find that, when we hold in our imagination the image of a certain object, we are more likely to see that object when flashed on a screen. By imagining the object, we gear ourselves up to look for it.

The act of looking for something is also subjectively experienced as part of the act of attending to the object when it is presented *unexpectedly*. But in this case what happens is that the afferent pattern of the object first stimulates the thalamus, which directs the efferent system to "look for" successively more accurate approximations to the activity of the primary projection area, until the efferent and afferent activities finally resonate by means of corticothalamic feedback loops (Bernstein et al. 2000). The system, we might say, is trying to figure out what the object is. The act of looking-for may thus be preceded by an afferent delivery of the corresponding signals, but the signals do not become an attentive consciousness of the object until the "looking-for" act is executed. Only then can it be said that I consciously "attend to" the object presented.

The action-based account of perception traces some of its roots to the "New Look" approach to perception of the 1950s (see Bruner and Klein 1960), but it is also important not to give up the ecological embeddedness of perception that the New Look sacrificed in order to isolate and operationalize its constructs. This seems to be a potential danger that the enactive/embodiment movement needs to guard against—not to isolate and operationalize its variables in such a way as to squeeze the holistic and subjective features out of them.

Another precursor is Neisser's notion of perceptual *schemata*. As Wertz (1987) summarizes, "Schemata are anticipatory plans that . . . control the activity of looking by directing the exploration of objects . . . Schemata . . . direct perceptual exploration, which samples the ambient array, which in turn modifies the schemata" (Wertz 1987). Hence Neisser: "Each exploratory eye movement will be made as a consequence of information already picked up, in anticipation of obtaining more" (Neisser 1976, 44). Gallagher (2005), who also is making an important contribution to bringing phenomenology and neuroscience together, makes a similar point with admirable clarity: "One of the important functions of the body in the contexts of perception and action is to provide the basis for an egocentric (or body-centered) spatial frame of reference . . . [t]his egocentric framework is required for the very possibility of action, and for the general structure of perceptual experience" (Gallagher 2005, 137).

Does this process lead to infinite regress, since perception presupposes schemata which presuppose prior perceptions? No, for two reasons. First, as Neisser stresses, infants are biologically predisposed to look for certain patterns, for example a mother's smiling face, and these initial schemata can then be modified through further perceptions. And secondly, as Merleau-Ponty emphasizes, there are bodily *a priori*; the body, because it is itself extended, also has a "virtual body," that is, it knows that every front has a back, every outside an inside, and these bodily *a priori* can function as schemata. As Gallagher puts it, to avoid the infinite regress, one requires a pre-reflective bodily awareness that is built into the structures of perception and action, but that is not itself egocentric (Gallagher 2005, 137). The schemata employed by the action-based approach, however, are not "intellectual" categories, in the sense in which Merleau-Ponty criticizes intellectualism. They are subjunctives embodied in a know-how whose categories resemble more Needleman's (1968) "existential *a priori*" than Kant's intellectual categories.

Such a view also seems consistent with the observations of Merleau-Ponty and the Gestalt psychologists that we see the whole of a situation before we see its parts. Merleau-Ponty (1942/67, 173) gives the example of noticing the disorder in a room before noticing the crookedness of a certain picture frame. Correlatively, we see the meaning of a situation before we see the physical details that convey the meaning, as in perceiving a cynical smile. The categories that equip and motivate us to look for organismically meaningful elements in the environment are the categories of know-how and the Gibsonian "action affordances" of objects, and only through the actual application of these categories to the act of perception can they be fleshed out in terms of the lines, colors, and shapes that stimulus-response oriented cognitive psychologists mistakenly regard as primary.

A criticism of Neisser's schemata was that they were very hypothetical, and could not be cashed out in terms of any biological facts. But more recent action theories and brain studies do cash them out, both in terms of neurophysiological findings that are at odds with the stimulus-response paradigm, and in terms of new biological notions more consistent with Merleau-Ponty's notion of self-organization in "psychophysical forms."

Notice the eschewal in this approach of each of the mechanistic, *partes extra partes* biases so often criticized by Merleau-Ponty. Because the organism must anticipate actions toward its environment in order for consciousness to occur, consciousness is not merely passively caused by incoming stimuli or unconscious computations performed on incoming stimuli. The body's organization of stimuli occurs prior to the reception of the stimuli, and if the body does not actively seek to appropriate and rearrange the physiological substrata for its own desired patterns of conscious activity, this consciousness can never occur.

Like Scheler (1961), we see life as a prerequisite for consciousness, because only a living being can direct its attention purposively in the way that conscious beings must do in order to be conscious rather than dumbly registering "data" as in a nonliving computer. And as in Merleau-Ponty's view, when we look for something, we *prepare ourselves* to see what we are looking for. As Merleau-Ponty says, "I give ear, or look, in the expectation of a sensation, and suddenly the sensible takes possession of my ear or my gaze, and I surrender a part of my body, even my whole body, to this particular manner of vibrating and filling space known as blue or red" (1941/62, 212). The organism must actively search for information in the environment before that information is consciously seen. Vision is active, not passive.

Thus we can also phenomenologically observe a difficulty in consciously imagining a blue wall while at the same time consciously and attentively looking *at* (that is, seeing) a pink wall. The efferent pattern corresponding to looking-for the blue wall is physiologically *incompatible* with the efferent pattern corresponding to looking-for the pink wall—they require two different patterns of efferent activity—yet the latter must be done if one is to *see* the pink wall. Attending to an imagined object and attending to a perceptual object that differs from it can therefore *conflict* with each other, due to the conflict between the corresponding efferent event-patterns; in such cases, we experience the task of simultaneously paying attention to that combination of mental images as being a difficult or impossible task.

We have argued that the organism must be emotionally motivated to look for relevant objects in the environment that could possibly have important action affordances. But the body's ways of categorizing motivational interests in the environment are not as clean-cut as the categories of perception. As Gendlin (1992a) puts it,

> To begin philosophy by considering perception makes it seem that living things can contact reality only through perception. But plants *are* in contact with reality. They *are* interactions, quite without perception. Our own living bodies also *are* interactions with their environments, and that is not lost just because ours also have perception. . . . Our bodies . . . interact as bodies, not just through what comes with the five senses. . . Merleau-Ponty . . . meant perception to include (latently and implicitly) also our bodily interactional being-in-the-world, all of our life in situations. . . . The body senses the whole situation, and it urges, it implicitly shapes our next action. It senses itself living-in its whole context—the situation. (Gendlin 1992a, 344–45)

If motivationally relevant anticipations are linked to the meaning-intentions that always accompany meaning-fulfillments, we must also be on guard against oversimplified misconceptions of the ways in which organismic interests motivate action and attention. And in this case too, the stimulus-response paradigm has badly misled us. The next section discusses ways to integrate the neuropsychology with the phenomenology of emotion and motivation in ways that are more faithful to the experienceable phenomena and free from the distorting prejudices of the "natural attitude."

4. Correcting the "Natural Attitude" toward Motivational Processes

When we realize the importance of emotion and motivation in grounding a coherent physiological account of the substrata of conscious experience, it becomes increasingly obvious how much naturalistic psychology has to learn from phenomenology. To understand consciousness and cognition as features of self-organizing systems requires that we understand what is so special about *some* self-organizing systems, such as humans, that leads to the familiar experience of phenomenal consciousness that we all have; and one exciting aspect is that, as

Cytowic (1993) suggests, *emotion and affect* may be among the properties of certain living systems that ground their peculiar ability to sustain what we call phenomenal consciousness. In Cytowic's view, "Consciousness *is* a type of emotion" (1993, 194, italics added). Affective tendencies, or motivations, are the key to bridging between the biological self-organizing system, which can be understood scientifically, and the experience of consciousness, which can be accessed through careful phenomenological reflection on one's own ongoing experiencing process. Thus if we can understand how emotion and motivation are features of some dynamical systems, and then understand the central role of emotion and motivation in constituting the difference between conscious and nonconscious processing, then we can understand human cognition and consciousness in scientific as well as phenomenological terms which at that point have become commensurable with each other.

Emotion and motivation can be understood as phenomena that lend themselves to *either* a conscious *or* a nonconscious status. In other words, they have to be combined with *something else* in order to be phenomenally conscious data of which we can be "aware." We have suggested here that this additional element consists of imagery (including motor and sensorimotor imagery), image schemata, or representation; the aims and objects of emotions must be represented in some sensory or proprioceptive or sensorimotor modality (even if only in the sense that an image helps to "symbolize" a feeling) in order for them to become conscious. Otherwise, they are unconscious, are structured quite differently from the way they would be if they were conscious, and give rise to very different behaviors from non-conscious processing, which is more piecemeal and less complete.

But emotion and motivation themselves must be understood in a way that is faithful to their phenomenological complexity, and not through the oversimplifications to which the natural attitude lends itself. We believe our account follows closely the phenomenological approach to affective experiencing developed by Eugene Gendlin (1962/1998, 1971, 1973, 1992a, b), which we see as connecting well with a self-organizational approach to the physiological substrates of the way affective processes relate to their intentional aims and objects. Gendlin emphasizes that, if we are to avoid confusing the *trigger* for an affective felt sense with its *intentional objects* (for instance confusing my son's failure to clean his room with what my anger is *really* about), we must begin by appreciating that what affects intend is never as simple as a trigger, or a simple behavior in relation to the trigger. Instead, the organism has a pattern of activity that it is trying to maintain through its self-organizing tendencies. When the organism is failing to engage in the pattern of activity that it is trying to engage in (for example, stagnation in my professional life), it initially senses that "something" is not right. But, until something triggers us to pay attention to the felt sense of this "wrongness" (the trigger may be my son's failure to clean his room), we lack an explicit thematization of what that "something" is. The felt sense of the privation of the desirable pattern may *implicitly* contain information about what is wrong, because there is a correspondence between what is wrong in the organism and what is missing from the environment that could fix it if present. But the organism cannot know exactly *what is* missing until it goes through a much more elaborate series of reflective processes, to "phenomenologically reduce" the meaning of the affect.

Every phenomenologist is aware of this distinction between a trigger and an intentional object, and the way these differ again from a causal object. A cookie may trigger the realization that the body wants something, but the cookie is not therefore the environmental stimulus that our body "wants"; the cookie only triggers us to pay attention to the *fact that* we are hungry, and then we can find something nutritious to eat that will get the body going in its optimal patterns again (the cookie may not even be a good object for this purpose). In some instances, the felt sense that the cookie triggers is not even a feeling of hunger, but a more general sense of dissatisfaction, which may be hastily and mistakenly *taken* for hunger. Similarly, when the sight of a naked woman triggers a man's sexual arousal, it would be wrong for him to assume that having sex with that particular woman is the aim of his emotion (and thus that she *per se* is the intentional object of it).

To avoid confusion, our point here is not to deny that a "trigger" in this sense can be the intentional object of a *perception,* or what the perceptual event is "about." The point is that we should not assume *a priori* that the intentional object of a given *perception* is the same as the intentional object of the concurrent *emotion.* Just because we perceive X and feel Y at the same time doesn't meant that X explains what Y is really "about." The natural attitude does encourage us to make this assumption without evidence, because it tends to construe the trigger as the cause of the emotional experience, and it tends to conflate the cause with the intentional object. In some cases, a trigger *may* be the intentional object of the emotion, but we should not assume this *a priori.*

According to Gendlin, we use metaphorical images to "pull up" the felt sense of a situation, in the way that typing a certain code pulls up a computer program (so that the imagery of my son's uncleaned room may especially well "pull up" or "symbolize" the feelings I will later realize are about my professional life). If entertaining that particular image makes us feel the felt sense more sharply, then we know that the metaphor is "working" for this purpose. But in the case of "pulling up" the felt sense, there are degrees of vividness (because we are dealing with holistic patterns, not linear, *partes extra partes* mechanisms), and the degree of vividness with which the image pulls up the felt sense is the measure of the adequacy of the image for "representing" the felt sense. This is how we know whether the trigger symbolically or metaphorically represents the felt sense to an adequate extent.

We then can attempt to identify the features in our intentional representations of the environment that are connected with the felt sense (for example the sense of "offness"). By paying attention to our bodies in the past, we have learned what kinds of situations it tends to feel certain ways in; so we can now ask ourselves "How *would* I feel different if this or that aspect of the environmental situation *were* changed?" This involves proprioceptive, sensory, and sensorimotor imagery, in the sense of imagining how I *would* feel under different circumstances from the ones I am now in; and it also involves still other proprioceptive, sensory, and sensorimotor imagery, in the sense that in order to imagine how I would feel different, I have to "represent" *those* different feelings in the same way that I do with this one, that is, with metaphorical imagery to focus my attention on the "what it's like" aspect of them. This is the process that Husserl (1962) calls "imaginative variation." We vary in our imagination aspects of the situation, until we hit on the one such that, if it were varied, we would no longer feel that way. (Of course there usually is not just *one* aspect that would make the imaged feeling change, but with experience at this sort of activity, we can become proficient at sorting it all out.)

A trigger stimulus also functions as a "Gibsonian affordance" (Newton 1996); in other words the trigger stimulus is *analogous* to a type of thing that the desired self-organizing pattern of activity *could* be performed in relation to—so that the cookie represents the type of thing that we *could* satisfy hunger in relation to; the person who angered us and whom we are tempted to murder represents the *type* of thing in relation to which we *could* activate murderous or angry feelings. The functioning of trigger stimuli as Gibsonian affordances offers an avenue to grounding an explanation of the neurophysiology of emotion more faithfully than the stimulus-response paradigm allows for. As we have seen, emotions play a role in action planning, and the "trigger" offers the possibility of the type of action that could be a possible expression of the emotion.

The phenomenology of emotion, like the phenomenology of other mental processes, should not neglect its paradoxical aspects. Emotions are perhaps the most extreme case of the paradox of agency, which we discussed earlier. This paradox is prominent, for example, in the direction of attention, which is difficult to coherently construe as either passive or active. We know that our emotions, which have definite biological correlates, in combination with sensory input which also has biological correlates, determine the direction of our attention, yet we also feel as if we are "free agents," and part of the action of this free agency is felt to be in the direction of conscious attention toward objects. At the same time, we feel that our attention is "pulled" by the objects, and that our consciousness of them is a passive causal reaction to forces external to us. Physical causation superficially seems as if it should exclude the possibility of agency, yet we experience ourselves as agents, and in some respects (such as the direction of attention) our agency seems to entail causal power on the part of our own conscious being. This situation must inevitably remain paradoxical as long as causation is viewed only in linear terms. But when we view it in terms of self-organizing systems, we can coherently integrate the causal manifold with Merleau-Ponty's notion of "psychophysical forms," and agency again becomes possible.

An implication of dynamical systems theory as applied to emotions is that a specific motivation, say the desire to raise my hand, results ultimately from the organism's self-organizing tendency. This self-organizing structure is therefore present, and embodies a tendency for me to want to raise the hand, even before the desire becomes pronounced enough to be a conscious awareness. Thus the "expectancy wave" accompanying the decision to raise the hand is measurable *before* I am aware of a decision or desire to raise it (Libet 1983; Young 1988, 164ff). Expectancy waves indicate that motivational feelings arise out of the organism's generally self-organizing nature.

The concept of self-organization is essentially the same as Merleau-Ponty's (1942/63) concept of a *purposeful* organism, in which a change in one part can be compensated for by changes in other parts where needed to maintain the continuity of the whole. If self-organization is the same as purposefulness, and if emotional motivations are purpose-directed activities, it follows that only self-organizing processes can be characterized by emotional motivations. And if there can be no consciousness without some emotionally motivated direction of attention, then it follows that only self-organizing processes can be conscious. Moreover, inaccessibility of consciousness to objectifying methods of empirical investigation stems largely from the fact that to experience a state of consciousness entails generating the emotional motivations that are a crucial part of the constitution of conscious states, and this in turn requires *being* the organism that generates those emotional motivations. Thus the reason why the phenomenological character of a state of consciousness cannot be inferred purely from observations made from the external standpoint that an experimentalist would use is that emotions are motivated *actions* that an organism performs, and to experience them *is* to perform them. A scientist observing a subject's brain, in order to be conscious of the observation, must perform the *motivations* in herself that direct her conscious attention; but by doing so she does not experience the *subject's* emotions. Her empirical observations may not yield knowledge of what the subject's consciousness "is like," but they do yield knowledge of what her *own* consciousness is like. The complex self-organizing process constitutive of the emotional motivations needed for the subject's phenomenal consciousness are experientially accessible only from the standpoint of the organism that executes them.

5. Conclusion

We have suggested that, within the revolutionary ferment in cognitive neuroscience, a trend is developing which would reject certain key modernist assumptions that have kept brain science stuck within the "natural attitude," and at the same time would facilitate a new brain science that can be used by phenomenological psychologists as a point of intersection between psychological and medical ways of investigating and treating the psyche. These key modernist assumptions which are now being questioned are: the assumption that subject and object are clearly distinct, with the former merely resulting from causal inputs from the latter; that the reality which ultimately must explain mental functioning is at bottom an atomistic-reductionism; that, as most philosophers since Descartes have assumed, *representational* conscious activities (thoughts and perceptions) are clearly distinguishable from *non*-representational ones (feelings and emotions); and, perhaps most important, that all reality, as mechanistic science conceptualizes it, is fundamentally *reactive* and *passive* rather than active—or in other words that nothing does anything unless caused to do it by some external force acting on it, that there is no such thing as a pattern of activity that organizes its own substrata rather than the other way around. In short, for modernist metaphysics, there has operated a "causal theory of perception," and by extension of consciousness per se, with no important or non-arbitrary distinction between non-living things and living ones (those which appropriate, rearrange, and reproduce the needed substrata in order to maintain a higher-order pattern of activity); yet the difference between conscious beings and non-conscious ones (such as nonliving computers) hinges crucially on this distinction.

Since consciousness is a higher-order process that must actively seek to appropriate and rearrange lower-level processes that are needed as substratum elements for its motivated pattern of activity, such a higher-order process cannot be explained as the causal result of the discrete actions of its own physiological substrates. It would be as misleading to explain consciousness as passively caused by the discrete mechanical interaction of particles of brain matter as it would be to explain a sound wave passing through a wooden door as being caused by the actions of the particles of wood in the door. Instead, it is the sound wave that causes the particles to vibrate in the pattern they do—a fact we would overlook if we were to content ourselves with explaining the pattern of the wave as being caused by the discrete movements of its substratum elements.

Another assumption of the natural attitude that also must be rejected with an enactive approach is the notion that consciousness plays no significant role in information processing—the epiphenomenalist notion that consciousness is merely the tip of an iceberg that consists of unconscious computational brain processes. Instead, consciousness *directs* much of this activity, and much of it could never take place without the direction of consciousness; yet it is important that consciousness itself is *embodied*—not in computational cerebral processes, but rather in *emotional and motivational* activities of the *whole* organism. It is the emotionally motivated, holistic process of action planning that directs the focus of conscious attention, not a computer-like computational process. It is not a stark stimulus-response or computer-like computational process that directs the focus of attention, but rather the emotionally motivated, holistic process of action planning by means of conscious, experience-based mental imagery and image schemata, including the rich complexity of motor, proprioceptive, and sensorimotor imagery.

References

Aftanas, L., A. Varlamov, S. Pavlov, V. Makhnev, and N. Reva. 2001. Event-Related Synchronization and Desynchronization during Affective Processing: Emergence of Valence-related Time-dependent Hemispheric Asymmetries in Theta and Upper Alpha Band. *International Journal of Neuroscience* 110(3–4), 197–219.

Aizawa, Ken. 2006. Paralysis and the Enactive Theory of Perception. In *Toward a Science of Consciousness 2006*, Abstract no. 3. Tucson: University of Arizona Press.

Akins, Kathleen. 1996. Of Sensory Systems and the 'Aboutness' of Mental States. *Journal of Philosophy* 91, 337–372.

Alexander, David, and Gordon Globus. 1996. Edge of Chaos Dynamics in Recursively Organized Neural Systems. In MacCormack and Stamenov 1996.

Anderson, C.M. 1998. Ibogaine Therapy in Chemical Dependency and Posttraumatic Stress Disorder: A Hypothesis Involving the Fractal Nature of Fetal REM Sleep and Interhemispheric Reintegration. *Multidisciplinary Association For Psychedelic Studies,* Vol. VIII, 5–14.

———. 2000. From Molecules to Mindfulness: How Vertically Convergent Fractal Time Fluctuations Unify Cognition and Emotion. *Consciousness and Emotion* 1, 193–226.

Anderson, Carl M., A. Polcari, C. McGreenery, L. Maas, P. Renshaw, and M. Teicher. 1999. Cerebellar Vermis Blood Flow: Associations with Psychiatric Symptoms in Child Abuse and ADHD. *Society for Neuroscience Abstracts,* 25 (part 2), 1637.

Archibald, S.J., C.A. Mateer, and K.A. Kerns. 2001. Utilization Behavior: Clinical Manifestations and Neurological Mechanismms. *Neuropsychology Review* 11:3, 117–30.

Asimov, Isaac. 1965. *The Human Brain.* New York: Mentor.

Aston-Jones, G., and F.E. Bloom. 1981. Activity of Norepinephrine-containing Locus Coeruleus Neurons in Behaving Rats Anticipates Fluctuations in the Sleep-Waking Cycle. *Journal of Neuroscience* 1, 876–886.

Aurell, Carl G. 1983. Perception: A Model Comprising Two Modes of Consciousness. Addendum: Evidence Based on Event-related Potentials and Brain Lesions. *Perceptual and Motor Skills* 56, 211–220.

———. 1984. Perception: A Model Comprising Two Modes of Consciousness. Addendum II: Emotion Incorporated. *Perceptual and Motor Skills* 59, 180–82.

———. 1989. Man's Triune Conscious Mind. *Perceptual and Motor Skills* 68, 747–754.

Aydede, Murat. 2001. Naturalism, Introspection, and Direct realism about Pain. *Consciousness and Emotion* 2, 29–74.

Ayer, A.J. 1946. *Language, Truth, and Logic.* London: Gollancz. (Revised second edition 1950.)

Bachmann, Talis. 2000. *The Microgenetic Approach to the Conscious Mind.* Amsterdam: John Benjamins.

Baron-Cohen, S., H. Tager-Flusberg, and D. Cohen, eds. 1993. *Understanding Other Minds: Perspectives from Autism.* Oxford: Oxford University Press.

Barresi, J., and C. Moore. 1996. Intentional Relations and Social Understanding. *Behavioral and Brain Sciences* 19:1, 107–110.

Barsalou, Lawrence. 1999. Perceptual Symbol Systems. *Behavioral and Brain Sciences* 23, 1.

Ben Ze'ev, Aaron. 2000. *The Subtlety of Emotions.* Boston: MIT Press.

———. 2002. Emotions Are Not Feelings. *Consciousness and Emotion* 3, 81–89.

Bernstein, Marica, Sara Stiehl, and John Bickle. 2000. Limbic Connectivities with Parietofrontal Circuits Controlling Saccadic Eye Movements: A Neurobiological Model for the Role of Affect in the Stream of Consciousness. In Ellis and Newton 2000a.

Bertalanffy, Ludwig von. 1933/1962. *Modern Theories of Development.* New York: Harper.

Bickhard, Mark. 1993. Representational Content in Humans and Machines. *Journal of Experimental and Theoretical Artificial Intelligence* 5, 285–333.

———. 2000. Motivation and Emotion: An Interactive Process Model. In Ellis and Newton 2000a.

Bickle, John. 1992. Multiple Realizability and Psychophysical Reduction. *Behavior and Philosophy* 20, 47–58.

———. 2002. *Philosophy of Neuroscience: A Ruthlessly Reductive Account.* Dordrecht: Kluwer.

———. 2005. Ruthlessly Reductive Neuroscience. *Presidential Address, Southern Society for Philosophy and Psychology* (March 25th, 2005).

Bickle, John, and R.D. Ellis. 2005. Phenomenology and Cortical Micro-Stimulation. In Smith and Thomasson 2005, 140–163.

Block, Ned. 1995. On a Confusion about a Function of Consciousness. *The Behavioral and Brain Sciences* 18, 227–247.

Boden, Margaret. 1982. Implications of Language Studies for Human Nature. In Simon and Scholes 1982, 89–104.

Borst, C.V., ed. 1970. *The Mind-Brain Identity Theory.* London: Macmillan.

Boudreaux, J.C., B.W. Hamill, and R. Jernigan, eds. 1987. *The Role of Language in Problem Solving 2.* Elsevier: North-Holland.

Brentano, Franz. 1960. The Distinction between Mental and Physical Phenomena. In Chisholm 1960.

Bruner, J.S., and G.S. Klein. 1960. The Functions of Perceiving: New Look Retrospect. In Wapner and Kaplan 1960.

Bullemer, P., and M.J. Nissen. 1990. Attentional Orienting in the Expression of Procedural Knowledge. Paper presented at a meeting of the Psychonomic Society, New Orleans (April 1990).

Bunge, Mario. 1979. *Ontology II: A World of Systems.* Dordrecht: Reidel.

Canadian Institute of Neurosciences, Mental Health, and Addiction. 2006. The Motor Cortex <http://thebrain.mcgill.ca/flash/d/d_06/d_06_cr/d_06_cr_mou/d_06_cr_mou.html#4>.

Caramazza, A., ed. 1990. *Cognitive Neuropsychology and Neurolinguistics: Advances in Models of Cognitive Function and Impairment.* New York: Plenum.

Chalmers, David. 1995. Facing Up to the Problem of Consciousness. *Journal of Consciousness Studies* 2, 200–219.

Changizi, M.A., A. Hsieh, R. Nijhawan, R. Kanai, and S. Shimojo. 2008. Perceiving-the-Present and Dynamic Geometrical Illusions. *Cognitive Science* 32:3, 459–503.

Charland, Louis, and Peter Zachar, eds. 2008. *Fact and Value in Emotion.* Amsterdam/Philadelphia: John Benjamins.

Chisholm, R.M., ed. 1960. *Realism and the Background of Phenomenology.* Glencoe: Free Press.

Churchland, Patricia S. 1986. *Neurophilosophy.* Cambridge: MIT Press.

———. 1988. Reduction and the Neurobiological Basis of Consciousness. In *Consciousness in Contemporary Science* (Oxford: Clarendon), 273–304.

Churchland, Paul M. 1985. Reduction, Qualia, and the Direct Introspection of Brain States. *Journal of Philosophy* 82, 8–28.

———. 1989. *A Neurocomputational Perspective: The Nature of Mind and the Structure of Science.* Cambridge: MIT Press.

Clark, Andy. 1997. *Being There.* Cambridge: MIT Press.

Clark, Andy. 2002. Is Seeing All It Seems? Action, Reason, and the Grand Illusion. *Journal of Consciousness Studies* 9, 5–6.

Clarke, P.G.H. 1974. The Organization of Visual Processing in the Pigeon Cerebellum. Journal of Physiology 243:1, 267–285.

Chomsky, Noam. 1965. *Aspects of the Theory of Syntax.* Cambridge: MIT Press.

Cohen, Asher, Richard Ivry, and Steven Keele. 1990. Attention and Structure in Sequence Learning. *Journal of Experimental Psychology: Learning, Memory, and Cognition* 16, 17–30.

Coles, M., G. Gratton, and M. Fabiani. 1990. Event-related Brain Potentials. In *Principles of Psychophysiology* (Cambridge: Cambridge University Press), 413–453.

Coopersmith, Stanley, ed. 1966. *Frontiers of Psychological Research.* San Francisco: Freeman.

Corbetta, M., F.M. Meizen, S. Dobmeyer, G.L. Schulman, and S.E. Petersen. 1990. Selective Attention Modulates Neural Processing of Shape, Color, and Velocity in Humans. *Science* 248, 1556–59.

Cornoldi, Cesare, and Mark McDaniel, eds. 1991. *Imagery and Cognition.* New York: Springer.

Courchesne, E. 1991. Neuroanatomic Imaging in Autism. *Pediatrics* 87:5, part 2, 781–790.

Courtemanche, R., J.P. Pellerin, and Y. Lamarre. 2002. Local Field Potential Oscillations in Primate Cerebellar Cortex: Modulation During Active and Passive Expectancy. *Journal of Neurophysiology* 88, 771–782.

Crick, F. and C. Koch. 1992. The Problem of Consciousness. *Scientific American* (September), 152–59.

Cytowic, Richard. 1993. *The Man Who Tasted Shapes.* New York: Warner.

Damasio, Antonio. 1989. Time-Locked Multiregional Retroactivation: A Systems Level Proposal for the Neural Substrate of Recall and Recognition. *Cognition* 33, 25–62.

———. 1994. *Descartes' Error.* New York: Putnam.

———. 1999. *The Feeling of What Happens.* New York: Harcourt Brace.

———. 2003. *Looking for Spinoza.* New York: Harcourt.

Damasio, Antonio, P.J. Eslinger, H. Damasio, G.W. Van Hoesen, and S. Cornell. 1985. Multimodal Amnesic Syndrome Following Bilateral Temporal and Basal Forebrain Damage. *Archives of Neurology* 42, 252–59.

Danto, A.C. 1968. *What Philosophy Is.* New York: Harper and Row.

Dascal, Marcelo. 1987. Language and Reasoning: Sorting Out Sociopragmatic and Psychopragmatic Factors. In Boudreaux, Hamill, and Jernigan 1987, 183–197.

Davidson, Donald. 1970. Mental Events. In Foster and Swanson 1970, 79–102.

Davidson, Julian, and Richard Davidson, eds. 1980. *The Psychobiology of Consciousness.* New York: Plenum.

Den Ouden, B., and M. Moen, eds. 1992. *The Presence of Feeling in Thought.* New York: Peter Lang.

Dennett, Daniel. 1969. *Content and Consciousness.* London: Routledge.

———. 1987. *The Intentional Stance.* Cambridge: MIT Press.

———. 1991. *Consciousness Explained.* Boston: Little, Brown.

———. 1996. *Kinds of Minds.* New York: Basic Books.

———. 2003. *Freedom Evolves.* New York: Viking.

Donoghue, J.P. 2002. Connecting Cortex to Machines: Recent Advances in Brain Interface. *Nature Neuroscience Supplement* 5 (November 2002), 1085–88.

Dretske, Fred. 1988. *Explaining Behavior: Reasons in a World of Causes.* Cambridge: MIT Press.

Edelman, Gerald. 1989. *The Remembered Present.* New York: Basic Books.

Ellis, Ralph D. 1980. Phenomenology and the Empiricist criteria for Meaning. *Philosophy Today* 24, 146–151.

———. 1986. *An Ontology of Consciousness.* Dordrecht: Kluwer/Martinus Nijhoff.

———. 1990. Afferent-Efferent Connections and "Neutrality-Modifications" in Imaginative and Perceptual Consciousness. *Man and World* 23, 23–33.

———. 1991. A Critique of Concepts of Non-Sufficient Causation. *Philosophical Inquiry* 13, 22–42.

———. 1995a. The Imagist Approach to Inferential Thought Patterns: The Crucial Role of Rhythm Pattern Recognition. *Pragmatics and Cognition* 3, 75–109.

———. 1995b. *Questioning Consciousness: The Interplay of Imagery, Cognition, and Emotion in the Human Brain*. Amsterdam: John Benjamins.

———. 1996. Ray Jackendoff's Phenomenology of Language as a Refutation of the Appendage Theory of Consciousness. *Pragmatics and Cognition* 4, 125–137.

———. 1997. Personalism, Purposeful Processes, and the Contemporary Natural and Cognitive Sciences. *Personalist Forum* 13, 49–67.

———. 1999a. Integrating Neuroscience and Phenomenology in the Study of Consciousness. *Journal of Phenomenological Psychology* 30, 18–47.

———. 1999b. Why Isn't Consciousness Empirically Observable? *Journal of Mind and Behavior* 20, 391–402.

———. 2000a. Consciousness, Self-organization, and the Process-Substratum Relation: Rethinking Nonreductive Physicalism. *Philosophical Psychology* 13, 173–190.

———. 2000b. Three Elements of Causation: Biconditionality, Asymmetry, and Experimental Manipulability. *Philosophia* 29, 1–21.

———. 2001a. Can Dynamical Systems Explain Mental Causation? *Journal of Mind and Behavior* 22, 311–334.

———. 2001b. Implications of Inattentional Blindness for 'Enactive' Theories of Consciousness. *Brain and Mind* 2, 297–322.

———. 2005. *Curious Emotions: Roots of Consciousness and Personality in Motivated Action*. Amsterdam: John Benjamins.

———. 2008. The Phenomenology of Alexithymia as a Clue to the Intentionality of Emotion. In Charland and Zachar 2008, 181–192.

Ellis, Ralph D., and Natika Newton. 1998a. Three Paradoxes of Phenomenal Consciousness. *Journal of Consciousness Studies* 5:4, 419–442.

———. 1998b. *Consciousness and the Brain: An Annotated Bibliography*. <www.consciousness-brain.org>.

———, eds. 2000a. *The Caldron of Consciousness: Affect, Motivation, and Self-Organization*. Amsterdam: John Benjamins.

———. 2000b. The Interdependence of Consciousness and Emotion. *Consciousness and Emotion* 1, 1–10

———, eds. 2004. *Consciousness and Emotion I: Agency, Conscious Choice, and Selective Perception*. Amsterdam: John Benjamins.

Engel, A.K., P. Fries, P. Konig, M. Brecht, and W. Singer. 1999. Temporal Binding, Binocular Rivalry, and Consciousness. *Consciousness and Cognition* 8:2.

Eslinger, Paul J., and Antonio R. Damasio. 1985. Severe Disturbance of Higher Cognition after Bilateral Frontal Lobe Ablation: Patient EVR. *Neurology* 35, 1731–741.

Eslinger, Paul J., G.C. Warner, L.M. Grattan, and J.D. Easton. 1991 "Frontal Lobe" Utilization Behavior Associated with Paramedian Thalamic Infarction. *Neurology* 41:3, 450–52.

Evans, G. 1986. *Varieties of Reference*. Oxford: Oxford University Press.

Evans, J.P., and H.M. Florman. 2002. The State of the Union: The Cell Biology of Fertilization. *Nature Cell Biol.* 4 (S1), S57–S63 / *Nature Med.* 8 (S1), S57–S63.

Farah, Martha. 1989. The Neural Basis of Mental Imagery. *Trends in Neuroscience* 12, 395–99.

Faw, Bill. 2000. Consciousness, Motivation, and Emotion: Biopsychological Reflections. In Ellis and Newton 2000a.

———. 2003. Pre-Frontal Executive Committee for Perception, Working Memory, Attention, Long-term Memory, Motor Control, and Thinking: A Tutorial Review. *Consciousness and Cognition* 12, 83–139.

Fodor, Jerry A. 1975.*The Language of Thought*. Cambridge: Harvard University Press.

———. 1987. *Psychosemantics*. Cambridge: MIT Press.

Foster, Lawrence, and Joe W. Swanson, eds. 1970. *Experience and Theory*. Amherst: University of Massachusetts Press.

Freeman, Walter. 1975. *Mass Action in the Nervous System*. New York: Academic Press.

———. 1987. Simulation of Chaotic EEG Patterns with a Dynamic Model of the Olfactory System. *Biological Cybernetics* 56, 139–150.

———. 2000. *How Brains Make Up Their Minds*. New York: Columbia University Press.

Fuchs, W. 1922. Eine Pseudofovea bei Hemianopikern. *Psychologische Forschung*.

Gallagher, Shaun, and Natalie Depraz, eds. 2002. Embodiment in Phenomenology and Cognitive Science, Special Issue of *Theoria et Historia Scientiarum: International Journal for Interdisciplinary Studies* (Spring).

Gallagher, Shaun, and Anthony Marcel. 1999. The Self in Contextualized Action. *Journal of Consciousness Studies* 6:4, 4–30.

Gallagher, Shaun, and Marc Jeannerod. 2002. From Action to Interaction. *Journal of Consciousness Studies* 9:1, 4–30.

Gallese, V., L. Fadiga, L. Fogassi, and G. Rizzolatti. 1996. Action Recognition in the Premotor Cortex. *Brain* 119, 593–609.

Gallese, V., and A. Goldman. 1998. Mirror Neurons and the Simulation Theory of Mindreading. *Trends in Cognitive Science* 2, 493–501.

Gazzaniga, Michael. 1986. *Mind Matters.* Boston: MIT Press.

Gendlin, Eugene. 1962/1998. *Experiencing and the Creation of Meaning.* Toronto: Collier-Macmillan.

———. 1971. A Theory of Personality Change. In Mahrer 1971.

———. 1973. Experiential Phenomenology. In Natanson 1973.

———. 1992a. The Primacy of the Body, Not the Primacy of Perception. *Man and World* 25, 341–353.

———. 1992b. *Thinking Beyond Patterns.* New York: The Focusing Institute. Also in Den Ouden and Moen 1992.

Gibson, James. 1986. *The Ecological Approach to Visual Perception.* Hillsdale: Erlbaum.

Gibson, Eleanor J. 1988. Exploratory Behavior in the Development of Perceiving, Acting, and the Acquiring of Knowledge. *Annual Review of Psychology* 39, 1–41.

Giorgi, Amedeo, ed. 1971a. *Duquesne Studies in Phenomenological Psychology,* Volume 1. Pittsburgh: Duquesne University Press.

Giorgi, Amedeo. 1971b. Phenomenology and Experimental Psychology I. In Giorgi 1971a, 6–16.

Glenberg, Arthur. 1996. What Memory Is For. *Behavioral and Brain Sciences* 20:1, 1–55.

Globus, Gordon. 1992. Towards a Noncomputational Cognitive Neuroscience. *Journal of Cognitive Neuroscience* 4, 299–310.

———. 1995. *The Postmodern Brain.* Amsterdam: John Benjamins.

———. 2003. *Quantum Closures and Disclosures.* Amsterdam: John Benjamins.

Goldman, Alvin. 1969. The Compatibility of Mechanism and Purpose. *Philosophical Review* 78, 468–482.

Goleman, Daniel. 1994. *Emotional Intelligence.* New York: Bantam.

Gottwald, B., Z. Mihajlovic, B. Wilde, and H.M. Mehdorn. 2003. Does the Cerebellum Contribute to Specific Aspects of Attention? *Neuropsychologia* 41:11, 1452–460.

Gould, J., and C. Gould. 1994. *The Animal Mind.* New York: Scientific American Library.

Gray, Jeffrey. 1990. Brain Systems that Mediate Both Emotion and Cognition. *Cognition and Emotion* 4, 269–288.

Griffiths, Paul E. 1997. *What Emotions Really Are*. Chicago: University of Chicago Press.

Grush, Rick. 2004. The Emulation Theory of Representation: Motor Control, Imagery, and Perception. *Behavioral and Brain Sciences* 27, 377–442.

Haines, D., E. Dietrich, G.A. Mihailoff, and E.F. McDonald. 1997. Cerebellar-Hypothalamic Axis: Basic Circuits and Clinical Observations. In Schmahmann 1997, 84–110.

Hanze, Martin, and Friedrich Hesse. 1993. Emotional Influences on Semantic Priming. *Cognition and Emotion* 7, 195–205.

Hardin, Lawrence. 1982. *Color for Philosophers*. New York: Hackett.

———. 2000. Red and Yellow, Green and Blue, Warm and Cool: Explaining Color Experience. *Journal of Consciousness Studies* 7, 113–122.

Hatsopoulos, N.G., M.T. Harrison, and J.P. Donoghue. 2001. Representations Based on Neuronal Interactions in Motor Cortex. *Progress in Brain Research* 130, 233–244.

Haugeland, J. 1985. *Artificial Intelligence: The Very Idea*. Cambridge: MIT Press.

Heidegger, Martin. 1927. *Being and Time*. Tübingen: Neomarius Verlag.

Heil, J., and A. Mele, eds. 1993. *Mental Causation*. Oxford, Oxford University Press.

Held, Richard and Alan Hein. 1958. Adaptation of Disarranged Hand-Eye Coordination Contingent upon Re-afferent Stimulation. *Perceptual and Motor Skills* 8, 87–90.

Helmholtz, Hermann. 1962. *Helmholtz's Treatise on Physiological Optics*. Translated by J.P.C. Southall. New York: Dover.

Hempel, C.G. 1965. Problems and Changes in the Empiricist Criterion of Meaning. In Nagel 1965, 16–27.

Hofstadter, Douglas R., and Daniel C. Dennett, eds. 1981. *The Mind's I: Fantasies and Reflections on Self and Soul*. New York: Penguin.

Horgan, Terrence. 1984. Jackson on Physical Information and Qualia. *Philosophical Quarterly* 34, 147–152.

———. 1992. Nonreductive Materialism and the Explanatory Autonomy of Psychology. In Wagner and Warner 1992.

Houk J.C., J.T. Buckingham, and A.G. Barto. 1996. Models of the Cerebellum and Motor Learning. *Behaviorial and Brain Sciences* 19, 368–383.

Hubel, David H., and Torsten N. Wiesel. 1959. Receptive Fields of Single Neurons in the Cat's Striate Cortex. *Journal of Physiology* 148, 574–591.

Humphrey, Nicholas. 1992. *A History of the Mind*. London: Chatto and Windus.

———. 2000. How to Solve the Mind-Body Problem. *Journal of Consciousness Studies* 7, 5–20.

Hurley, Susan. 1998. *Consciousness in Action*. Cambridge: Harvard University Press.

Husserl, Edmund. 1900/1913. *Logical Investigations*. Translated by J.N. Findlay. New York: Humanities Press.

———. 1913/1931. *Ideas*. Translated by W.R. Boyce Gibson. London: Collier, 1931; from *Ideen zu einer reinen Phänomenologie und phänomenologischen Philosophie*, 1913.

———. 1917/1991. *On the Phenomenology of the Consciousness of Internal Time*. Translated by John B. Brough. Bloomington: Indiana University Press.

———. 1954. *Crisis of European Sciences*. Evanston: Northwestern University Press.

———. 1962. *Phänomenologische Psychologie*. Den Haag: Martinus Nijhoff. Original German edition, 1900.

Huttenlocher, Janet. 1968. Constructing Spatial Images: A Strategy in Reasoning. *Psychological Review* 75, 286–298.

Hutto, Daniel. 1999. *The Presence of Mind*. Amsterdam: John Benjamins.

———. 2000. *Beyond Physicalism*. Amsterdam: John Benjamins.

Imamizu, H., S. Miyauchi, T. Tamada, Y. Sasaki, R. Takino, B. Putz, T. Yoshioka, and M. Kawato. 2000. Human Cerebellar Activity Reflecting an Acquired Internal Model of a New Tool. *Nature* 403 (6766), 192–95.

Ito, Masao. 1993. Movement and Thought: Identical Control Mechanisms by the Cerebellum. *Trends in the Neurosciences* 16, 448–450.

———. 2000. Neurobiology: Internal Model Visualized. *Nature* 403, 153–54.

Ito, Y., M.H. Teicher, C.A. Glod, and E. Ackerman. 1998. Preliminary Evidence for Aberrant Cortical Development in Abused Children: A Quantitative EEG Study. *Journal of Neuropsychiatry and Clinical Neurosciences* 10, 298–307.

Jackendoff, Ray. 1987. *Consciousness and the Computational Mind*. Cambridge: MIT Press.

———. 1996. How Language Helps Us Think, *Pragmatics and Cognition* 4, 1–34.

Jackson, Frank. 1986. What Mary Didn't Know. *Journal of Philosophy* 83, 291–95.

James, William. 1890/1950. *The Principles of Psychology*. New York: Dover.

Jarvilehto, Timo. 1999. Efference knowledge. *Psycoloquy* 9 <www.cogsci.soton.ac.uk/psyc-bin/newpsy?article=9.83andsubmit=View+Article>.

Jaynes, Julian. 1976/1990. *The Origin of Consciousness in the Breakdown of the Bicameral Mind*. New York: Houghton-Mifflin.

Jeannerod, Marc. 1994. The Representing Brain: Neural Correlates of Motor Intention and Imagery. *Behavioral and Brain Sciences* 17, 187–244.

———. 1997. *The Cognitive Neuroscience of Action*. Oxford: Blackwell.

Johnson, Mark. 1987. *The Body in the Mind*. Chicago: University of Chicago Press.

Johnson-Laird, Philip N., and R.M.J. Byrne. 1991. *Deduction*. Hillsdale: Erlbaum.

Joseph, Rhawn. 1982. The Neuropsychology of Development: Hemispheric Laterality, Limbic Language, and the Origin of Thought. *Journal of Clinical Psychology* 38, 4–33.

Juarrero, Alicia. 1999. *Dynamics in Action: Intentional Behavior as a Complex System*. Cambridge: MIT Press/Bradford.

Kandel, Eric, and James Schwartz. 1981. *Principles of Neural Science*. New York: Elsevier-North Holland.

Katz, J. 1992. Psychophysical Correlates of Phantom Limb Experience. *Journal of Neurology, Neurosurgery, and Psychiatry* 55, 811–821.

Kauffman, Stuart. 1993. *The Origins of Order*. Oxford: Oxford University Press.

Kelso, J.A. 1995. *Dynamic Patterns: The Self-Organization of Brain and Behavior*. Cambridge: MIT Press/Bradford.

Kim, Jaegwon. 1992. Multiple Realization and the Metaphysics of Reduction. *Philosophy and Phenomenological Research* 52, 1–26.

———. 1993. The Nonreductivist's Troubles with Mental Causation. In Heil and Mele 1993, 189–210.

———. 1998. *Mind in a Physical World: An Essay on the Mind-Body Problem and Mental Causation*. Cambridge: MIT Press.

Kimura, Doreen, and Y. Archibald. 1974. Motor Functions of the Left Hemisphere. *Brain* 97, 337–350.

Kitcher, Philip. 1985. *The Nature of Mathematical Knowledge*. Oxford: Oxford University Press.

Krebs, Charles. 1998. *A Revolutionary Way of Thinking: From a Near Fatal Accident to a New Science of Healing.* Melbourne: Hill and Content.

Kurthen, M. 2001. Consciousness as Action: The Eliminativist Sirens Are Calling. *Behavioral and Brain Sciences*, 24:5, 990–91.

Lakoff, George, and Mark Johnson. 1987. *Women, Fire, and Dangerous Things.* Chicago: University of Chicago Press.

Langacker, R.W. 1987. *The Foundations of Cognitive Grammar,* Volume 1. Stanford: Stanford University Press.

Lauterbach, E.C. 1996. Bipolar Disorders, Dystonia, and Compulsion after Dysfunction of the Cerebellum, Dentatorubrothalamic Tract, and Substantia Nigra. *Biological Psychiatry* 40:8, 726–730.

Lavy, Edith, and Marcel van den Hout. 1994. Cognitive Avoidance and Attentional Bias: Causal relationships. *Cognitive Therapy and Research* 18, 179–194.

LeDoux, Joseph. 1996, *The Emotional Brain.* New York: Simon and Schuster.

Legrenzi, P., V. Girotto, and P.N. Johnson-Laird. 1993. Focussing in Reasoning and Decision Making. *Cognition* 49, 37–66.

Lethin, Anton. 2002. How Do We Embody Intentionality? *Journal of Consciousness Studies* 9:8, 36–44.

———. 2004. Exposing the Covert Agent. In Ellis and Newton 2004, 157–180.

Levine, D.L.. 2007. Persistent Hand Movement Representations in the Brains of Amputees. *Brain* 130:2 <e65; doi:10.1093/brain/awl321>.

Levine, Joseph. 1983. Materialism and Qualia: The Explanatory Gap. *Pacific Philosophical Quarterly* 64, 354–361.

L'hermitte, F., B. Pillon, and M. Serdaru. 1986. Human Autonomy and the Frontal Lobes. Part I: Imitation and Utilization Behavior: A Neuropsychological Study of 75 Patients. *Annals of Neurology* 19, 326–334.

Liberman, A.M., F.S. Cooper, D. Shankweiler, and M. Studdert-Kennedy. 1967. Perceptions of the Speech Code. *Psychological Review* 74, 431–461.

Libet, Benjamin. 1999. Do We Have Free Will? *Journal of Consciousness Studies* 6, 47–58.

Libet, Benjamin, A.G. Curtis, E.W. Wright, and D.K. Pearl. 1983. Time of Conscious Intention to Act in Relation to Onset of Cerebral Activity (Readiness-Potential): The Unconscious Initiation of a Freely Voluntary Act. *Brain* 106, 640.

Loeber, R.T., A.R. Sherwood, P.F. Renshaw, B.M. Cohen, and D.A. Yurgelun-Todd. 1999. Differences in Cerebellar Blood Volume in Schizophrenia and Bipolar Disorder. *Schizophrenia Research* 37:1, 81–89.

Logan, G.D. 1980. Attention and Automaticity in Stroop and Priming Tasks: Theory and Data. *Cognitive Psychology* 12, 523–553.

Luria, Alexander R. 1973. *The Working Brain*. New York: Basic Books.

———. 1980. *Higher Cortical Functions in Man*, second edition. New York, Basic Books.

MacCormack, Earl, and Maxim Staminov, eds. 1996. *Fractals of Brain, Fractals of Mind*. Amsterdam: John Benjamins.

Machamer, P., and R. Turnbull, eds. 1978. *Studies in Perception*. Columbus: University of Ohio Press.

Mack, Arien, and Irvin Rock. 1998. *Inattentional Blindness*. Cambridge: MIT Press/Bradford.

Mackie, John L. 1974. *The Cement of the Universe*. Oxford, Oxford University Press.

Macrides, Foteos, H.B. Eichenbaum, and W.B. Forbes. 1982. Temporal Relationship between Sniffing and the Limbic Theta Rhythm during Odor Discrimination Reversal Learning. *Journal of Neuroscience* 2, 1705.

Mandelbrot, B.B. 1983. *The Fractal Geometry of Nature*. New York: Freeman.

———. 1999. *Multifractals and 1/f Noise: Wild Self-Affinity in Physics (19630l970)* (Volume N). New York: Springer.

Marhenke, Paul. 1950. The Criterion of Significance. *Proceedings and Addresses of the American Philosophical Association*, XXIII.

Mahrer, Alvin, ed. 1971. *Creative Developments in Psychotherapy*. Cleveland: Case Western Reserve University Press.

McHugh, D.E., and A.T. Bahill. 1985. Learning to Track Predictable Target Waveforms Without a Time Delay. *Investigative Ophthalmology and Visual Science* 26, 932–37.

Meltzoff, A., and A. Gopnik. 1993. The Role of Imitation in Understanding Persons and Developing Theories of Mind. In Baron-Cohen, Tager-Flusberg, and Cohen 1993, 335–366.

Mensch, James. 1996. *Knowing and Being*. University Park: Pennsylvania State University Press.

Merleau-Ponty, Maurice. 1941/1962. *Phenomenology of Perception*. Translated by Colin Smith. New York: Humanities Press.

———. 1942/1963. *The Structure of Behavior.* Translated by A. Fischer. Boston: Beacon. Original French edition 1942.

———. 1964. *The Primacy of Perception.* Evanston: Northwestern University Press.

Millikan, R. 1984. *Language, Thought, and Other Biological Categories.* Cambridge: MIT Press.

Milner, A.D., and M.A. Goodale. 1995. *The Visual Brain in Action.* New York: Oxford University Press.

Milner, A.D., and M.D. Rugg, eds. 1992. *The Neuropsychology of Consciousness.* London: Academic Press.

Minsky, Marvin. 1986. *The Society of Mind.* New York: Simon and Schuster.

Monod, Jacques. 1971. *Chance and Necessity.* New York: Random House.

Moore, G.E. 1900/1956. *Principia Ethica.* Cambridge: Cambridge University Press.

Ernest Nagel, ed. 1965. *Meaning and Knowledge.* New York: Harcourt, Brace.

Nagel, Thomas. 1974a. Physicalism, *Philosophical Review* 74, 339–356.

———. 1974b. What Is It Like to Be a Bat? *Philosophical Review* 83, 435–450.

Natanson, Maurice, ed. 1973. *Phenomenology and the Social Sciences.* Evanston: Northwestern University Press.

Natsoulas, Thomas. 1978. Consciousness. *American Psychologist* 33, 269–283.

———. 1981. Basic Problems of Consciousness. *Journal of Personality and Social Psychology* 41, 132–178.

———. 1990. Reflective Seeing: An Exploration in the Company of Edmund Husserl and James J. Gibson. *Journal of Phenomenological Psychology* 21, 1–31.

———. 1993. What Is Wrong with Appendage Theory of Consciousness. *Philosophical Psychology* 6, 137–154.

———. 2000. On the Intrinsic Nature of States of Consciousness: Further Considerations in the Light of James's Conception. *Consciousness and Emotion* 1, 139–166.

Nauta, Walle J. 1971. The Problem of the Frontal Lobe: A Reinterpretation. *Journal of Psychiatric Research* 8, 167–187.

Needleman, Jacob. 1968. *Being in the World: Selected Papers of Ludwig Binswanger.* New York: Harper and Row.

Neisser, Ulric. 1976. *Cognition and Reality.* San Francisco: Freeman.

———. 1994. Ecological Psychology. Lecture at the Southern Society for Philosophy and Psychology.
Newman, J., and A. Grace. 1998. Newly Elucidated Circuitry Subserving the Selective Gating of Fronto-Hippocampal Systems Contributing to the Stream of Consciousness: A Model for the Modulation of Attention by Affective States and Episodic Representations. *Consciousness Research Abstracts: Toward a Science of Consciousness*, Tucson, 1988, p. 78.
Newton, Natika. 1982. Experience and Imagery. *Southern Journal of Philosophy* 20, 475–487.
———. 1989a. On Viewing Pain as a Secondary Quality. *Nous* 23:5, 569–598.
———. 1989b. Visualizing *Is* Imagining Seeing: A Reply to White. *Analysis* 49, 77–81.
———. 1989c. Error in Action and Belief. *Philosophia* 19, 363–401.
———. 1991. Consciousness, Qualia, and Reentrant Signalling. *Behavior and Philosophy* 19, 21–41.
———. 1992. Dennett on Intrinsic Intentionality. *Analysis* 52, 18–23.
———. 1993. The Sensorimotor Theory of Cognition. *Pragmatics and Cognition* 1, 267–305.
———. 1996. *Foundations of Understanding*. Amsterdam: John Benjamins.
———. 2000. Conscious Emotion in a Dynamic System: How I Can Know How I Feel. In Ellis and Newton 2000a, 91–108.
———. 2001. Emergence and the Uniqueness of Consciousness. *Journal of Consciousness Studies* 8, 47–59.
———. 2002. Representation in Theories of Embodied Cognition. In Gallagher and Depraz 2002.
Nisbett, R., and L. Ross. 1980. *Human Inference: Strategies and Shortcomings of Social Judgement*. Englewood Cliffs: Prentiss-Hall.
Noë, Alva. 1999. Thought and Experience. *American Philosophical Quarterly* 36, 257–265.
Noë, Alva, Evan Thompson, and Pessoa Luiz. 2000. Beyond the Grand Illusion: What Change Blindness Really Teaches Us about Vision. *Visual Cognition* 7, 93–106.
Norman, Daniel. 1981. Categorization of Action Slips. *Psychological Review* 88, 1–15.
O'Brien, G., and J. Opie. 1998. A Connectionist Theory of Phenomenal Experience. *Behavioral and Brain Sciences* 22, 127–148.
Olds, James. 1977. *Drives and Reinforcement: Behavioral Studies of Hypothalamic Functions*. New York: Raven.

O'Regan, J.K. and A. Noë. 2001. A Sensorimotor Account of Vision and Visual Consciousness. *Behavioral and Brain Sciences* 24:5, 883–917.

Ornstein, Robert, and Richard Thompson. 1984. *The Amazing Brain*. Boston: Houghton-Mifflin.

Panksepp, Jaak 1998. *Affective Neuroscience*. New York, Oxford.

———. 2000. The Neuro-Evolutionary Cusp between Emotions and Cognitions: Implications for Understanding Consciousness and the Emergence of a Unified Mind Science. *Consciousness and Emotion* 1, 17–56.

Pardo, J.V, P.J. Pardo, K.W. Janer, and M.E. Raichle. 1990. The Anterior Cingulate Cortex Mediates Processing Selection in the Stroop Attentional Conflict Paradigm. *Proceedings of the National Academy of Sciences* 87, 256–59.

Perlis, Donald. 1995. Consciousness and Complexity: The Cognitive Quest. *Annals of Mathematics and Artificial Intelligence* 15, 309–321.

Petersen, S.E., P.T. Fox, A.Z. Snyder, and M.E. Raichle. 1990. Activation of Extrastriate and Frontal Cortical Areas by Visual Words and Word-like Stimuli. *Science* 249, 1041–44.

Polanyi, Michel. 1958. *Personal Knowledge: Toward a Post-Critical Philosophy*. Chicago: University of Chicago Press.

Popper, Karl, and John Eccles. 1977. *The Self and Its Brain*. Berlin: Springer.

Posner, Michael I. 1990. Hierarchical Distributed Networks in the Neuropsychology of Selective Attention. In Caramazza 1990, 187–210.

———. 1980. Orienting of Attention. *Quarterly Journal of Experimental Psychology* 32, 3–25.

Posner, Michael I., and Mary K. Rothbart. 1992. Attentional Mechanisms and Conscious Experience. In Milner and Rugg 1992, 187–210.

———. 1998. Attention, Self regulation, and Consciousness. *Philosophical Transactions of the Royal Society of London* B. 353, 1915–1927.

———. 2000. Developing Mechanisms of Self Regulation. *Development and Psychopathology* 12, 427–441.

Posner, Michael I., and S.E. Petersen. 1990. The Attention System of the Human Brain. *Annual Review of Neuroscience* 13, 25–42.

Pribram, Karl. 1980. Mind, Brain, and Consciousness: The Organization of Competence and Conduct. In Davidson and Davidson 1980, 47–64.

———. 1991. *Brain and Perception: Holonomy and Structure in Figural Processing.* Hillsdale: Erlbaum.

Prigogine, I. 1996. *The End of Certainty: Time, Chaos, and the New Laws of Nature.* New York: Free Press.

Putnam, Hilary. 1993. Functionalism. Paper presented at a meeting of the American Philosophical Association, Atlanta, December 28th, 1993.

Pylyshyn, Z.W. 1973. What the Mind's Eye Tells the Mind's Brain: A Critique of Mental Imagery. *Psychological Bulletin* 80, 1–23.

Ramachandran, V.S., and S. Blakeslee. 1998. *Phantoms in the Brain: Probing the Mysteries of the Human Mind.* New York: Morrow.

Rawson, David. 1932. The Story of the Cerebellum. *Canadian Medical Association Journal* 26:2, 220–25.

Restak, Richard. 1984. *The Brain.* New York: Bantam.

Rhodes, Gillian, and Tanya Tremewan. 1993. The Simon then Garfunkel Effect: Semantic Priming, Sensitivity, and the Modularity of Face Recognition. *Cognitive Psychology* 25, 147–187.

Richardson, John. 1991. Imagery and the Brain. In Cornoldi and McDaniel 1991, 1–46.

Runeson, Sverker. 1974. Constant Velocity—Not Perceived as Such. *Psychological Research* 37, 3–23.

Ryle, Gilbert. 1949. *The Concept of Mind.* New York: Barnes and Noble.

Sartre, Jean-Paul. 1966. *The Psychology of Imagination.* New York: Washington Square Press.

Scheler, Max. 1961. *Man's Place in Nature.* Boston: Beacon Press.

Schües, Christina. 1994. The Anonymous Powers of the Habitus. *Study Project in the Phenomenology of the Body Newsletter* 7, 12–25.

Schmahmann, Jeremy, ed. 1997. *The Cerebellum and Cognition.* New York: Academic Press.

Schmahmann, Jeremy, Carl M. Anderson, Natika Newton, and Ralph D. Ellis. 2001. The Function of the Cerebellum in Cognition, Affect, and Consciousness: Empirical Support for the Embodied Mind. *Consciousness and Emotion* 2, 273–309.

Searle, John. 1981. Minds, Brains, and Programs. In Hofstadter and Dennett 1981.

———. 1984. *Minds, Brains, and Science.* Cambridge: Harvard University Press.

———. 1992. *The Rediscovery of the Mind*. Cambridge: MIT Press.
———. 2000. Consciousness, Free Action, and the Brain. *Journal of Consciousness Studies* 7, 3–22.
Sedikides, Constantine. 1992. Mood as a Determinant of Attentional Focus. *Cognition and Emotion* 6, 129–148.
Segal, M. 1985. Mechanisms of Action of Noradrenaline in the Brain. *Physiological Psychology* 13, 172–78.
Sellars, Wilfrid. 1965. The Identity Approach to the Mind-Body Problem. *Review of Metaphysics* 18, 430–451.
———. 1978. Berkeley and Descartes: Reflections on the Theory of Ideas. In Machamer and Turnbull 1978.
———. 1980. Behaviorism, Language, and Meaning. *Pacific Philosophical Quarterly* 61, 3–25.
Sheets-Johnstone, Maxine. 1998. Consciousness, a Natural History. *Journal of Consciousness Studies* 5:3, 260–294.
Simon, T.W., and R.J. Scholes, eds. 1982. *Language, Mind, and Brain*. Hillsdale: Erlbaum.
Smith, David Woodruff, and Amie L. Thomasson, eds. 2005. *Phenomenology and Philosophy of Mind*. Oxford: Oxford University Press.
Sperry, R.W. 1966. The Great Cerebral Commissure. In Coopersmith 1966, 60-70.
Spitz, R.A., and K.M. Wolf. 1946. Anaclitic Depression: An Inquiry into the Genesis of Psychiatric Conditions in Early Childhood. *P.A. Study of the Child*, II. New York: International University Press.
Springer, Sally, and Georg Deutsch. 1989. *Left Brain, Right Brain*. New York: Freeman.
Srebro, Richard. 1985. Localization of Visually Evoked Cortical Activity in Humans. *Journal of Physiology* 360, 233–246.
Stamenov, Maxim, and Vittorio Gallese, eds. 2002. *Mirror Neurons and the Evolution of Brain and Language*. Amsterdam: John Benjamins.
Staub, F., J. Bogousslavsky, P. Maeder, M. Maeder-Ingvar, E. Fornari, J. Ghika, F. Vingerhoets, and G. Assal. 2006. Intentional Motor Phantom Limb Syndrome. *Neurology* 67, 2140–46.
Stippich, C., H. Ochmann, and K. Sartor. 2002. Somatotopic Mapping of the Human Primary Sensorimotor Cortex during Motor Imagery and Motor Execution by Functional Magnetic Resonance Imaging. *Neuroscience Letters* 331, 50–54.
Studdert-Kennedy, M., and D. Shankweiler. 1970. Hemispheric Specialization for Speech Perception. *Journal of the Acoustical Society of America* 48, 579–594.

Sudnow, D. 1978/1999. *Ways of the Hand*. Cambridge: MIT Press/Bradford.
Summerfield, C., T. Egner, M. Greene, E. Koechlin, J. Mangels, and J. Hirsch. 2006. Predictive Codes for Forthcoming Perception in the Frontal Cortex. *Science* 24, 314:5803, 1311–14.
Sundararajan, Louise. 2000. Background-Mood in Emotional Creativity: A Microanalysis. *Consciousness and Emotion* 1:2, 227–243.
Swanson, W.J., and V.D. Vacquier. 1998. Concerted Evolution in an Egg Receptor for a Rapidly Evolving Abalone Sperm Protein. *Science* 281, 710–12.
Thelen, Esther, and Linda Smith. 1994. *A Dynamic Systems Approach to the Development of Cognition and Action*. Cambridge: MIT Press/Bradford.
Thelen, E., G. Schoner, and C. Scheier. 2001. The Dynamics of Embodiment: A Field Theory of Infant Perseverative Reaching. *Behavioral and Brain Sciences* 24, 1–86.
Thomas, Nigel. 1989. Experience and Theory as Determinants of Attitudes toward Mental Representation. *American Journal of Psychology* 102, 395–412.
Tucker, Don. 1981. Lateral Brain Function, Emotion, and Conceptualization. *Psychological Bulletin* 89, 19–43.
Tye, Michael. 1983. On the Possibility of Disembodied Existence. *Australasian Journal of Philosophy* 61:3, 275–282.
Varela, Francisco, Evan Thompson, and Eleanor Rosch. 1991/1993. *The Embodied Mind*. Cambridge: MIT Press.
Velliste, M., S. Perel, M.C. Spalding, A.S. Whitford, and A. B. Schwartz. 2008. Cortical Control of a Prosthetic Arm for Self-Feeding. *Nature* doi:10.1038
Wagner, S., and R. Warner, eds. 1992. *Beyond Materialism and Physicalism*. Notre Dame: University of Notre Dame Press.
Wapner, S., and B. Kaplan, eds. 1960. *Perspectives in Psychological Theory*. New York: International University Press.
Warrington, E.K. 1985. Visual Deficits Associated with Occipital Lobe Lesions in Man. *Pontificiae Academiae Scientiarum Scripta Varia* 54, 247–261.
Watt, Douglas. 1998. Affect and the 'Hard Problem': Neuro-developmental and Corticolimbic Network Issues. *Consciousness Research Abstracts: Toward a Science of Consciousness*, Tucson 1998, 91–92.
———. 2000. The Centrencephalon and Thalamocortical Integration: Neglected Contributions of Periaqueductal Gray. *Consciousness and Emotion* 1, 91–114.

Watts, Allan. 1966. *The Book: On the Taboo against Knowing Who You Are.* New York: Pantheon.
Wegner, Daniel. 2003. *The Illusion of Conscious Will.* Cambridge: MIT Press.
Weiskrantz, L. 1988. *Thought Without Language.* Oxford: Clarendon.
Wertz, Frederick J. 1987. Cognitive Psychology and the Understanding of Perception. *Journal of Phenomenological Psychology* 18, 103–142.
Whitehead, Alfred N. 1925. *An Enquiry Concerning the Principles of Natural Knowledge.* New York: Dover.
Wider, Kathleen. 1997. *The Bodily Nature of Consciousness: Sartre and Contemporary Philosophy of Mind.* Ithaca: Cornell University Press.
Winson, Jonathan. 1986. *Brain and Psyche.* New York: Random House.
Wohlschläger, A., and H. Bekkering. 2002. The Role of Objects in Imitation. In Stamenov and Gallese 2002, 101–114.
Woodruff-Pak, D.S. 1997. Classical Conditioning. In Schahmann 1997, 342–366.
Yarbus, Alfred L. 1967. *Eye Movement and Vision.* New York: Plenum.
Young, John Z. 1988. *Philosophy and the Brain.* Oxford: Oxford University Press.

Index

abstract thought, ix, 31–34, 44–47, 50, 59–60, 68–9, 79, 108, 123, 128, 137
access consciousness (versus phenomenal consciousness), x, 216
action imagery, 27, 55ff, 60ff, 84, 87, 90–91, 115–16, 137, 164ff
and mirror neurons, 187–88
afferent nervous pathways, xxx, 7, 39–44, 79, 122–24, 139ff, 164–67, 179, 193–96, 200, 204ff, 220, 228–29
affordance, xvii, xxii, 6, 7, 27–29, 34–35, 39, 43–47, 53, 60, 70, 84–86, 98, 137, 164, 168, 189–190, 196–200, 202ff, 226, 230, 232, 235
agency, x, xxvii, xxix, 42, 85, 99, 112ff, 144, 167, 178, 187, 198ff, 207ff
Aizawa, Ken, 19, 239
akinetic mutism, 31, 209
Akins, Kathleen, 104, 239
alexithymia, 47, 163–64
amoebas, 155
amphetamines, 181
amygdala, 7, 36, 47, 209
anaesthesia, 5, 24
Anderson, Carl, 37, 67, 239, 255
anger, 8, 13, 40, 126, 164, 174, 235
anhedonia, 182
anterior cingulate cortex, 7, 32, 36, 44–47, 165–66, 204–09
anthropomorphism, 201
anticipatory perceptual imagery, xiv, xviii, xxii, xxx, 6, 15–17, 30, 39ff, 58, 64ff, 84–85, 99–132, 136ff, 157ff
appendage theory of consciousness, 125, 163, 202, 244, 252

Area V4 (of temporal cortex), 32, 127
art (and use of representation), 58ff
artificial intelligence systems, 208ff
aspect shifts, 113, 186
assimilation effect (in color perception), 185
attention, xii–xiv, xvii–xxx, 6–8, 17, 32, 35–36. 40–41, 43ff, 58, 64–65, 79, 84, 99, 108, 112ff, 164ff, 197ff, 220, 226ff
Aurell, Carl G., xviii, 7, 32, 39, 44, 45–46, 118, 124, 127, 205–06, 220, 227–240
Aydede, Murat, 176, 240

Bachmann, Talis, 36, 41, 124, 140
background conditions (for causal relations), xxiii, 86, 91–97, 138, 211–12, 222–23
Barsalou, Lawrence, 171, 175, 240
basal ganglia, 198
basins of attraction, 86, 125, 209, 216
being in the world, 102, 119, 232
Ben Ze'ev, Aaron, xxiv, 179, 240
Bertalanffy, Ludwig von, xii, 208, 240
Bickhard, Mark, 53–54, 64, 67, 89, 240
Bickle, John, 58, 71, 89–95, 211, 240, 241
binding via syncronized oscillations, 192
binocular vision, 157ff
blindsight, xxii, 46, 129, 169
Block, Ned, x, 28, 83, 98, 158, 214–15, 241

259

Boden, Margaret, 30, 198, 241
body image versus body schema, 222ff
body map (in parietal cortex), 41, 52, 69
boundaries (permeability of, in dynamical systems), 72–73
brain stem, 27, 38ff, 79, 181, 204–05, 209
brainstem-hypothalamic loops, 38ff
Brentano, Franz, 50–51, 241
Bruner, Jerome, 229, 241
Bunge, Mario, xi, 64, 241

causal theories of word reference (inadequacies of), 170ff
causation (*see also* mental causation, dynamical causation), 88, 117, 146, 208, 236
and causal closure, 88, 89ff, 212
cerebellum, xxii, 37ff, 53, 59, 61, 64, 69, 84, 137, 165–67, 198; cerebellar cortex, 37; cerebellar nuclei, 37; cerebellum's loops with the thalamus and hypothalamus, 39ff
Chalmers, David, xxvi, 4, 10, 14, 19–22, 67, 75, 83, 100, 139, 210, 213–15, 225, 241
Changizi, M.A., xviii, 15, 36, 111, 131, 142, 184, 190, 227, 241
chaos theory, 65, 70, 89ff, 209
Chinese Room argument, 29–30
choice (willed action), xv, xxv, 1, 23, 35, 84, 90–91, 113, 160
Chomsky, Noam, 69, 242
Churchland, Patricia, 134, 242
Churchland, Paul, 3, 5, 134, 242
circularity objection (against enactivism), viii, xx–xxi, 58, 126, 181, 201
Clark Kent–Superman principle, 18, 19ff
Clark, Andy, x, xxvi, xxvii, 26–31, 101, 133, 140, 198, 242
cognition, vii–x, xx, xxvii, 26ff, 36ff, 115–16, 119, 198–200, 222
coherence of theories, viii, xi–xii, xxiii, xxvi, xxix, xxv, xxix, 3, 8–11, 23–24, 70, 217, 220–21, 225, 232, 236
complex dynamical systems, xi, 27, 47, 73, 78, 86, 89ff, 222
computation (trivial versus important senses), 151
computational model (see also information–processing paradigm), 5, 25, 219
confabulation, 169
consciousness, definitions of, 9–12, 17, 24, 33, 49–51, 59, 101, 138ff, 184ff
construction of experienced world, 103, 192, 228
consummatory versus appetitive emotion, 181
corollary discharge (*see also* efference copy), 43, 167, 198
corticothalamic loops, 7, 124, 127, 229
creativity, 54, 56,
curiosity, 35, 48, 121, 124, 189, 202
Cytowic, Richard, 70, 124, 220, 233, 242

Damasio, Antonio, 242–43, 245
Danto, Arthur, 2, 243
Dascal, Marcelo, 34
Davidson, Donald, 63, 101, 243
Dennett, Daniel, xxv, 14, 23, 51, 90–91, 112, 124, 169, 188, 195, 243, 247, 253, 255
depth perception, 182ff; paradox of, 158ff
derivatively unconscious processes, 124–25
digital delay (in sound recording), 111
Donoghue, J.P., xvi–xviii, xix, 28, 87, 151, 166, 243, 247, 255
dopamine, 181
doxic modalities (of similar contents), 180ff
dreaming, x, 71, 88, 182
Dretske, Fred, 170, 243
dualism, xxiv, 9, 67, 75, 87, 91, 101, 139, 149, 160, 210–12, 218, 225
duck-rabbit illusion, 113
dynamical causation, 89ff, 208, 212, 236
dynamical emergence (versus metaphysical emergence), 139ff
dynamical system, *see* self-organization

Index   261

early cerebellar activation (in perception), 38ff
early hippocampal ERP (event related potential), 38ff
early selection for attention, 36
Eccles, John, 154, 254
ecological psychology, x, xii, 229
Edelman, Gerald, 103, 109, 208, 243
efference copy, 69, 167, 177, 192, 198
electric eels, 5
eliminativism, 134, 188
embeddedness of mental processes, 26, 229
embodiment, ix, 25ff, 49ff, 170ff, 198, 221ff
embryonic brain cell transplant, 224–25
emergence (and emergent properties), xxiii, xxviii, 63, 68, 75–78, 85, 101, 138–39, 158–59, 183–191, 193, 222
emotion, viii–xii, xxii, xxiv, xxx, 5, 7–10, 13, 18, 226–27, 31–38, 40, 44–47, 49, 53, 59–60, 65–67, 70–71, 76, 78ff, 114–17, 119ff, 164ff, 174ff, 183, 189, 202ff, 225ff
emotional agnosias, 47
emotional triggers, 234ff
emotions distingished from motivations (*see also* emotion, motivation), 125ff
empiricist criteria for meaning, 5
emulation theory (of representation), 56ff
enactivism, viii–ix, xii, xx, xxvii, xxix–xxx, 25–27, 47, 49, 62, 64, 81, 85–87, 138, 160, 196, 200, 203, 216, 228–29, 238
encoding (*see also* isomorphism), 146
epiphenomenalism, xxiv–xxv, xxix, 2, 13ff, 87ff, 215, 219, 238
epistemology, xxvii, 1, 5, 17–20, 134, 188–89, 213–15, 217–220
error, 60ff
event related potential (ERP), 38ff
existential a priori, 119, 230
expectancy waves (*see also* readiness potential), xv, 90, 209
explanation, various meanings of, 6, 10–13, 19, 22–23, 64–65, 74, 83, 101, 139–141, 150, 151, 210

explanatory gap, xxvi, xxix, 14–15, 22, 25, 83–84, 100–01, 121, 136, 141, 144, 150, 157, 183, 199
extended reticular thalamic activating system, 44–45
extensional versus intentional meanings, 140–41, 214–16

Farah, Martha, 118, 124, 245
Faw, Bill, 32, 46, 126, 220, 245
feedback loops, xxiii, xxvi, 42–43, 61, 63, 69, 79, 87, 153, 167, 199, 201, 109, 229
feeling of confidence, 33–34, 128, 152
felt sense (*see also* Gendlin), 8, 34, 110, 127, 190, 234–35
first-person and third-person definitions (of conscious processes), xxvii, 10–11, 138ff
Fodor, Jerry A., 34, 51, 68, 170, 175, 245
fractals, 65
free will, 9, 221
freedom and determinism, paradox of, 160
Freeman, Walter, x, xxvii, 64, 208–09, 245
frontal inhibition, *see* frontal cortex, inhibition, inhibitory cortex
GABA, 71, 181
Gallagher, Shaun, x, xxx, 26, 135, 221–22, 230, 245, 253
Gallese, Vittorio, 107, 187, 245, 256, 258
Gazzaniga, Michael, 206, 246
Gendlin, Eugene, 8, 34, 126, 232–34, 246
Gestalt psychology, 230–31
Gibson, Eleanor, x, 246
Gibson, James, ix, 70, 196, 198, 230, 235, 246, 252
Glenberg, Arthur, 26, 171, 246
Globus, Gordon, 89, 209, 218, 246
goals (of action), xix, 11, 28, 36, 55, 65–77, 80–1, 114, 122, 125–26, 146–49, 157, 171, 180–82, 191
Goldman, Alvin, 101, 107, 245, 246

Goleman, Daniel, 46, 246
Griffiths, Paul, 173, 179, 245, 246
Grush, Rick, xx, 56–59, 246

hard problem of consciousness, xxvi–xxvii, 1, 4, 10, 24, 67, 83, 99, 160, 210–15
Hardin, Lawrence, 185, 247
Hebbian synapses, 51
Heidegger, Martin, 118–19, 247
hemianopsia (pseudo-fovea in), 224
hemispherectomy, 223–24
heroin, 178
higher order thought (HOT) theory, xxii–xxiii
hippocampal-cerebellar loops, 39ff
hippocampus, 36ff
holograms, 129
homeostasis, xi, 26, 78, 80, 126, 182–83, 209
homunculus, xiv, xxii, 3–6, 115, 163–64
Horgan, Terrence, 95, 247
Hubel, David H., 118, 204–05, 247
humanistic psychology, xxvii
humor, 185
Humphrey, Nicholas, x, xxx, 26, 135, 195–200, 204, 210–11, 247
hunger, 69, 124, 126–27, 234–35
Hurley, Susan, 26, 198, 248
Husserl, Edmund, 3, 15, 23, 50, 110, 117–18, 143, 217–221, 228, 235, 248, 252
Huttenlocher, Janet, 31, 59, 248
Hutto, Daniel, ix, 49, 248
hypothalamus, xxii, 36ff, 209

identity (personal; *see also* psychophysical identity), 70
illusion, 12, 21, 42ff, 76, 90, 103–07, 134, 157, 169
illusory choice model (inadequacies of), 91ff
image schema, 28, 39, 46, 120, 228, 233, 238
imaginability argument, 21, 161

imagination (phenomenological description of), 227ff
imagination, vii–xii, xv–xx, xvi, 8, 14, 18–23, 29–34, 36–37, 41–44, 55–56, 58–60, 115–16, 120ff, 128ff, 135ff, 142ff, 149ff, 175ff, 203ff, 220, 229, 231
imaginative variation (in phenomenological approach), 235–36
inattentional blindness, xiii, xvii, 41, 64, 84, 150
indexicals, problem of, 16–17
ineffability of consciousness, 98, 100ff, 114ff, 139–140, 159, 189
infant conceptual learning, 50
information processing (conscious versus non-conscious), vii–viii, xii–xiv, xviii–xxiv, 4–8, 10, 14, 17–18, 31–32, 35–36, 38, 47, 64, 66, 70–71, 83–84, 99–100, 118–19, 123ff, 129, 135–36, 147–48, 151ff, 163, 202, 204–05, 219, 220, 231, 238
information-processing paradigm (see also computational model), 5, 25, 219
inhibition, xi, xvii, xxvii, 27, 36ff, 107, 166
inhibitory neurotransmitters (*see also* inhibition), xv, xvi
intentionality, viii–xi, xxviii, xxix, 25ff, 49–51, 60–64, 67–68, 80, 85, 98, 106–07, 146–47, 155, 169ff, 200
interactionism (variant of dualism), 87, 211
interactivism, 89
intermodal schema, 107
interoception, 164
intrinsic intentionality, 51
introspection and private access, 163ff
introspection, xxx, 3, 163ff
involuntary attention, 45–46, 189
ionized molecules, 90, 124
isomorphism, xiv, xxii, xxvii, 4, 6, 10–12, 50, 55ff, 69, 86–87, 123, 146ff
Ito, Masao, xv, 31, 37, 43–44, 56, 69, 91, 137, 248

Jackendoff, Ray, 60, 126, 147, 198, 244, 248
Jackson, Frank, xxix, 13, 20, 74, 84–87, 136, 211–15, 244, 247
James, William, 15, 169, 191, 199, 248, 249, 251, 252
Jarvilehto, Timo, 195, 249
Jaynes, Julian, 66, 249
Jeannerod, Marc, 66, 249
Johnson, Mark, 31, 137, 175, 199, 249, 250
Johnson-Laird, Philip N., 57, 249
Joseph, Rhawn, xi, 126, 148, 207, 249
Juarrero, Alicia, x, xi, 64, 67, 73, 249

Kalman filter (in emulation theory of representation), 57ff
Kauffman, Stuart, xi, xxvii, 6, 64, 67, 72–73, 125, 138, 145, 182, 208, 211, 249
Kelso, J.A., xi, 64, 67, 73, 141, 145, 249
Kim, Jaegwon, xxiii, 112, 207, 222, 249
knowledge argument, xxix, 13, 17, 20, 22, 24, 84–85, 87, 184, 210–12, 215
Kuhn, Thomas S., ix

Lakoff, George, 57, 175, 199, 250
language, xi, 23, 27, 33ff, 50ff, 69, 128, 152, 170–75, 207
LeDoux, Joseph, xxiv, 8, 250
left brain versus right brain, 68
Lethin, Anton, 124, 130, 204, 205, 250
Levine, Joseph, xxvi, xxix, 14, 42, 83, 100, 139, 213, 250
liar paradox, 185
Libet, Benjamin, xv, 90, 133, 209, 236, 250
limbic system, xxii, 32, 36, 44–46, 124, 135, 208, 216, 220, 226–27
limbic-frontal-cerebellar loops, 45ff
linear systems (*see also* dynamical systems), 88
lived body (in phenomenological approach), 218ff
living systems, vii, xii, xxi, xxvii, 35, 47, 63ff, 78ff, 87–89, 139, 145–46, 170, 196, 201, 208, 221, 223, 231–33, 238
localizability of consciousness, 16–17
logic, *see* abstract concepts
looking-for, xviii, 7, 17, 45–46, 120, 122, 127, 131, 150, 176–78, 203, 226–231
Luria, Alexander, 124, 130, 195, 200, 204–06, 220, 227, 251

MacCormack, Earl, 208, 239
Mack, Arien, xiii, xiv, xviii, 7, 35, 36, 41, 43–45, 64, 84, 120, 141, 150, 203, 206–08, 251
Mackie, J.L., xxiii
macro-action, xi, xxvii–xxviii, 25ff, 62ff, 98
Mandelbrot, B.B., 65, 251
marasmus, 66
meaning intention (in Husserl), 143, 228
Medieval causal theories of perception, 3–5
mental causation, viii, xxviii–xxix, 14ff, 17, 22, 24, 117, 208, 212, 236
mental versus non-mental, vii–x, xii, xviii, xx–xxiii, xxvii, xxix–xxx, 12, 27–28, 29–30, 31, 44, 49ff, 63ff, 81, 106, 116, 147, 151, 164, 175, 196ff
mentality, definitions of, xx–xxi
Merleau-Ponty, Maurice, ix, xxx, 23, 37, 47, 50, 54–55, 69, 108, 123–25, 141, 168, 170–74, 187, 195–96, 208, 218–224, 227, 230–32, 236, 251
micro-action, xi, xxvii–xxviii, 25ff, 62ff, 98
microgenesis of perception, 41ff
micro-reductionism, 89, 95ff
microstimulation (of cortical areas), 71
mind-body problem, viii–xii, 1, 11, 18, 25, 66–67, 80–81, 83ff, 98, 118, 135ff, 195, 197, 208, 210ff
Minsky, Marvin, xi, 252
mirror neurons, 107, 187–88
mismatch negativity (in event related potential studies), 38ff
misrepresentation (and error), 52–53, 60ff

modularity of brain systems, 206
Monod, Jacques, xi, xii, 6, 64, 72, 125, 208, 211, 252
moods, intentionality of, 176ff
morphine, 179
motivation, vii–xi, xiv, xix, xxii, 7–9, 33ff, 49, 64ff, 78ff, 117ff, 132ff, 180, 189, 202, 205–06, 209, 220ff
motor area, *see* motor cortex
motor control systems (and representation), 57ff
motor cortex, xi, xvii, xxii, 32, 36ff, 53, 57, 59, 69, 84, 90, 107, 127, 136ff, 165–67, 177–78, 187, 198, 204, 207
motor imagery (see action imagery)
multiply realizable causal structures, 88, 93ff, 125, 208

Nagel, Thomas, x, 60, 188, 247, 252
Natsoulas, Thomas, xi, 252
natural attitude (in phenomenological approach), 217ff
natural attitude in emotion theory, deficiencies of, 232ff
natural language, 27, 34, 50–51, 175
natural selection, 11, 66, 104, 155
Necker cube, 186
Neisser, Ulric, x, 230ff, 252
neural groups, xxvii, 24, 51–52, 56
neural nets, 33
neurotransmitters, xv–xvi, xxii, 27, 39–40, 46, 71, 80, 137, 209
New Look movement in perception research, 229
Newton, Isaac, viii
Noë, Alva, ix, xxvii, 81, 135, 253–54
norepinephrine, 181
novelty, emergence of from contradiction, 191

occipital lobe, xii, 4, 7, 32, 38ff, 118, 124, 127, 130, 150, 164, 205, 226
occular motor control, 167
ontogenesis, 207
open thermodynamic systems (versus closed systems), 72ff

operant conditioning, 129
operational definition (*see also* ostensive definition), 2, 10, 229
opioid pleasure, intentionality of, 176
organic and inorganic systems (*see also* living systems), 89ff
ostensive definition, (*see also* operational definition), 33–34, 128, 184, 189–190, 193
overecausation, xxiii

PAG (periaqueductal gray area), 38ff
pain, xxii, 3–5, 23, 42–43, 130, 163, 175–77, 178–79, 196–98
Panksepp, Jaak, x, 35, 47, 86, 173, 175–76, 182, 189, 198, 216, 254
paradox of agency, *see* agency
paralysis, xix, 42–43, 64, 167
parietal "body mapping" (*see also* body map), 69
parietal lobe, 4, 38ff, 69, 91, 167, 187, 204–06, 226, 229
parietal P300 electrical potential, 38ff, 206
perceived location (of objects), xviii
perception, xix, 3, 6, 12, 38ff, 52ff, 64, 71, 76–77, 103ff, 130, 141, 157–50, 165, 168ff, 183ff, 196ff, 227ff
perceptual activity theory of imagery, 122
perceptual model of consciousness, xxix, 25, 135–36, 179–180
Perlis, Donald, 103, 254
persistent vegetative state, 46, 209
phantasm, 3–6
phantom limb, 12, 42–43, 195,
phenomenal consciousness, x, xxvii, 11, 50, 62, 70, 81, 86, 99ff, 156ff, 186ff, 191ff, 212ff, 232ff
phenomenal time (*see also* specious present), 15
phenomenological reduction, 218
phenomenology, ix–x, xxvii–xxx, 15–17, 50, 67, 75, 85, 132, 166–68, 175ff, 217ff
physicalism, 18, 189, 218
planning versus production errors, 61

plasticity (see also shunt mechanism, background conditions, feedback loops), 86, 89, 224
Polanyi, Michel, 54, 171, 254
Popper, Karl R., 154, 254
Posner, Michael 7, 32, 35–36, 44, 118, 120, 122, 124–25, 127, 204–06, 220, 229, 254–55
postmodernism, 218
potential representations, xxviii, 28, 55, 85
pragmatic meanings (in linguistics), 34
preconscious, xix, xx–xxi, 6, 28, 45–46, 6787, 116, 121, 125-132, 148
Pribram, Karl, 70, 235
privileged access, 168ff
propositional attitude, 51
proprioception, 27, 32–33, 45, 59, 78–79, 85, 99, 106–08, 115–16, 122, 124, 126–28, 132, 136–38, 164, 167, 189, 222, 226, 233, 235
prosthetic devices, xvi
protention (in Husserlian sense), 110, 117, 143
proto-desire, 139ff, 145ff, 153ff
proto-intentionality, 27–29, 68
proto-representation, 139ff, 145ff, 153ff
psychophysical forms (in Merleau-Ponty's approach), 220ff
psychophysical identity theories, 87, 210–12, 225

quantum theory, xxiii, 73, 89, 90–92

Ramachandran, V.S., 42–43, 167, 255
Raphe nuclei, 209
readiness potential, xv, 90, 209
re-entered signals (and "re-entrant" activation), 109, 129, 253
reflective versus prereflective experience, 165ff
reflexive motor movements, 28
representation, ix, xix–xx, xxiv, xxvii–viii, xxix, 10–12, 17, 27–28, 38, 42, 47, 49ff, 54ff, 86ff; action representation, xxix, 27–28, 54ff, 60ff, 85ff, 175ff; Akin's view of, 104; and emotion, 79ff, 124ff, 132ff; and parietal body mapping, 69ff; as unifying process, 68ff; causal theory of, 10–12, 51–54, 84ff, 146; Chomsky's theory of, 69; emulation theory of, 56ff; Meltzoff-Gopnik account, 106ff, 190; multi-modal, 59ff, 106, 190; multi-temporal, 191ff; Noë's theory of, 81; of other persons, 187ff; of self, 182ff
Restak, Richard, 207, 224, 255
Richardson, John, 220, 229, 255
robots, vii, xvi–xvii, 29–30, 35, 64, 88, 141–42, 201–02, 215–16
Rock, Irvin, xiii, xiv, xviii, 7, 35, 36, 41, 43–45, 64, 84, 120, 141, 150, 203, 206–08, 251
Rosch, Eleanor, ix, x, xxix, 44, 85, 207, 253–54, 257
Rothbart, Mary, 7, 32, 35–36, 43, 118, 120, 122, 124–25, 127, 204–06, 220, 229, 254–55
Ryle, Gilbert, 169, 255

saccade, xiii
Sartre, Jean-Paul, 50, 169, 228, 255, 258
Scheler, Max, 231, 255
Schmahmann, Jeremy, 37, 44, 59, 61, 166, 247, 255
Schües, Christina, 141–42, 255
Searle, John, 29, 30, 64, 68, 112, 255
secondary qualities, 9, 77, 102, 105, 114, 117
sedimented preconscious processes, xvii, 28–29, 151–52
seeking system, 35, 175–76, 189
selective attention, 35, 121
self-organization, vii–viii, ix–xix, xxiii, xxvii–xxviii, 6–11, 18, 23, 26, 30, 47, 49, 58, 62, 63ff, 72ff, 89ff, 99, 101, 135, 138–39, 145, 153–54, 160, 180–82, 188–89, 200–02, 207ff, 220, 224, 231–33, 236
self-similarity (in dynamical systems), 63ff
self-talk, role of in cognitive development, 207

Sellars, Wilfrid, 3, 256
semantic properties, 51
sensations, 196ff
sense of ownership (of bodily movement), 199ff
sensorimotor image, xxvii, 31–33, 45, 55–56, 59, 116, 126–28, 136–37, 148, 155, 167, 174–75, 177, 200–06, 226, 233–35
sensorimotor imagery (see action representation, action imagery)
Sheets-Johnstone, Maxine, 26, 175, 256
shunt mechanisms, xxiii, 86, 212
sleep versus waking, x, 44, 70–71, 177
smell, 33, 103
solipsism (and objective reality), 60ff
spatiality, paradox of, 16–17, 102ff
specious present, 15, 17, 99, 109–112, 117, 130, 144, 157, 159
Staminov, Maxim, 208, 251
stimulus-response paradigm, xxiv, 5, 119, 184, 220, 226, 231–32, 235, 238
stroke recovery, 6, 21, 212, 223–24
subjunctives, 30, 91, 123, 144, 207, 230
subliminal priming studies, 120, 247, 251, 255
sub-personal level, xxvii
Sundararajan, Louise, 164, 257
supplementary motor area, 41, 84, 90, 165–66, 207
supramodal body scheme, 106
symbolization function of emotional intentionality, 233–34

taste, 193
teleology, 11, 17–18, 62, 74–75, 89
temporality, experience and paradox of (*see also* ìthicknessî of temporal experience, specious present), 16, 17, 109ff, 112, 117ff
thalamus, 7, 35ff, 205, 209, 226, 229
Thelen, Esther, ix–xi, 26, 49–50, 52–54, 64, 73, 87, 146, 182, 195, 208, 257

theory-of-mind model of infant interpersonal perception, 106ff
thickness of temporal experience (*see also* temporality, specious present), 99, 110–11, 117, 153, 191–93, 197–99
thirst, xxi, 132–33
Thomas, Nigel, 122, 257
Thompson, Evan, ix, x, xxix, 44, 85, 207, 253–54, 257
top-down connectivity, xix, 89ff
trigger stimulus (in emotion), 8, 39, 51–52, 98, 166, 172, 176, 181, 226–27, 233–35
Tucker, Don, 207, 257

unconscious motor imagery, xvii–xviii, 28
unconscious proto-mental processes, xiii, xv–xxii, 5, 23, 26–28, 34–35, 41–47, 64, 66ff, 81, 124–29, 151, 169, 175ff, 219
understanding, ix–xii, xxii–xxvii, xxx, 4–7, 13, 20, 24ff, 39ff, 54ff, 70, 86, 123, 127–28, 137, 155, 171, 200
utilization behavior, xv–xvii

Varela, Francisco, ix, x, xxix, 44, 85, 207, 253–54, 257
virtual body (in phenomenological theory), 230
voluntary attention, 177

Watt, Douglas, 9, 17, 46, 70, 179, 182, 195, 220, 258
Wegner, Daniel, xxv, 14, 90–91, 112, 258
Weiskrantz, Lawrence, 169, 258
Wertz, Frederick J., 47, 218, 228, 230, 258
Whitehead, Alfred N., 6, 145, 258
widely distributed brain processes, ix, xxii, 44, 206
Wiesel, Torsten N., 204–05, 118, 247
word reference, causal theories of, 170

working versus long-term memory, 192
World III objects (in Popper-Eccles sense), 154
worms and insects, 155

Zawinul, Joe, and creativity in jazz improvisation, 56
zombie argument, 14–15, 17, 19, 136, 161, 202, 215

www.ingramcontent.com/pod-product-compliance
Lightning Source LLC
Chambersburg PA
CBHW030108010526
44116CB00005B/148